Good Bottled Beer Guide

Jeff Evans

Sponsored by

Safeway

BOOKS

Contents

Published by CAMRA Books, 230 Hatfield Road,
St Albans, Hertfordshire AL1 4LW.
Tel. (01727) 867201 Fax (01727) 867670
e-mail: camra@camra.org.uk

© CAMRA Books 2003
ISBN 1-85249-185-X
Author: Jeff Evans
Design: Rob Howells
Cover photograph: Thomas Dobbie

Great effort has gone into researching the contents of this book, but no responsibility can be taken for errors.

Foreword

Safeway is proud to sponsor the CAMRA *Good Bottled Beer Guide* for the second time.

So much has happened since the last edition, including the disappearance of some of the biggest names in British brewing and the closure of several breweries, but it's certainly not all bad news.

I believe beer has started to reclaim its glory as the pre-eminent choice of drink for British imbibers. It has far more to offer with food than does wine, it presents a greater range of styles from more countries than wine, and it is slowly losing its 'bad boy' image. And we all know its understated health benefits.

One of the nicest elements of my job is meeting new people: brewers, maltsters, hop-growers, journalists, importers and pub and bar owners, often as fellow judges at beer competitions. At both the Great British and Great American Beer Festivals in London and Denver in 2002, I was lucky to be in the company of the world's finest brewers, witnessing how the Americans were learning from their British counterparts and vice-versa, and all in the presence of the Belgian, Czech and German brewers. This exemplifies how we collectively brew, sell, drink and write about beer, and we do so, more than for any other reason, because we enjoy it.

The change it has had on me is to metamorphose from buyer of beer at a supermarket group into a tyro brewer, and the more people I meet in brewing, the more I realise how much there is to learn.

Safeway will continue to play its part to help beer through whole- or part-sponsorship of events like the Great British Beer Festival and the British Guild of Beer Writers' annual dinner, and initiatives like the Beer Academy and the SIBA *Wheat Beer Challenge*. For your part, please continue to enjoy your beer: I will.

Glenn Payne
Category Buyer, Beer
Safeway Stores

Introduction

Casting my mind back seven years, I remember proposing to CAMRA's publishing directors that I write a book on real ale in a bottle. Is there scope for such a book?, I was asked. How many bottled real ales are there in circulation? Oh, about a hundred, I replied. Gasps of amazement all around the room.

If this seems an extreme reaction, you have to remember that, when CAMRA came into existence in the early 1970s, bottle-conditioned beer, like cask-conditioned beer, was on its last legs. There were only five beers known to be in regular production that fermented in the bottle, just like real ale ferments in the cask at the pub. All other beers were filtered, pasteurised or, usually, both. Guinness Extra Stout, Worthington's White Shield, Eldridge Pope's Thomas Hardy Ale, Gale's Prize Old Ale and Courage's Imperial Russian Stout were the resilient survivors, flying in the face of the same 1960s convenience consumerism that had landed us with sliced white bread and the frozen roast lunch. In 1996, to suggest that the number of bottle-conditioned beers had swelled to three figures was remarkable. One can only wonder what the directors' reaction would have been if I'd been able to foretell that this fourth edition would feature more than 500.

Bottle is beautiful

So, where has this growth come from? Generally, you can point to the 'bottle is beautiful' school of brewery marketing that has seen the can relegated to industrial status while glass glows appealingly in the aisles. You can also thank enlightened importers for shipping in continental wheat beers like Hoegaarden, that have made British drinkers realise that yeast in a bottled beer is not necessarily a bad thing. Improved technology and better control of yeasts have encouraged some major companies – who, after all, have big reputations to lay on the line – to take the risk of offering a living bottled beer to the public, and this, in turn, has inspired smaller brewers to join the fray. And it is in this microbrewing sector that real progress has been made.

Frustrated by the ever-tightening pub market, in which buyers at pub group head offices continually ignore beers from small producers in favour of heavily-discounted national brands, many microbreweries have diversified into bottle. Their product is, in many ways, ideal for this medium. Their cask ales are sold on the basis of quality and craftsmanship, with the concept of 'localness' adding a further gloss. In bottle, they can sit alongside farmhouse cheeses, breads from village bakeries, country fruit wines and home-made chutneys in regional craft centres and at farmers' markets.

Producing reliable, quality live beer is a challenge, but the benefits of getting it right make it all worthwhile. Through prolonged fermentation, the bottle-conditioning process produces a beer with full, fresh flavours and a clean, natural sparkle. Pasteurisation is an easy option and in most instances, in my opinion, produces an inferior beer. I fail to understand why brewers spend money on the best ingredients, take great care in brewing a finely balanced, flavoursome beer and then blast it with heat. I've tasted excellent cask ales that have been pasteurised for the bottle to the point where you wouldn't know they were the same original brew. I've also tasted delicate Czech lagers that have been wrecked by 'cooking' in the pasteuriser.

Heating up the beer certainly stamps out any unwanted bacteria, but it also, more often than not, leads to a stale, wet cardboard taste, the result of oxygen damaging the beer. In bottle-conditioned beers, while oxidation is not always eradicated, it is certainly far less common, because the living yeast in the bottle can eat up much of any oxygen that is present.

A certain idiosyncrasy

Supermarkets have made a great play in recent years on stocking food products that have individuality, from producers that take time to create foods with flavour, depth and a certain idiosyncrasy. With a few notable exceptions, such stores, however, have been slow to recognise the merits of bottle-conditioned beer. When asked why, they tell you that customers complain about beer that is cloudy or hard to pour. It's a handy excuse to justify filling shelves with filtered, pasteurised beer, but does the cheese counter get away with only stocking cellophane-wrapped Cheddar and Dairylea these days? Greater education for customers is needed, it is true, so that, when they pick up a real ale in a bottle, they know what they're going to get. The *Good Bottled Beer Guide* challenges major retailers to get the message across and reminds them that CAMRA is always there to help.

There is, however, another part of the industry that must do its bit, too. If real ale in a bottle is to continue to grow then brewers must ensure they provide a thoroughly reliable product. No one is asking for beer to taste exactly the same every time you open a bottle: quite the opposite, in fact, because comparing how flavours have developed in different bottlings of the same beer is part of the joy. However, the customer has a right to expect a drinkable beer every time.

Research for this book has revealed that bottle-conditioned beer quality is better than ever, but that there are brewers who perhaps still haven't thought through the process clearly enough. The likes of Fuller's and Young's wouldn't dare compromise their reputations by sending out beer that might prove unacceptable in the bottle. They have the resources, of course, to get their vision of bottle conditioning right, but, big or small, the same issues confront all breweries looking to bottle, namely scrupulous cleanliness of both equipment and yeast, and a realistic assessment of shelf life. Gone are the days when, because a beer contained yeast, it could get away with having no best before date. Only strong, full-bodied ales, in my view, happily survive years in a bottle.

Catching the eye

For its fourth edition, the *Good Bottled Beer Guide* has again unearthed some cracking beers. Many tried and tested favourites remain but there's also evidence that the imagination of the brewers has been running wild as they re-think methods of brewing and discover new combinations of ingredients. Malts of all grainy, colourful characters, hops trawled from across the world, even off-beat ingredients like fruits and honey: all put their stamp on beers in this book. From re-creations of historic, once-forgotten beer styles, to cutting-edge organic ales, the choice is astonishing.

Furthermore, there have been some very welcome developments concerning those five, classic bottle-conditioned beers that CAMRA discovered at its inception. After the demise of Courage's Imperial Russian Stout and the sacrificing of Guinness Extra (now Guinness Original) to the pasteuriser, we can still celebrate the longevity of Gale's Prize Old Ale and the new lease of life that White Shield is enjoying back home in Burton. The fact that the beer has been drafted into the wider Worthington's portfolio, where it will hopefully benefit from the marketing expertise of Coors, is a major boost for the real ale in the bottle sector.

One final thrill comes with the news that Thomas Hardy's Ale is back in production – not at its original Dorset site, but at least in the capable and enthusiastic hands of O'Hanlon's in Devon. I look forward to reviewing this beer in the next edition, but how many other beers that may feature, even I won't hazard a guess.

Jeff Evans
Newbury, July 2003

Brewing Bottles

As well as the letter B, Beer begins with malt, often described as 'the soul of beer'. Malt is barley grain that has been partially germinated to help release sugars needed for the brewing process and then kilned to prevent further germination. The degree of kilning also dictates the character of the malt; the more 'baked' the malt, the darker the colour and the roastier the taste. Some malts are toasted black for bitter, coffeeish flavours; others are just lightly crisped for a sweeter, nuttier taste.

At the brewery, the malt is crushed and then combined in a vessel called a mash tun with hot water (known as 'liquor' in the trade), which has usually been treated to remove unsuitable chemicals or to emulate the brewing waters of towns like Burton upon Trent. (To give some examples of how water affects the finished beer, the best pale ales are made from hard water, while the finest pilsners are based on a much softer liquor.) In traditional lager brewing countries, this infusion mash is replaced by a decoction system, in which parts of the mash are temporarily pumped into a separate vessel and subjected to a higher temperature as a means of extracting the best brewing sugars.

On the hop

After roughly an hour and a half's mashing and stirring, a thick, sweet liquid called wort is formed. This is run off from the mash tun (or the equivalent lauter tun in lager breweries) and diverted into a boiler known as a copper, leaving behind the spent grain, which is sprayed – or 'sparged' – to extract any last sugars. In the copper, the wort is boiled up with hops which add bitterness and sometimes herbal, spicy, citrous or floral characters. Like malts, hops come in many varieties. Some are very bitter; others milder. Some make themselves known in the aroma; others are expressed in the taste. Hops also act as a preservative. They can be added as whole hop flowers or as compressed pellets. Some brewers use hop oils (concentrated extract), but these can be astringent. The hops are added at various stages of the boil (or even later in the brewing process – a method known as 'dry hopping' – for extra aroma). Sometimes 'adjuncts' are introduced in the copper or mash tun. These include sugars, which add to the fermentability of the wort, and maize, which helps produce a good head on the finished beer, but such additives are opposed by purists.

After an hour or two in the copper, the hops are strained out and the hopped wort is run off and cooled,

How real ale in a bottle is brewed

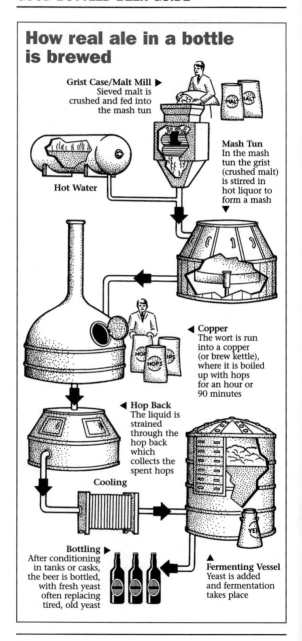

Grist Case/Malt Mill ▶
Sieved malt is crushed and fed into the mash tun

Hot Water

Mash Tun
In the mash tun the grist (crushed malt) is stirred in hot liquor to form a mash ▼

◀ Copper
The wort is run into a copper (or brew kettle), where it is boiled up with hops for an hour or 90 minutes

◀ Hop Back
The liquid is strained through the hop back which collects the spent hops

Cooling

Bottling ▶
After conditioning in tanks or casks, the beer is bottled, with fresh yeast often replacing tired, old yeast

▲ Fermenting Vessel
Yeast is added and fermentation takes place

My Beer's Got Bits in It

An obvious characteristic of real ale in a bottle is that it contains a sediment. The sediment is largely comprised of yeast and natural proteins and is certainly not harmful. However, in these days when style so often outpoints substance in the eyes of the public, finding bits in beer still causes some alarm. So it is ironic but very welcome that a trendy continental wheat beer like Hoegaarden – designed to be drunk cloudy – is now convincing people there is nothing wrong with a beer that is not sparkling-bright after all.

before being pumped into a fermenting vessel, where yeast is added ('pitched') and fermentation begins.

Yeast is a single-celled fungus that turns the sugars in the wort into alcohol and carbon dioxide (the gas that gives beer its natural effervescence). Each yeast, however, also has its own character which is skilfully harnessed and preserved by brewery chemists. Many breweries use the same yeasts for decades, ensuring that the brewery maintains its own style and individuality.

During the first few days of fermentation, the yeast works furiously with the wort, growing quickly and covering the top with a thick, undulating duvet of foam. Most is skimmed off, but some sinks into the brew and continues to work, eating up the sugars and generating more carbon dioxide and alcohol. Lager beers are known as 'bottom fermenting', because the yeast they use sinks to the bottom of the wort, rather than lying on the top. A few days later, this 'primary fermentation' is deemed over and bottle-conditioned beers and other, 'processed' bottled beers go their separate ways.

Life and death

Processed, or 'bright', beers are chilled, filtered and pasteurised, effectively killing off and removing any yeast still in the brew. They are then put into bottles and carbonated. Some of these beers are given time at the brewery beforehand to mature. Other beers follow a halfway-house system whereby the beer is sterile filtered to remove the yeast, but is not pasteurised. These, strictly speaking, do not condition in the bottle and generally have a fairly short shelf-life, but they do have a fresher taste than heavily pasteurised beers.

For bottle-conditioned beers, however, the next stage varies from brewery to brewery. Some breweries adopt the simplest form of bottle conditioning. They just siphon the beer from a cask or tank into the bottle, yeast and all. This can be a rather hit and miss affair, as not enough yeast may get into the bottle to ensure a good secondary fermentation and the beer may be rather flat when opened. Other breweries take greater pains to ensure their beers have just the right level of fizz. They fine or filter out the tired old yeast and replace it with fresh yeast, which may be a special strain that works well in bottles. The technically precise check the yeast count under the microscope to guarantee that the right amount of yeast is present.

Some brewers 'kräusen' the beer ready for bottling. This involves adding an amount of partially fermented wort to the beer to give the yeast new sugars to react with and so generate more life. Others prime the beer, using sugar solutions which again provide the yeast with something new to feed on. Once capped and labelled, bottles are often warm-conditioned at the brewery for a few weeks before going on sale, to ensure that the secondary fermentation gets off to a good start.

There's Something Wrong with My Beer

If you want boring consistency, choose a pasteurised beer (but look out for the wet paper or cardboard notes that all too often indicate that pasteurised beer has become oxidised). If, on the other hand, you want the ultimate bottled beer experience, choose bottle-conditioned beer. However, by definition, real ale in a bottle is a living product and part of the trade off for the ripe, deep flavours is the fact that sometimes things can go wrong.

Most often this is a result of lack of care at the brewery or during bottling. The most successful bottle conditioners have learned that absolute sterility in the brewhouse is paramount, to avoid unwanted bacteria turning the beer sour. These bacteria may not have much effect in a cask beer, which is drunk within a month or so, but left to their own devices in a bottle for several months, they can cause havoc. When this is the case, it is usually obvious from the first sniff and, believe me, you won't feel inclined to take a sip!

Scrupulous bottlers ensure that any yeast in the bottle is clean and pure and they bottle under the most rigid circumstances, keeping out damaging oxygen. Sometimes, however, the bottler's work is all in vain as failure to look after the bottles somewhere in the supply chain (or even in your own larder!) can lead to disappointment. Remember to keep bottles upright, cool and away from the glare of bright lights.

Tasting Times

There's a widespread perception that drinking in the pub is okay, because it's a fun, gregarious activity, but that drinking at home is a sad step on the lonely road to ruin. Let me dispell that myth immediately: if you have just flipped the cap on a bottle of beer and have settled back into your armchair, I can tell you that you are not alone. Many drinkers are doing the same thing. However much they love the camaraderie of the boozer, they understand that, in many ways, someone who is serious about beer is often better placed to appreciate its qualities at home.

This is because you have complete control. You can give your beer your undivided attention, you can savour the aromas and delicate flavours of the drink in your hand without the smell of chips and cigarette smoke getting in the way, and you can dictate exactly how your beer is served. You even have a greater choice of beers to call upon, so you needn't stick to a pint of the usual. If you're adventurous, you can go the whole hog and set yourself up a little tasting session.

Beer lovers may be united by their love of the drink but they are divided by beers themselves. Some prefer their ales hoppy and bitter; other like their lagers buttery and floral. As a bit of fun, why not put together a small selection of bottles that will illustrate this diversity? You could opt for completely different beer styles, as an insight into the heritage of beer. Choose a mild, a bitter, a stout, a porter and a barley wine, as a flavour of traditional British brewing, and then, on another occasion, cast your eyes beyond these shores for a wider understanding of the beer world. Pick up a pilsner, a German wheat beer, an American craft beer, a Trappist ale and a Belgian fruit beer. Alternatively, you could major on IPAs, drawing together a range of beers that follow that style, or do the same for imperial Russian stouts. What about lining up a choice of beers seasoned with different hops, so that you can try to figure out the flavour characteristics of each strain?

The more the merrier

Tasting is a fun pastime for one, but there's no denying it's even better among friends. Beer is the world's most sociable drink, so consider dragging a few mates out of the pub to share a tasting with you now and again. Impress them with the range of beers you've laid on and get everyone talking about the wonders of beer. Just as you don't need to be a wine buff to enjoy wine, you don't need to be a beer bore to discuss hops and malt either. If you want to be serious, provide pen and paper for tasters to make notes, but otherwise make it a light-hearted occasion.

It goes without saying that the first thing to organise is your range of beers. Try to follow a pattern, along the lines suggested on the previous page. Ideally, choose about half a dozen beers (tasting more may confuse the palate), make sure that you buy enough beer to go around and keep some bottles in reserve in case your friends demand more! Ensure the beers have been stored properly and that the sediment in each bottle has been given time to settle. Cool the beers to the appropriate temperatures, so that they are served in the best possible condition.

Keeping some bottle-conditioned beers in the fridge for too long, or at too low a temperature, may result in a hazy beer (as harmless proteins become visible), but most beers can be cooled effectively in a standard domestic fridge within an hour or so. For ales, which should be poured cool but not cold (or if you have too many beers to go in the fridge), a larder, cellar or garage may be even better. Buckets of cool water provide another alternative. For lagers and wheat beers more drastic chilling is usually required. Guidance is offered for each beer in this book.

Choosing your glass

Next provide the glassware. You don't need to go down the Belgian route of having the right shaped glass for every beer, however appealing that may be. You could just settle for a large wine glass that will allow you to swirl the beer and assess the aromas properly. When tasting a range of beers, it is often useful to re-try early samples, so a number of glasses per taster may be required. Some off-licences will hire out glassware – even plastic tumblers will do at a push, though not ideal – but, as an alternative, you can simply have a couple of glasses for each taster and rinse them out as you go along, keeping enough beer back for refills.

Make sure that the glasses are not warm. One of the most annoying and all too common failings of bar staff is serving beer in a glass that has just come out of the dishwasher and is still warm to touch. The heat not only negates any cooling the beer has had but also speeds up flavour loss and oxidation. A useful procedure is to fill each glass with cold water and leave it to stand, emptying it only when you're ready to pour the beer. This cools the glass and the wetness helps control the froth if the beer is lively.

Another advantage of drinking at home is that you can dictate not only your own glassware but also the

Buying and Storing

Because it is a living, working product, real ale in a bottle needs a little extra attention before you drink it. Just like cask ale in a pub, it benefits from care and respect, but a few ground rules make it simple:

Buy fresh stock
Although bottle-conditioned beers sometimes mature beautifully in the bottle (particularly strong, malty ales), buy the freshest beer you can (check the best before dates) and, with only a few exceptions, drink it sooner, rather than later.

Keep it dark
Most beer bottles are dark brown. This is for a purpose. The opacity of the glass protects the beer from being 'sunstruck' – a chemical reaction caused by bright light that leads to unpleasant flavours and 'skunky' aromas. To help the bottles do their job, store them in as near a light-free zone as possible. Be particularly careful with clear or green glass bottles, which may look nice but are woefully inadequate in protecting beer.

Keep it cool
Low temperatures preserve beer. When it comes to serving temperatures, follow the advice on the label.

Keep it upright
Unless the bottle has a cork, in which case it is best stored lying down, to keep the cork moist, bottled beers should be stored vertically. If you do lay down a beer, remember to put it back upright a few days before drinking to allow the sediment to settle.

amount of beer you put into it. Swirling a small quantity in a wine glass is a much easier way of assessing the aroma of a beer than sticking your nose into a brim-full pint. Bottle-conditioned beer, of course, contains a sediment so you may find it useful to decant each beer into a jug first. Open the bottles carefully, squeezing the cap with a bottle opener to allow the first hiss of carbonation to escape. Then slowly remove the cap and allow the beer to stand for a minute or so to vent off a little more carbonation. Pour gently, allowing the beer to trickle in at an angle, thus helping to keep the foam under control (too much foam, if not appropriate for the beer, can change its balance, as hop flavour, in particular, transfers to the head; lagers and wheat beers often benefit from a good foam top). If emptying the bottle, hold it and the jug/glass up to the light as you pour. You can then see when the sediment is nearing the neck of the bottle and stop pouring.

As a general rule, start your tasting with the weakest beer and work upwards in strength, perhaps keeping dark beers with a strong roasted malt content back to the end, to avoid swamping the palate. The first stage of tasting comes not with the mouth, or the nose, but with the eye. There is no doubt that you can be positively or negatively led towards a beer simply from liking or disliking its appearance. The colour and clarity may be appealing or unattractive, but a greater factor is the carbonation. A flat, lifeless beer looks very unappetising and an overly-gassy beer can be similarly daunting.

Swirl and sniff

Go for the aroma next. Give your beer a good swirl then take a deep sniff. You may need a few sniffs to really sort out the complex scents which arise. These come from the various ingredients used in the brew (malt, hops, etc.), but also result from the brewing process, which throws up the most unlikely characteristics, like exotic fruits. These aromatic emissions are known as esters and arise from the activity of the yeast. In lower gravity beers, the fruitiness is usually light and citrous; in stronger, heavy beers more pronounced fruity characteristics like banana and pear drops may be apparent.

It is fascinating to pour out a selection of beers and assess all their aromas first, before drinking any of them. By the time you have assessed the last beer, the aroma of the first is likely to have developed somewhat as the beer has become exposed to the air and carbonation has begun to dissipate. Sniff again and see what you find this time. When you actually get around to drinking some beer, the aroma element is still active, particularly when you swallow and the aroma escapes from the back of your throat through your nose.

When tasting beer, give it time in your mouth for full appreciation. You may be tempted to knock it back, but it pays to wash the beer over your tongue, allowing each taste-sensitive part to do its job and pick up the salt, sour, sweet and bitter characteristics and other flavours. You will also be able to judge the body (is it light or heavy, smooth or rough, creamy or grainy?) and the degree of condition (the amount of dissolved carbon dioxide in the beer). Without good condition, a beer is unappealing and flat on the tongue; too much condition and the beer can be sharp and prickly to drink.

Most beer descriptions centre on malt and hops, these

being the main components of the beer. Malt is usually sweetish (from the maltose sugar it contains) and can have a grainy, nutty or biscuity taste. Dark malts bring roasted flavours, including coffee and chocolate. Malt can also be responsible for dryness in a beer. Hops provide bitterness but much more besides. They can taste peppery, spicy, herbal, fruity, citrous, floral and grassy. On top of malt and hops, fruity esters introduce all sorts of intriguing flavours.

Bear in mind, however, that everyone's taste perceptions differ. Your detection (of bitterness, hoppiness, sweetness, maltiness, etc.) may not be as great as your friends' but your tasting experience may be wider, allowing you to recall and compare exotic flavours, like kiwi fruit, mangoes or black cherries, that they have never encountered. This book may help start the debate. What I have attempted to do for the featured beers is pick out the flavours that were obvious to me. But the tasting notes are merely a snapshot. As the merit of bottle-conditioned beers lies in the fact that they mature in the bottle, the notes should only be used as a guide to the broad flavourings and the general style of the beer. Taste for yourself and see what you can find.

Don't spit: swallow

Thankfully, beer tasting, unlike wine tasting, requires you to swallow and not spit, as the aftertaste is important. How often have you sat in a pub and enjoyed the lingering taste in your mouth after a good gulp of beer? You probably recognise, too, that this aftertaste is not quite the same as the beer tastes when in the mouth. This is because certain attributes (particularly bitterness) last longer or become more apparent later. Between each beer, it is always a good idea to rinse your palate with water, so provide jugs and separate glasses (still, bottled water has the cleanest taste). You may also think about putting out a plate of plain crackers, which can help cleanse the mouth of strong flavours.

Finally, one aspect of beer tasting that is often overlooked is quantity. There's no question that your opinion of a beer can change the more you drink (even before you reach the intoxication stage). So why confine beer tastings to the odd sip? After sampling the range, drink up the bottles – unlikely to be a problem with friends in tow – and then make up your mind. See how your perceptions have altered since the first mouthful.

When you've organised one tasting, you can easily follow it up with more. The possibilities are endless – far more menu combinations even than McDonald's – and every new bottle opened is a voyage of discovery.

Exotic Treats

The dramatic rise in the number of bottled real ales brewed in the UK is mirrored by an ever-expanding range of quality imported brews. Indeed, the UK has arrived late in recognising the value of bottle conditioning. In other countries, Belgium in particular, bottle-conditioned beer has been revered for decades. These Belgian classics lead the way in this survey of exotic treats that are now relatively easy to find.

Who would have thought that one of the most popular beers with young British drinkers would be a spiced wheat beer from Belgium? **Hoegaarden** (5%), bittersweet, easy-drinking and flavoured with coriander and curaçao, may be mass market and owned by the mighty Interbrew group but its influence in encouraging young people to look at 'beers with bits in' should not be underestimated. The brewery also produces **Hoegaarden Grand Cru** (8.7%), strong, flowery and bittersweet.

Dentergems Witbier (5%), from the Riva brewery in Dentergem, is one of Hoegaarden's competitors and is similarly cloudy, but drier. **Brugs Tarwebier** (4.8%) is another *witbier*, now owned by Scottish & Newcastle subsidiary Alken-Maes. It has a quenching, scented, bitter lemon taste, and a dry 'tonic water' finish. Making inroads into this market are two heavily-sponsored, 5% Dutch beers. **Wieckse Witte** is owned by Heineken and, with its light lemon, slightly toffeeish flavour and spicy bitterness, is vying for Hoegaarden's crown with **Korenwolf**, imported by Coors. The latter takes its name from the imaginative Dutch term for a hamster (literally 'corn wolf') and is brewed with four different cereals.

Abbey habits

Spiced wheat beers aside, Belgium is primarily noted for strong, robust ales, many with a monastic background. **Chimay** 7% (with a red cap) is a fruity, malty and crisp beer from a Trappist brewery near the border with France. Its two brothers are quite different in character. Chimay 8% (with a white cap) is extremely hoppy and filled with bitter orange fruit, while Chimay 9% (with a blue cap) is full, smooth and malty with fruit notes and a renowned port-like finish. **Westmalle Dubbel** (7%) comes from the largest Trappist brewery and is particularly complex. Spice, banana, dark fruits and other items have been detected and there is a distinct trace of almonds. **Orval** (6.2%) originates in the monastery of the same name in the Belgian Ardennes. It is a world classic, a fascinating amber ale that is both bitter and fruitily acidic. Also in the verdant Ardennes is the **Rochefort** brewery. Its beers are numbered rather than named. The one called **8** is light-drinking for its 9.2%, tasting spicy, peppery and fruity. Stand back, or better sit down, for **10**, which at 11.3% is a dreamy way to round off a day, offering a peppery and dry taste, with some background fruit.

Only beers brewed by Trappist monks qualify to wear the Trappist habit; beers in the same vein produced elsewhere (sometimes under licence from a monastic order) have to make do with the 'Abbey beer' classification. Schaapskooi, brewer of La Trappe, was one of the stalwart Trappist production centres, and the only one in the Netherlands, but then the brewery was bought by Dutch giant Bavaria and the Trappist title had to be surrendered. **La Trappe Dubbel** (6.5%) is still brewed at the brewery, and is sweet, malty and winey. Look also for its **Tripel** (8%) and even **Quadrupel** (10%). However, the Trappist quota had already been upped by the arrival into brewing of monks at **Achel**, on the Belgian/Dutch border. Its range of new beers includes the 8% **Blonde** – a peppery, bittersweet, dryish beer.

Thanks to filtered beers like Leffe and Grimbergen, Abbey beers are featuring in many trendy UK bars. These two are owned, respectively, by Interbrew and S&N. Heineken was one big European brewer that did not have an Abbey brand to call its own until a couple of years ago. Then it bought up the Belgian Affligem brewery. Much investment has taken place at the site (which, like most Abbey breweries, is some distance from the cloisters that provide the name). The first step towards conquering Britain has come with **Affligem Blonde**, a 6%, softly malty ale with a clean, crisp spiciness, that has been marked down in strength for its UK audience (it is 6.8% at home).

Among other abbey treats are **Tripel Karmeliet** (8%)

Reading the Labels

To discover which beers from other countries are bottle conditioned, look for the words that mean 'with yeast' or 'bottle-fermented'. In German, seek out *mit hefe*, *Flaschengärung* or *naturtrüb* ('naturally cloudy'), but avoid *hefefrei* and *ohne hefe* as these mean yeast-free. For Belgian beers you need the benefit of two languages. In French and Flemish respectively, the words to find are *sur levure*, *sur lie* or *op gist* (all meaning 'with yeast sediment'), or *refermentée en bouteille*, *fermentation en bouteille*, *hergist in de fles* and *nagisting in de fles* ('bottle-fermented'). Dutch and Flemish are very similar, so on Dutch beer labels spot the words *op gist* or *met gist*.

---

from Bosteels brewery, better known for its 8% beer, Kwak. The flavour combines sweet malt, strong toffee, hints of lemon, an oaty creaminess and spicy hops. **Abbaye des Rocs** (9%) does not originate in an abbey, as it name implies, but in a modern brewery established in the 1980s, close to the French border. The beer is rich, fruity and spicy. The brewery also produces a strong wheat beer (6%) called **Blanche des Honnelles**.

It's easy to think that every Belgian beer has a holy background, but this is not so: some have alternative connections. Famous **Duvel** (8.5%) is the 'devil of a beer' from the Moortgat brewery, north of Brussels. It has a full zesty bitterness, subtle pear fruit and a surprisingly light body for its strength. **Barbār** (8%) is a honey beer brewed by Lefèbvre, south-west of Brussels. Despite the honey, the beer is bitter rather than sweet, with heavy fruit and malt flavours. **Delirium Tremens** (9%) comes in a stone-effect bottle and should not be dismissed as a gimmick. Brewed near Ghent by Huyghe, it has a complex, mouth-numbing taste which mixes fruit cocktail flavours with hop bitterness. **Gouden Carolus Classic**, at 8.5%, comes from Het Anker ('The Anchor') brewery in Mechelen and is mellow and toffeeish.

Among the newer breweries in Belgium is **Achouffe**. Oddbins have been supporters of their big, Champagne-like bottles, of which the most popular are probably **La Chouffe**, an 8% coriandered blonde with bitter fruit notes, and the ruby **McChouffe**, an attempt to merge Belgian and Scottish styles, resulting in a malty, 8.5% brew.

Silly season

One other Belgian style emerging in the UK is the *saison* – a summer ale. The two most prominent examples come from Silly and Dupont. **Silly**, as has been pointed out time and again, is simply the name of the brewery's town and its 5% beer is similarly no joke. Deep raisiny, figgy fruit flavours and plenty of malt would imply that this is a rather heavy beer. Instead, it drinks sweet and light. **Vieille Provision**, to give the Dupont *saison* its full title, is a touch stronger at 6.5%, and closer to what is expected from a summer beer, crisp, herbal and gently bitter with an orange acidity.

Most of the connoisseur beers of France tend not to be bottle conditioned. Many *bières de gardes* (literally, 'beers for keeping'), which have been matured at the brewery, like Jenlain, Ch'ti and Trois Monts, fall into this category. However there are bottle-conditioned products in circulation. They tend to follow the Belgian wheat and Abbey footprints, with highlights including **Gavroche**

(8.5%) from the St-Sylvestre brewery and Breton beers like **Britt Blanche** (4.8%), a spicy wheat beer, the amber **Coreff** (5%) from Deux Rivières brewery, and **Lancelot** (6%) and **Duchesse Anne** (6.5%), from the Lancelot brewery. Jenlain's brewers, Duyck, also turn out an organic, naturally fermented beer called **La Fraîche de L'Aunelle** (5.5%), while the Bécu brewery has a choice of beers under the **L'Atrébate** banner, of which the spicy, malty, 7% Brune has impressed most.

German wheats and other treats

Germany's great bottle-conditioned offering is the *weissbier*. As a style this was all but dead a few decades ago, but it has bounced back. **Schneider Weisse** (5.4 %) is one of the most highly rated such wheat beers. Brewed just north of Munich, it is spicy, dry and very fruity (banana), with a touch of sourness. **Aventinus** (8%), another Schneider beer, is an amazingly complex but very drinkable beer with a full, smooth, fairly sweet and malty taste, well supported by bananas and spice.

Carrying the *weissbier* torch in the UK have been beers such as **Schöfferhofer** (5%), brewed by the German national brewer Binding, which has a pleasant clove-spice edge, and the likes of **Erdinger** and **Franziskaner**. **Weihenstephaner Hefe Weissbier** (5.4%) comes from what is claimed to be the world's oldest brewery, just north of Munich, and is appley, with banana and clove. The brewery's **Dunkel** (5.3%) is a dark wheat beer, featuring malt, cloves and a slight sourness. The award-winning **Hopf Weisse** (5.3%), also from Bavaria, is imported by Cains, while Refresh UK is now pushing **Löwen Weiss** (5.2%) from Munich's Löwenbräu brewery. There are also 'own label' wheat beers brewed in Germany for various UK supermarkets. However, when choosing German wheats, remember that beers labelled *kristalweissbier* are filtered, but *hefeweissbier* and *hefeweizenbier* mean the beer contains yeast.

Few examples of American bottle-conditioned beers, sadly, make their way across the Atlantic. **Sierra Nevada** claims its excellent beers are bottle-conditioned, but there is very little yeast in the bottles. The same applies to the gloriously hoppy, 5.9% **Goose Island IPA**, from Chicago. However, look for **Bridgeport** and **Deschutes** breweries, both in Oregon, with their IPA and Bachelor ESB (5.7%) respectively, plus other brews.

Galbraith's well-regarded beers from New Zealand are about to break in the UK, but the last word goes to **Coopers Sparkling Ale** (5.8%), from Adelaide. Served cloudy, it packs a fresh fruity taste and is one beer that reflects positively on the Australian brewing industry.

Green for Go?

As the number of organic beers listed in this book reveals, British brewers are increasingly doing their bit for the environment. But brewing organically is no easy option.

Ingredients grown free of pesticides remain rare and costly. The number of organic varieties of barley available to the brewer is still small and, when it comes to the malting process, coloured malts, in particular, have been slow to come on stream. Hops, too, belong to a seller's market. New Zealand Hallertau are the most popular, although there are now a small number of organic hop growers in Britain, to add more variety.

At the brewery, even assuming that raw ingredients are of good quality and affordable, there are other factors to deter the brewer. Strict demarcation has to be observed between organic and non-organic goods moving in and out, and there's a wealth of paperwork to complete. Even wetting the malt presents a challenge. Burtonising is officially ruled out and only certain minerals are allowed to help adjust the pH of the brewing liquor.

Despite such difficulties, it's clear that many brewers show a strong commitment to the cause of ecology. It's easy to be cynical and suggest that maybe some see a commercial advantage in wearing green clothes. But, considering the low level of organic beer sales at present, and the hassle involved, they must have remarkable foresight if this is the case. Anyone who shares their concern for the environment will be happy to pay a few pennies extra for a bottle and lend some support. But if, beyond such goodwill, the success of organic brewing has to fall back on the tried and tested benchmark of taste, the evidence from researching this book is that beers produced in this way will certainly not be found wanting.

Organic Brewers

The following brewers produce organic beers featured in this book. Many have official organic accreditation; others simply declare that they use organic ingredients. See the relevant entries for further details.

Alewife	North Yorkshire
Bartrams	O'Hanlon's
Black Isle	Old Chimneys
Bragdy Ceredigion	Organic
Bragdy Ynys Môn	Pitfield
Butts	Quay
Hopdaemon	Refresh UK

Beer on the Table

It's some years now since the late, lamented Inspector Morse chastised poor Sgt Lewis for asking him if he was going to have anything to eat on a lunchtime. 'Beer is food, Lewis', he gruffly retorted. And indeed it is. But Lewis certainly had a point. Man cannot live by beer alone, as some of Britain's biggest breweries have been stressing in the past year or so as they have made considerable efforts to persuade drinkers that beer and food make a worthy match.

Taking a leaf out of the Belgians' book, where *cuisine à la bière* has developed over centuries, brewers like Coors, Scottish Courage, Hall & Woodhouse and particularly Greene King, with its 'Beer to Dine For' campaign, have been banging the drum for beer, employing top chefs to make the case that, as drinks go, beer takes some beating as a companion for food.

Compare and contrast

The first thing they've had to do is to suggest that wine and food, as a combination, is old hat and that the sommelier's days may be numbered. On reflection, it is indeed surprising that wine has such a grip on the market. After all, the best that wine, with its dominant fruitiness, can do is offer contrast to the food on your plate. Beer, on the other hand, can certainly provide a counterpoint but it can also marry beautifully with the flavours in your meal. There are so many different characteristics to beer, from hoppy or malty to spicy or chocolatey, fruity or creamy and so on, that there is literally a beer for each dining occasion.

Let's munch our way through a typical few courses. Beginning with an aperitif, what could perk up the palate better than a sharp, hoppy bitter or a tart and spritzy Belgian fruit beer? For starters, a malty ale is a perfect balance for a rich pâté, and the floral, citrous notes of a genuine pilsner are a treat with delicate fish or even something more complex like smoked salmon. Disraeli, after a heavy night in the House, once famously dined on oysters and stout, which, like Darby and Joan or Morecambe and Wise simply belong together.

Main course beef demands a robust ale – a hoppy Northern bitter, perhaps – whereas roast pork may appreciate the appley flavours of a Bavarian-style wheat beer. Lamb is best offset by something with a malty, spicy character – a French *bière de garde*, has been suggested – and chicken and light poultry are enhanced by the lemon notes of a German *helles* lager or a wheat beer from the same country. For spicy foods there are now spicy beers. Hop Back, for example, brews Taiphoon, containing lemongrass, specifically to balance Thai and other oriental dishes. For barbecues look towards the dark, smoky maltiness of a German *rauchbier* or a strong mild. Even salads have more zip with a crisp, floral bitter to wash them down.

When it comes to puddings and cheeses, wine is way out of its depth. A fruity bitter with a ploughman's lunch merely hints at the fun to be had matching beer with more complex cheeses. A ripe Stilton comes even more alive with a glass of old ale at its side. Belgian fruit beers work nicely with fruity tarts, or even white chocolate, while anyone who has yet to try a glass of stout with a chocolate pudding has missed out on one of the great culinary treats. After dinner, wind down with the beer equivalent of a port, a heady Trappist ale perhaps, a barley wine, or the complexities of a *weizenbock*, such as Schneider's Aventinus from southern Germany.

Quantity is what puts off most people when drinking beer with food. The thought of having to sink a pint with each course or down a bottle per person can be daunting and will, of course, diminish the appetite and blunt the palate. But that's where bottled beers come into their own. You can easily share a bottle or two among friends and some brewers now provide larger bottles just for this purpose. The other advantage of bottles is that you can load the table with plenty of variety, keeping your guests guessing and sharpening up their appetites with something new and exciting for each course.

Menu planning

The table opposite illustrates some noted beer and food combinations you may wish to consider, and throughout this book brewers have offered their own suggestions for food marriages with their beers. You may find it useful, if you're planning to stage a beer dinner, to choose dishes that allow beers to progress from light to dark, quaffable to heavy, throughout the meal. But be adventurous and remember that taste is entirely personal.

If you plan to cook with beer, marinading meats and fish, or splashing into stews and sauces, you may find it better to serve a different beer with the dish. The same beer you've added to the saucepan may just get lost in the flavour balance and you'll probably need a little more variation to bring out the best in what you've cooked.

White wine with fish and red wine with meat is now a discredited maxim, but it may not be long before the even simpler 'wine with food' idea goes the same way. 'Bon appétit', as French brewers say.

The Flavour Match

Before Dining
Aperitifs	Pilsners; milds; hoppy bitters; Belgian wheat beers and fruit beers

Starters
Soups:	
Vegetable	Pale bitters
Meaty	Malty ales
Shellfish	Stouts; porters; Belgian wheat beers
Fish	Pilsners; German lagers; light bitters; Belgian wheat beers
Pâté	Milds; strong dark lagers
Quiches/soufflés	Light bitters

Main Courses
Beef	Full-bodied bitters
Pork	Pilsners; Bavarian wheat beers; strong dark lagers
Lamb	Spicy, malty ales; dark lagers
Chicken	Lagers; wheat beers
Turkey	Malty ales
Duck	Kriek
Game	Malty ales; Trappist ales
Meat pies	Full-bodied bitters
Sausages	Full-bodied bitters; dark lagers; Bavarian wheat beers
Barbecue	Smoked beers; dark lagers
Oriental	Wheat beers; ginger/spiced beers
Curries	Strong IPAs; premium lagers
Salads	Floral-hopped bitters; nutty, malty ales; wheat beers
Pizzas	Malty lagers
Ploughman's	Hoppy, fruity bitters

Cheeses
Mild	Light bitters
Stronger	Full-bodied ales
Mature/blue	Trappist ales; old ales; barley wines

Desserts
Chocolate/coffee	Porters; stouts; Belgian fruit beers
Red berry	Porters
Apple/banana	Bavarian wheat beers
Creamy	Stouts
Spiced	Bavarian wheat beers

Guests of Honour

'Why does the *Good Bottled Beer Guide* only feature *bottle-conditioned* beers?' is a question occasionally asked. The simple answer is that, just as the CAMRA *Good Beer Guide* focuses only on draught real ales (cask-conditioned beers), its companion volume concentrates only on real ale in a bottle (bottle-conditioned beers). Real ale, defined in the *Oxford English Dictionary* as 'beer which has been brewed and stored in the traditional way, and which has undergone a secondary fermentation in the container from which it is dispensed', is a living, maturing product. It is not filtered, pasteurised or artificially carbonated. It usually has a lighter texture, more depth of flavour and an appetising freshness, if cared for properly. CAMRA firmly believes that this process produces the best possible beers and its major guidebooks inevitably reflect this conviction. It is the Campaign for Real Ale, after all.

Nevertheless, CAMRA's policy on bottled beers does extend a little wider than the technical strictures of bottle conditioning effectively allow. CAMRA also recognises the skills and traditions that lie behind a handful of other bottled beers from the British Isles. These beers, while regrettably not naturally fermenting in the bottle, do at least have a remarkable tale to tell. They are the last survivors of fading beer styles and should be encouraged to remain in production.

Monastic tradition

Consider Greene King's **Strong Suffolk** Vintage Ale. This 6% ABV beer harks back to the monastic tradition of blending beers. The main element of the brew is a dark, vinous beer known as 5X that has been allowed to stagger up to 13% alcohol and then rest for two years under the influence in 100-barrel oak vats. The vats are covered by a layer of marl – a chalky soil found around the brewery's Suffolk home – which helps seal the beer from wild yeasts. When ready, it is blended with a young, fresh brew called BPA to create a wonderfully complex bottled beer. Neither 5X nor BPA are sold individually.

While the tradition of ageing and blending young and old beers remains in other countries – highlighted in Belgium by the classic sour red beer, Rodenbach, for instance – it has all but died out in the UK. It could be argued that the beer would taste even better, and have more of a future if bottle conditioned, but CAMRA is certainly not going to ignore a beer of such heritage and quality only to see it wither and die. Not that there is much evidence of this at present. Greene King is firmly committed to the beer and in recent years has added new vats for 5X production.

A similar beer is brewed in Dublin. Guinness Original may no longer be bottle conditioned in the UK, and is thus a shadow of its former self, but the Irish giant does brew a remarkable stronger version, known as **Foreign Extra Stout**. Like Strong Suffolk, the beer is a blend of young and aged ales and at 7.5% is a profound, full-bodied drink with rich roasted notes but also a hint of lactic sourness from the mature beer at its heart. Foreign Extra Stout was first exported from Ireland at the turn of the 19th century. For some reason, it was not sold in the UK for many years, but it made a welcome return in the 1990s. Travellers will find an even stronger version (8%) on sale in other European countries.

In Scotland, a taste of local brewing from the past lives on in **Traquair House Ale**. This 7.2%, dark ale was developed by the late laird, Peter Maxwell Stuart, at his family home in the Borders. Traquair House had a brewery in the 18th century, Peter restored it in 1965 and this beer harks back to the Scottish art of producing strong, complex, malty ales, as well as keeping alive the concept of country house brewing.

Vintage Harvest

One further beer to mention belongs to a different tradition. **Harvest Ale**, from Lees in Manchester, is already a world classic, despite only being launched in 1986. The beer is brewed every October/November, with new season Maris Otter malt and Golding hops boiled for three hours in the copper to produce a reddish-brown colour. Although not bottle conditioned, its formidable 11.5% alcohol allows the beer to mature in the bottle, so that various vintages can be compared. To ignore this particular beer on the grounds that it does not ferment in the bottle would be foolish. Apart from tasting magnificent, it showcases the culture of brewing celebratory beers from the year's first crops of barley and hops. It is also one of the few genuine barley wines in circulation and thus a flagship for this stuttering style.

Rules are there to be broken, the old adage says, but CAMRA does not do so lightly. Please do not confuse these four remarkable beers with run of the mill beers that have been filtered and pasteurised purely for convenience, at the expense of taste. Strong Suffolk, Foreign Extra Stout, Traquair House Ale and Harvest Ale may not qualify for the *Good Bottled Beer Guide* on technical grounds, but they are there in spirit and certainly deserve these honourable mentions.

How the Guide Is Organised

The *Good Bottled Beer Guide* contains details of all known bottle-conditioned beers being brewed in the UK at the time of going to press. The beers are listed by brewery (which is briefly described), and within each brewery beers are listed in increasing order of strength. For each beer the following information is given: alcohol by volume percentage (ABV – the beer's strength), bottle size and ingredients. Suggested serving temperatures have been simplified to 'cold', 'cool' and 'room temperature', as gauging the precise temperature of a beer is always difficult. Cool is estimated to be around 12°C, or the correct temperature for cask ale in a pub.

Beers featured in this book are mostly sold locally, through farmers' markets, small grocers, craft shops and delicatessens. Some breweries also sell direct to the public, but this may be by the case only, and some offer a mail order service, which is mentioned if relevant. Otherwise beers can be obtained through specialist off-licences or mail order companies, many of which are listed in the Beer Shops section at the back of the book. If a beer has a listing with a major retailer (supermarket or off-licence chain), this is indicated in the entry. However, where beers are actually sold is inevitably subject to change, so it is suggested that readers contact the breweries for up to date details of retailers.

The tasting notes are purely the views of the author. Because bottle-conditioned beers are likely to change character during their shelf life, the flavour balance and level of condition may vary. These notes are therefore offered only as a basic guide. For more details of all the breweries featured, and for information about the cask beers they produce, see CAMRA's annual *Good Beer Guide*.

Acknowledgements

Much appreciation is offered to numerous people for their assistance in the compilation of this book. These include CAMRA's brewery liaison officers, brewers who kindly forwarded details of their beers and sample bottles, CAMRA's Research Manager, Iain Loe, and beer importer James Clay (for help with beers from overseas).

Any brewers who would like to make sure their beers are featured in the next edition are welcome to contact Jeff Evans, via CAMRA at: 230 Hatfield Road, St Albans, Hertfordshire AL1 4LW (e-mail: camra@camra.org.uk).

ALEWIFE

Alewife Brewery, Starston, Harleston, Norfolk IP20 9NN.
Tel. (01379) 855267
E-mail: alewifebrewery@yahoo.co.uk
Web site: www.alewifebrewery.co.uk
Mail order service

This tiny brewery was set up by Jane Taylor in 2000 after encouragement from friends who admired her home brewing skills. She named the brewery – based in a little village off the A143 in Norfolk – after the historic alewife, a woman brewer who in centuries past produced beer at home as part of her household duties and placed a broom by the gate to show when her ale was ready. The broom now forms part of the brewery's logo. Jane seldom brews draught beer, because of the weight of casks, but focuses instead on bottles and runs a mail order service from her web site. The malts used in her beers are organically produced.

HARVEST ALE

ABV 4.5%　　　**Bottle size** 500 ml　　　**Serve** cool
Ingredients Pale malt; crystal malt; Challenger hops

This was Jane's first commercial beer and it remains her most popular. She bottles it direct from a cask or the conditioning tank, like her other beers.

DARK SKIES STOUT

ABV 4.6%　　　**Bottle size** 500 ml　　　**Serve** cool
Ingredients Pale malt; chocolate malt; Styrian Golding hops

A stout first produced in early 2001. It makes a perfect match for curries and other spicy food, according to Jane.

FESTIVAL ALE

ABV 6.5%　　　**Bottle size** 500 ml　　　**Serve** cool
Ingredients Pale malt; chocolate malt; roasted barley; Golding hops

Originally a celebration beer for the new millennium, Festival Ale, says Jane, makes a great accompaniment for a slice of rich fruit cake. The beer is matured for several months before bottling.

HUNTERS MOON

ABV 6.8%   **Bottle size** 500 ml   **Serve** cool
Ingredients Pale malt; crystal malt; hops undeclared

Brewed only for special occasions, this complex, potent
brew incorporates a mix of English hops.
Tasting Notes
A complex ruby ale with a creamy, malty nose laced
with a hint of bubblegum. Dark malt and a sharp,
raspberry fruitiness feature in the mouth, with fruit and
chocolate lingering in the finish.

B&T

**B&T Brewery Ltd., The Brewery, Shefford, Bedfordshire
SG17 5DZ. Tel. (01462) 815080 Fax (01462) 850841**
Mail order service

This Bedfordshire brewery was founded as Banks &
Taylor in 1981 and rescued from receivership by new
ownership in 1994, when the company name was
shortened to B&T. Key brewery personnel were
maintained to ensure consistency, and the name Banks
& Taylor is still used on the bottle labels. Bottling takes
place on site after one month's maturation in the cask.
The beer is allowed to drop bright and then re-seeded
with new yeast and primed with sugar. The brewery
won the *Tesco Beer Challenge* in 2002 with a bottled
version of its cask ale called SOS. The beer was brewed
by B&T and bottled by Brakspear, but the demise of the
Henley brewery coincided with the end of the exclusive
Tesco contract and this bottled beer is no longer
available.

BLACK DRAGON MILD

ABV 4.3%   **Bottle size** 500 ml   **Serve** cool
Ingredients Mild ale malt; crystal malt; black malt; roasted
barley; wheat malt; Golding hops

Brewed initially as a cask beer for CAMRA's May Mild
Month celebrations in 2001, Black Dragon found its
way into bottle later the same year.
Tasting Notes
A near-black beer that pours with a beige head. Dark
malts lead in the aroma before a bittersweet, roasted
malt and barley taste supported by fruity hop. Bitterness
builds in the dry, roasted finish.

DRAGONSLAYER

ABV 4.5%   **Bottle size** 500 ml   **Serve** cool
Ingredients Pearl pale malt; wheat malt; Challenger and
Golding hops

Taking its name from the legend of St George,
Dragonslayer was first brewed in cask form in 1992. Its
light and fruity character makes it a particularly suitable
accompaniment for white meats and pasta dishes, say
the brewers. The best before date is set at six months.
Tasting Notes
A straw-coloured ale with a spicy, fruit cocktail aroma.
To taste, it is bittersweet, malty and fruity, yet at the
same time crisp, with a little spicy hop and a trace of
liquorice. Dry, spicy hop and malt finish.

EDWIN TAYLOR'S EXTRA STOUT

ABV 4.5%   **Bottle size** 500 ml   **Serve** cool
Ingredients Pearl pale malt; brown malt; roasted barley;
Challenger hops

Named after the great-grandfather of brewery founder
Martin Ayres, Edwin Taylor's Extra Stout has been on
sale in cask form since 1991. This bottle-conditioned
version was launched in 1998 and is said to be ideal
with oysters and strong meats like game. Before
bottling, the beer is given a month longer to mature in
cask than the other beers. A seven-month best before
date is stamped on each bottle. The aforementioned Mr
Taylor was, as the label grandly declares, involved in
brewing in London in the 1890s. His great-grandson is
happy to chuckle about the more modest reality of his
profession – he was a drayman for Fremlins.
Tasting Notes
A near-black beer with a beige foam head. The aroma is
chocolatey and coffeeish, preluding a nicely balanced
taste of sweet malt, coffee, hop and roast bitterness.
Lingering, dry, roast finish.

OLD BAT

ABV 6%   **Bottle size** 500 ml   **Serve** cool
Ingredients Pearl pale malt; crystal malt; brown malt;
Fuggle hops

Originally known by the jokey name of 2XS (drink 2XS,
get it?) when first appearing in cask in 1990, this strong
bitter was renamed Old Bat when the first bottles

appeared back in 1998. The best before date is set at ten months. Good with cheese, according to the brewers.

Tasting Notes
A chestnut-coloured strong ale with a very malty and fruity (bananas) aroma, backed by a little savoury yeastiness. The same banana notes come through in the taste, which is malty and sweet. The finish is sweetish, malty and fruity, but with a little bitterness for balance.

BLACK OLD BAT

ABV 6.5%   **Bottle size** 500 ml   **Serve** cool
Ingredients Pearl pale malt; crystal malt; black malt; Fuggle hops

This winter brew is described by B&T as a 'barley wine-type porter', which perhaps sums up its complexity. It was new in cask and bottle in 1998 and is another beer to try with strong meats and cheeses. A ten months' best before period is posted on the bottle.

BALLARD'S

Ballard's Brewery Ltd., The Old Sawmill, Nyewood, Rogate, Petersfield, Hampshire GU31 5HA.
Tel. (01730) 821301/821362 Fax (01730) 821742
E-mail: carola@ballardsbrewery.org.uk
Web site: www.ballardsbrewery.org.uk

Founded in 1980 at Cumbers Farm, Trotton, Ballard's has been trading at Nyewood in West Sussex since 1988 and bottle conditioning for a number of years. Recently, it has been producing special beers for the British Museum, to tie-in with exhibitions. These have included Queen of She-Beer and Rhinoceros (Albrecht Dürer showcase) and have been sold in the museum's Digby Trout restaurant and cafeteria, as well as in the usual Ballard's outlets. All the beers are fined in a conditioning tank, sterile filtered and re-seeded with dried yeast before bottling.

BEST BITTER

ABV 4.2%   **Bottle size** 500 ml   **Serve** cool
Ingredients Pearl pale malt; crystal malt; Fuggle and Golding hops

Ballard's first ever draught beer, and its consistent best seller, was only introduced in bottled form in 2001. As for most of the other beers, the best before date is set at nine months post-bottling. One to drink with plain English cooking, according to the brewery founder, Carola Brown.

Tasting Notes
An amber beer with a malty, fruity nose. The taste is quite dry and bitter with a little malt sweetness to start and some ale-fruit character. Dry, bitter finish.

NYEWOOD GOLD

ABV 5%   **Bottle size** 500 ml   **Serve** cool
Ingredients Pearl pale malt; torrefied wheat; Phoenix hops

It's amazing what you learn just by drinking beer. For instance, 'Nye', as in the brewery address and the name of this beer, is apparently a collective noun for a group of pheasants – which, of course, appear on the label. This beer was first brewed for the 1997 *Beauty of Hops* competition, where it took top honours in the category for Phoenix hops. The same draught beer then claimed the *Best Strong Bitter* prize at the *Champion Beer of Britain* contest in 1999. It was a logical progression to bottle it for the first time the same year. Ballard's recommends serving Nyewood Gold at a slightly lower temperature than its other beers and perhaps enjoying a glass with a fish dish or a curry.

Tasting Notes
A golden ale with a soft malt and fruit nose before a bittersweet taste of malt, fruit and hop. Mellow, bittersweet, fruity finish, with soft malt lingering.

WASSAIL

ABV 6%   **Bottle size** 500 ml   **Serve** cool
Ingredients Pearl pale malt; crystal malt; Fuggle and Golding hops

Wassail is a drinking salutation, translating as 'Be whole' from Old English. This beer of the same name first appeared in cask in 1980, and in bottle in 1996, and is now produced every two months or so. The label shows Hengist, the 5th-century leader of the Jutes, toasting Vortigern, King of the Britons. Rowena, Hengist's daughter, who seduced Vortigern, is also depicted. The brewery suggests taking a glass or two with cheese, or with strong meats such as game or beef.

Tasting Notes
A russet-coloured strong ale with a meaty, malt and

fruit nose. Soft in the mouth, it tastes fruity, malty and alcoholic. The gently bitter, fruity, hoppy finish leaves a little tingle on the gums.

FOXY

ABV 9.3%   **Bottle size** 275 ml   **Serve** cool
Ingredients Pearl pale malt; crystal malt; Fuggle and Golding hops

Foxy is the latest in the Ballard's series of 'Old Bounder' beers. The brewery has been producing these for 15 years now and, until recently, adopted the novel approach of matching the alcohol by volume percentage to the last two digits of the year for which the beer was brewed. Old Bounder itself appeared in 1988, at 8.8%, and the last beer to follow this pattern was Pleasure Domes, at 10%, in 2000. However, with duty so high on such strong beers, the brewery decided to move back to the year before the series began, producing Early Daze (8.7%) and then jumping ahead to Alchemist (9.2%), before creating this 9.3% beer. The first batch of each of these beers rolls out on the first Sunday in December (as part of a charity 'beer walk') and the brew is then repeated as required throughout the next 12 months. There is a draught version, too (available over Christmas), which is aged for at least two months before dispatch to the pub. Although each bottle carries a nine-month best before date, the beer is likely to remain drinkable for much longer. Enjoy it with game, beef or cheese, add a little to a Christmas pudding, or mull it with spices and a little sugar.
Tasting Notes
A ruby ale with a malty, toffeeish, fruity nose. Malt leads in the taste which is largely bitter with a light toffeeish sweetness. Bitter, malty, toasted finish.

Availability of Beers
Beers in this book are mostly sold locally, through farmers' markets, small grocers, craft shops and delicatessens. Some breweries also sell direct to the public, but this may be by the case only, and some offer a mail order service, which is mentioned if relevant. Otherwise beers can be obtained through specialist off-licences or mail order companies, many of which are listed in the Beer Shops section at the back of the book. If a beer has a listing with a major retailer (supermarket or off-licence chain), this is indicated at the end of the entry.

BARTRAMS

**Bartrams Brewery, Rougham Estate, Rougham,
Bury St Edmunds, Suffolk IP30 9LZ.
Tel. (01449) 737655
E-mail: captainbill@lineone.net**

Marc Bartram set up his own brewery in an industrial
unit in 1999 and moved into new premises in summer
2003. An earlier Bartrams Brewery operated in
Tonbridge, Kent, between 1894 and 1920. It was run by
Captain Bill Bartram, whose image Marc wanted to use
on his beer labels and pump clips. No photograph was
found, however, so Marc grew a beard, became Captain
Bill and now features on all his beers. Each beer is
filtered and re-seeded with fresh yeast prior to bottling.
Marc now hopes to gain Soil Association accreditation
for the beers he brews using organic ingredients.

MARLD

ABV 3.4%   **Bottle size** 500 ml   **Serve** cool
Ingredients Mild ale malt; amber malt; roasted and flaked
barley; Galena and Golding hops

As for most of Marc's beers, the informative label on
this dark ruby mild declares all ingredients and also
original gravity figures.
Tasting Notes
Spicy malt and a hint of chocolate in the aroma are
followed by a malty taste, with a faint fruit note, before
a lightly roasted, dry finish in which bitterness grows.

PREMIER BITTER

ABV 3.7%   **Bottle size** 500 ml   **Serve** cool
Ingredients Maris Otter pale malt; crystal malt; chocolate
malt; Challenger, Fuggle and Golding hops

Caricatures of PMs Thatcher and Churchill have
featured on the pumpclips for the cask version of this
ale, as did the contenders at the last General Election.

LITTLE GREEN MAN

ABV 3.8%   **Bottle size** 500 ml   **Serve** cool
Ingredients Pale malt; Pacific Gem and Hallertau hops;
coriander

A more quaffable version of the 4% Green Man (see

below), like its inspiration produced with organic ingredients.

Tasting Notes
A golden, bitter ale influenced throughout by the peppery, orangey notes of subtle coriander and hops. Dry, bitter, spicy and hoppy finish.

RED QUEEN

ABV 3.9%   **Bottle size** 500 ml   **Serve** cool
Ingredients Maris Otter pale malt; crystal malt; chocolate malt; Challenger, Fuggle and Golding hops

A rich amber-coloured session ale.

Tasting Notes
Chocolate maltiness gives way to a little hop spice and citrous notes in the aroma, before balanced malt and bitterness combine in the taste, together with a clean, sweet, hoppy-citrous edge. Bitterness grows in the lightly fruity, hoppy finish.

GREEN MAN

ABV 4%   **Bottle size** 500 ml   **Serve** cool
Ingredients Pale malt; Pacific Gem, Hallertau and Perle hops; coriander

A golden best bitter made with organic ingredients. Marc may change the organic ingredients he uses slightly, depending on what becomes available in that form.

Tasting Notes
A fuller-bodied version of Little Green Man, with more malty sweetness in the taste. Sappy hops lose ground to a peachy/orangey fruitiness in the nose but re-emerge in the mouth. Dry, bitter, lightly fruity and spicy, hop finish.

PIERROT

ABV 4%   **Bottle size** 500 ml   **Serve** cool
Ingredients Maris Otter pale malt; caramalt; Fuggle, Golding, Saaz and Tettnang hops

An intriguing ale inspired by a visit Marc made to a Croatian brewery.

Tasting Notes
A golden ale with a complex, hoppy nose, hops and bitterness well balanced by malt in the taste and plenty of body for its strength. Long, hoppy finish. A hint of

bubblegum throughout adds a something of a Belgian ale character.

THE BEE'S KNEES

ABV 4.2%   **Bottle size** 500 ml   **Serve** cool
Ingredients Maris Otter pale malt; carapils malt;
Challenger, Ahtanum and Fuggle hops; wildflower honey;
coriander

As for Pierrot above, a very pale-coloured malt forms the basis of the mash for this honey-flavoured beer.
Tasting Notes
An amber beer with a floral, honeyed, hoppy aroma. There's a honey softness throughout the taste, which is otherwise crisp and bitter, with good malt balance. Dry, bitter finish with the smoothness of honey.

CATHERINE BARTRAM'S IPA

ABV 4.3%   **Bottle size** 500 ml   **Serve** cool
Ingredients Pale malt; First Gold and Fuggle hops

One Catherine Bartram was apparently a survivor of the Siege of Lucknow (1857–8) and her diary helped paint a picture of what went on during the conflict. Her Indian connections inspired this India Pale Ale.
Tasting Notes
A golden ale with an initial malty aroma which soon gives way to light, fruity hop. Tangy hop leads over malt in the taste and dominates the dry and increasingly bitter aftertaste.

JESTER QUICK ONE

ABV 4.4%   **Bottle size** 500 ml   **Serve** cool
Ingredients Maris Otter pale malt; crystal malt; chocolate malt; Ahtanum hops

A sweet, reddish bitter using American hops. Its name comes from the 'signature' (a drawn Jester) used by one of the local artists who produce Marc's pumpclips.

STINGO!

ABV 4.5%   **Bottle size** 500 ml   **Serve** cool
Ingredients Pale malt; Hallertau and Perle hops; honey; coriander

Another honey beer, made using organic ingredients. A

Norwich Beer Festival winner in its cask version.
Tasting Notes
A sweetish and fruity bitter with a hoppy nose and a
floral honey note on the swallow. Light honey softens
the mostly bitter finish.

CAPTAIN BILL BARTRAM'S BEST BITTER

ABV 4.8%　　**Bottle size** 500 ml　　**Serve** cool
Ingredients Maris Otter pale malt; crystal malt; Fuggle and
Golding hops

A tawny beer named after the brewery's inspiration.
Tasting Notes
Red berry fruits lead in the nose, edging out lightly
toasted, slightly treacly malt. Fruit, malt and bitterness
are all to the fore on the palate and nicely balanced.
Toasted malt, hops, lingering fruit and just a hint of
almond contribute to the finish.

THE CAPTAIN'S CHERRY STOUT

ABV 4.8%　　**Bottle size** 500 ml　　**Serve** cool
Ingredients Mild ale malt; crystal malt; black malt;
chocolate malt; smoked malt; Galena, Fuggle and Golding
hops; cherries

A multi-award-winning ruby beer, based on the stout
below but flavoured with cherries. Marc is obviously
pleased with the way in which he processes the fruit
and includes it in this beer and the Damson Stout
mentioned below, but he declines to reveal his secret.
Tasting Notes
Cherry fruit leads over dark, lightly smoky malt in the
aroma. The flavours of Captain's Stout are all here, too,
but with light cherry adding a touch more sweetness.
Subtle cherry lingers in the aftertaste, which is
bittersweet, smoky and marked by roasted malt.

CAPTAIN'S STOUT

ABV 4.8%　　**Bottle size** 500 ml　　**Serve** cool
Ingredients Mild ale malt; crystal malt; black malt;
chocolate malt; smoked malt; Galena, Fuggle and Golding
hops

A ruby-coloured stout made using Bavarian smoked
malt and (in part) American hops.
Tasting Notes
Biscuity dark malt leads in the lightly smoky aroma

with just a hint of vanilla. There is plenty of roasted
malt character in the taste, with coffee notes and a
whiff of smoke, but a light, sweet fruitiness ensures it is
not too bitter or heavy. Bittersweet, roasted malt and a
lingering smokiness run into the finish.

DAMSON STOUT

ABV 4.8%   **Bottle size** 500 ml   **Serve** cool
Ingredients Mild ale malt; crystal malt; black malt;
chocolate malt; smoked malt; Galena, Fuggle and Golding
hops; damsons

A variation on the Cherry Stout featured above.

BEER ELSIE BUB

ABV 4.8%   **Bottle size** 500 ml   **Serve** cool
Ingredients Maris Otter and Halcyon pale malt; amber
malt; torrefied wheat; Challenger, Golding and Fuggle hops;
wildflower honey; coriander

A strong honey beer originally brewed for a pagan
wedding and now produced for other pagan festivals,
including Halloween. The back label features an
amusing, not entirely (if at all) truthful, account of how
the beer got its name.
Tasting Notes
A dark golden ale with a mellow honey note to the
citrous, floral nose. Slightly earthy bitterness leads over
spicy orange in the mouth, with more honey emerging
softly on the swallow to linger lightly in the bitter,
hoppy aftertaste.

XMAS HOLLY DAZE

ABV 5%   **Bottle size** 500 ml   **Serve** cool
Ingredients Maris Otter pale malt; crystal malt; Golding
and Fuggle hops

A light-coloured bitter only on sale at Christmas.

NEW YEAR DAZE

ABV 5.2%   **Bottle size** 500 ml   **Serve** cool
Ingredients Maris Otter pale malt; crystal malt; roasted
malt; Golding and Fuggle hops

A deep reddish bitter made available only over the
Christmas and New Year period.

BARUM

**Barum Brewery Ltd., Pilton, Barnstaple, Devon
EX31 1PD. Tel. (01271) 329994 Fax (01271) 321590
E-mail: info@barumbrewery.co.uk
Web site: www.barumbrewery.co.uk**

Barum was founded in 1996 with the purchase of the
Combe Brewery in Ilfracombe. Relocated to near
Barnstaple, it now produces a wide range of beers. The
four bottle-conditioned beers are bottled direct from
casks by Keltek Brewery.

ORIGINAL

ABV 4.4%   **Bottle size** 500 ml   **Serve** cool
Ingredients Pipkin pale malt; crystal malt; roasted malt;
Fuggle, Challenger and Golding hops

Barum's first ever beer: a dark golden ale.

BREAKFAST

ABV 5%   **Bottle size** 500 ml   **Serve** cool
Ingredients Pipkin pale malt; roasted malt; wheat malt;
Challenger and Golding hops

Barum brewery's enigmatic slogan is: 'Beer's not just for
breakfast anymore', so they just had to call one of their
beers Breakfast. The label shows a cartoon chef frying
up a pint.
Tasting Notes
A heavily-hopped amber ale with a fruity aroma, a taste
full of tangy, fruity hops and a bitter finish with the
same characteristics.

CHALLENGER

ABV 5.6%   **Bottle size** 500 ml   **Serve** cool
Ingredients Pipkin pale malt; roasted malt; wheat malt;
Challenger hops

As its name suggests, this is a single-varietal hop beer,
focusing on Challenger hops.

BARNSTABLASTA

ABV 6.6%   **Bottle size** 500 ml   **Serve** cool
Ingredients Pipkin pale malt; crystal malt; chocolate malt;
wheat malt; Challenger and Golding hops

Reflecting both its strength and the proximity of Barnstaple in its name, Barnstablasta is a winter beer, as implied by the Santa Claus on the label who is about to be flattened by a falling grand piano.

Tasting Notes

A ruby/brown beer with an aroma of light chocolate, malt and fruit. The big, sweet taste features tangy, fruity hops and there's more than a hint of roasted malt in the lingering, fruity hop finish.

BATEMAN

George Bateman and Son Ltd., Salem Bridge Brewery, Wainfleet, Lincolnshire PE24 4JE.
Tel. (01754) 880317 Fax (01754) 880939
E-mail: enquiries@bateman.co.uk
Web site: www.bateman.co.uk

The Bateman brewery was established by the current chairman's grandfather back in 1874. Boardroom turbulence led to worries over its future in the 1980s, but the family retained control and secured the company's independence in a famous financial battle. It remains one of the UK's most revered breweries. All Bateman's own bottled beers are filtered, but it has occasionally turned out a bottle-conditioned beer for other parties, such as the ale for Booths listed below, which is bottled by Wessex Craft Brewers.

POUR WITH CARE

ABV 4.5%   **Bottle size** 500 ml   **Serve** cool
Ingredients Maris Otter pale malt; crystal malt; wheat malt; Challenger and Golding hops

Booths is a family-owned grocery chain based in North-West England, founded more than 150 years ago. Its 25 stores stock well over 100 bottled ales, many of them bottle conditioned, which earned the group the British Guild of Beer Writers' *Beer Supermarket of the Year* award in 2000. This 'own label' beer – launched in 2001 – is the brainchild of beer buyer Dave Smith, who hopes its descriptive title will encourage supermarket shoppers to try bottle-conditioned beer and understand more about serving this style of beer. At the bottlers, excess yeast is sedimented out in conditioning tanks before packaging, with no further yeast added.

Tasting Notes

A red-amber ale with a malty, banana-toffee nose. The

taste is slightly salty, with loads of banana and toffee-malt flavour and a good, bitter balance. Bitterness increases in the drying, banana-malt finish.
Major stockist Booths

BATH

**Bath Ales Ltd., The Old Barn, Siston Lane, Webbs Heath, Bristol BS30 5LX. Tel. (0117) 961 5122
Web site: www.bathales.com**

Founded in 1995 near Wincanton and moved to a new 15-barrel site in 1999, Bath Ales now runs a handful of excellent pubs in the Bath and Bristol areas. The bottle-conditioned beers mentioned below are brewed and bottled under contract by Hepworth & Co in Horsham.

GEM

ABV 4.8%   **Bottle size** 500 ml   **Serve** cool
Ingredients Maris Otter pale malt; Challenger and East Kent Golding hops

Conceived as a beer for sale to restaurants and the hotel trade, Gem is considerably stronger than the 4.1% cask beer that bears the same name. The label carries the Bath Ales emblem of a hare, drawn in the style of the many chalk figures that adorn hillsides in the West Country. Challenger hops are used in the brew kettle, with Goldings introduced later for aroma.
Tasting Notes
A dark amber bitter with a fruity nose (hints of pineapple and a little pear drop). The same fruitiness features in the taste but is not so dominant when balanced with malt sweetness and perfumed, hoppy bitterness. Dry, bittersweet, scented-hop finish.

FESTIVITY

ABV 5%   **Bottle size** 500 ml   **Serve** cool
Ingredients Maris Otter pale malt; crystal malt; chocolate malt; roasted barley; wheat malt; Challenger and Bramling Cross hops

A gold medallist as a cask beer in CAMRA's *Champion Winter Beer of Britain* contest in 2002, and runner-up overall, Festivity was launched in bottle in summer 2003 to draw attention to Bristol's bid to become *European City of Culture*.

BELVOIR

**Belvoir Brewery Ltd., Woodhill, Nottingham Lane,
Old Dalby, Leicestershire LE14 3LX.
Tel./Fax (01664) 823455
E-mail: sales@belvoir-brewery.go-plus.net
Web site: www.belvoirbrewery.co.uk**

Established in 1995 by Colin Brown, who used to brew with both Shipstones and Theakston, this brewery sits in the Vale of Belvoir (pronounced 'beaver'). As well as three regular cask ales, three bottled beers are now in production, each being filtered and re-seeded with fresh yeast prior to bottling on site.

BEAVER BITTER

ABV 4.3%   **Bottle size** 500 ml   **Serve** cool
Ingredients Maris Otter pale malt; crystal malt; chocolate malt; Challenger, Progress, Bramling Cross and Golding hops

One of the brewery's first ever cask beers, Beaver Bitter makes a play on the often-mispronounced name of the brewery and its attractive, rural setting.

PEACOCK'S GLORY

ABV 4.7%   **Bottle size** 500 ml   **Serve** cool
Ingredients Maris Otter pale malt; crystal malt; Target, Progress and Golding hops

The agricultural pastures of the Vale of Belvoir are overlooked by the battlemented Belvoir Castle (seat of the Duke of Rutland) and there the grounds are home to a fine collection of peacocks. Their splendour is echoed in the name of this brew which was launched as a cask beer back in 1997.

OLD DALBY

ABV 5.1%   **Bottle size** 500 ml   **Serve** cool
Ingredients Maris Otter pale malt; crystal malt; chocolate malt; Challenger, Progress, Bramling Cross and Golding hops

Old Dalby is the name of the village where Belvoir Brewery has set up home. Another beer first introduced in cask in 1997, it is generally only made available in the winter months.

BIRD IN HAND

**Wheal Ale Brewery, c/o The Bird in Hand,
Trelissick Road, Hayle, Cornwall TR27 4HY.
Tel. (01736) 753974
E-mail: george@birdinhand-hayle.co.uk
Web site: www.birdinhand-hayle.co.uk**

The Bird in Hand is a large brew pub situated alongside
the Paradise Park bird gardens in Hayle. The brewery is
housed in outbuildings alongside the beer garden and
produces a few cask beers, plus the bottle-conditioned
beer below. This was introduced in summer 2001 and is
bottled at Keltek Brewery.

SPECKLED PARROT

ABV 5.5%   **Bottle size** 500 ml   **Serve** cool
Ingredients Maris Otter pale malt; crystal malt; Fuggle and
Golding hops

There are no prizes for guessing the inspiration for the
name of this strong ale, which ties in neatly with the
bird park next door. Also sold in cask form.
Tasting Notes
A red-brown beer with an aroma of malt, banana-toffee
and estery fruit, plus a spicy yeast note. The full,
smooth body has loads of malt, traces of banana and an
earthy, spicy yeastiness. Plenty of bitterness means it is
not too sweet. Toasty, malty, bitter finish.

BLACK ISLE

**Black Isle Brewery, Old Allangrange, Munlochy, Highland
IV8 8NZ. Tel. (01463) 811871 Fax (01463) 811875
E-mail: greatbeers@blackislebrewery.com
Web site: www.blackislebrewery.com**
Mail order service

Converted farm buildings in the Highlands of Scotland
provide a home for Black Isle Brewery, which was set up
1998. The Black Isle itself is not an island but a
peninsula across the Moray Firth from Inverness, with
an ancient history of barley production and a
spectacular coastline. The brewery runs a busy mail
order service, selling the following organic beers by the
case and also two other bottled beers (filtered but not
pasteurised). The beers listed below are kräusened in a
conditioning tank prior to bottling.

ORGANIC BLONDE

ABV 4.5%   **Bottle size** 500 ml   **Serve** cool
Ingredients Pale malt; wheat malt; Hersbrucker and
Hallertau hops

Previous sold as both a cask ale and a filtered bottled
ale, this full-bodied beer goes very well with smoked
trout and also raspberries, according to brewer David
Gladwin.
Tasting Notes
A golden brew featuring spicy hops and slowly
emerging apricot fruit in the aroma. The fruit increases
on the palate, with apricot and lemon notes shining
through against a backdrop of bittersweet spicy hops.
Dry, bitter fruit finish.
Major stockist (all beers) Safeway in Scotland

ORGANIC PORTER

ABV 4.5%   **Bottle size** 500 ml   **Serve** cool
Ingredients Pale malt; crystal malt; chocolate malt; wheat
malt; oat flakes; Hallertau and Golding hops

A Salisbury Beer Festival champion in 2002 under its
original cask name of Wagtail, this dark brew is
suggested by David as a perfect match for seafood like
oysters and crab, and perhaps a good old farmhouse
Cheddar.
Tasting Notes
A dark ruby porter with a mellow, creamy, coffeeish
nose. The taste is also creamy and coffeeish but
bittersweet, with a very restrained hoppy fruitiness
behind. Bitter, roasted finish.

ORGANIC SCOTCH ALE

ABV 4.5%   **Bottle size** 500 ml   **Serve** cool
Ingredients Pale malt; crystal malt; peat-smoked malt;
wheat malt; Hallertau and Styrian Golding hops; bog myrtle

A beer to savour with haggis and black pudding! It's the
first time any brewer has recommended these dishes to
this book as an accompaniment for his beer. Apart from
peat-smoked malt (more familiar to whisky drinkers),
the unusual ingredient in Scotch Ale is bog myrtle. It
may sound like the moaning ghost who hides in a
lavatory in the Harry Potter books, but this is an
aromatic marshland shrub (also known as sweet gale)
that was often used to season beer before the arrival of

hops some 500 years ago. The beer was first produced
in 2002.
Tasting Notes
A red-coloured ale with a big malty nose backed up
with a hint of mint toffee, spice and smoke. The taste is
spicy, smoky and malty with a cool 'peppermint' note.
Toasted malt on the swallow grows in the finish with
lingering cool spice, smoke and bitterness.

ORGANIC WHEAT BEER

ABV 4.5%   **Bottle size** 500 ml   **Serve** cool
Ingredients Pale malt; wheat malt; Hersbrucker and
Hallertau hops; coriander; orange peel

Brewed initially in 2001 as a cask beer, this Belgian-style
wheat beer was runner-up in 2002's *Wheat Beer
Challenge*. David Gladwin suggests that it should served
with fresh Scottish mussels.
Tasting Notes
A hazy, golden beer with lemon, orange and spice in
the aroma. The taste is peppery, spicy and full of bitter
citrous character, before a dry, slightly perfumed,
bittersweet, orange and lemon finish.

BLACKAWTON

**Blackawton Brewery, Unit 7, Peninsula Park,
Channon Road, Saltash, Cornwall PL12 6LX.
Tel. (01752) 848777 Fax (01752) 848999
E-mail: blackawtonbrewery@talk21.com**

Blackawton Brewery was set up in 1977, one of the first
of the new wave of microbreweries founded after the
early successes of CAMRA. Until 2001 it was the longest
established brewery in Devon, but then it was sold and
the new owners moved it just across the River Tamar to
Cornwall. The brewery moved yet again in 2003, but
this time just around the corner to larger premises. The
beers are bottled for Blackawton by Keltek Brewery. A
third bottle, Dragonheart (5%), based on a cask ginger
beer, may be introduced in the near future.

WINTER FUEL

ABV 5%   **Bottle size** 500 ml   **Serve** cool
Ingredients Pale malt; crystal malt; chocolate malt;
torrefied wheat; Progress and Golding hops; mace; ginger;
lemons

The label of this seasonal warmer declares that it conceals a 'secret wintery twist'. Now the secret is out: brewer Steve Brooks adds whole lemons to the copper for a citrous edge and seasons the beer not only with hops but with Christmas spices, too.

Tasting Notes

A light ruby ale with an aroma of Christmas cake spices. The taste is malty but spicy with a ginger warmth poking through. Bitter, Christmas spice finish.

HEAD STRONG

ABV 5.2%   **Bottle size** 500 ml   **Serve** cool
Ingredients Pale malt; crystal malt; wheat malt; Progress, Challenger and Styrian Golding hops

Head Strong is one of the beers Steve inherited when the company was purchased and it dates right back to the brewery's formative days (first mentioned in the *Good Beer Guide*'s 1979 edition). Steve, however, has personalised the beer a little by adding Challenger hops.

Tasting Notes

A dark golden beer with a citrous aroma. Spicy/citrous hops dominate the taste until toasted malt emerges along with estery notes. Bitter, roasted malt finish.

BLUE ANCHOR

Blue Anchor Inn, 50 Coinagehall Street, Helston, Cornwall TR13 8EL. Tel./Fax (01326) 565765
Mail order service

Famous as one of the four home-brew houses still in operation when CAMRA accepted the challenge of preserving British brewing heritage in 1971, The Blue Anchor is one of the country's classic pubs. The thatched building began life as a monks' resting place in the 15th century. Its brewery has been refurbished in recent years and now prepares its celebrated 'Spingo' beers for the bottle. Bottling takes place at Keltek Brewery, after the beers have been matured in casks.

JUBILEE ALE

ABV 4.5%   **Bottle size** 275 ml   **Serve** cool
Ingredients Pipkin pale malt; Golding hops

An IPA brewed for The Queen's Golden Jubilee in 2002 but maintained as part of the regular range.

BLUE ANCHOR

SPINGO MIDDLE

ABV 5%   **Bottle size** 275 ml   **Serve** cool
Ingredients Pipkin pale malt; Golding hops

Spingo has been on tap at The Blue Anchor for
centuries, the pub claims. The origin of the name is the
Old English 'stingo', a term for strong beer.
Tasting Notes
A dark amber, robust ale with an earthy, spicy malt
aroma. The distinctive taste merges earthy maltiness
and spice, before a dry, thick, bittersweet, spicy finish. A
'don't mess with me' sort of beer.

SPINGO SPECIAL

ABV 6.6%   **Bottle size** 275 ml   **Serve** cool
Ingredients Pipkin pale malt; Golding hops

This is a stronger version of Spingo Middle and, like its
stablemate, may be found in dishes like beef in Spingo
and Spingo burgers at the pub.
Tasting Notes
A powerful ruby ale with an earthy, appley, spicy nose.
Sweet malt is well to the fore in the mouth, allowing
the earthy, bitter spiciness to provide a nice contrast.
Bittersweet, fruity, spicy aftertaste.

CHRISTMAS SPECIAL

ABV 7.6%   **Bottle size** 275 ml   **Serve** cool
Ingredients Pipkin pale malt; crystal malt; Golding hops

A seasonal draught ale available for a longer period in
bottle.
Tasting Notes
A strong ruby ale with a peppery, malt and fruit nose
and the distinctive Blue Anchor spiciness in the sweet
and malty taste. Red fruit and oranges lurk in the
background before a sweetish, fruity finish.

EASTER SPECIAL

ABV 7.8%   **Bottle size** 275 ml   **Serve** cool
Ingredients Pipkin pale malt; Golding hops

Just in case Spingo Special is not strong enough for your
taste, the Blue Anchor thoughtfully provides an even
more potent version on draught around Easter time and
in bottle for a while longer.

BOGGART

**Boggart Hole Clough Brewing Company,
Unit 13, Brookside Works, Clough Road, Moston,
Manchester M9 4FP. Tel./Fax (0161) 277 9666
E-mail: mark@boggart-brewery.co.uk
Web site: www.boggart-brewery.co.uk**

The peculiar name of this brewery comes from the
peculiar name of the park next door. Mark Dade is the
founder. A former brewer at Marble Brewery, he set up
on his own in 2001.

STEAMING

ABV 9%   **Bottle size** 500 ml   **Serve** cool
Ingredients Pale malt; wheat malt; Galena and Challenger
hops

Both these bottled beers are available in cask form but
are not typical of the Boggart selection, which features
half-a-dozen or more brews in the 3–5% range.
Steaming was first brewed and bottled in late 2001 and
is now a regular product.

ROCKET FUEL

ABV 14%   **Bottle size** 330 ml   **Serve** cool
Ingredients Pale malt; amber malt; wheat malt; Nugget
and Liberty hops

Brewed every six months or so, this powerful, take-no-
prisoners ale was introduced in May 2003.

BORVE

**Borve Brew House, Ruthven, Huntly, Moray AB54 4SR.
Tel. (01466) 760343**

Borve was founded in 1983, on the Isle of Lewis, but
moved to the mainland five years later, setting up shop
in a former school. The school is now a pub, with the
brewhouse adjacent. The recent illness of brewer
Gregory Hughes has seen a temporary halt to
production, but he hopes to be able to supervise
production of the bottled beers again in the near future.
These bottled beers are virtually identical to the draught
products, except for being coarse filtered (to leave some
yeast in suspension) rather than fined. There are no

primings and all bottled beers are part-matured on site before shipping. Sell-by dates are set at six months.

BORVE ALE

ABV 4%   **Bottle size** 330 ml   **Serve** cool
Ingredients Pale malt; crystal malt; chocolate malt; roasted barley; Target hops

The brewery's original tipple, Borve Ale was first presented to Scots drinkers in 1983 as a cask beer. This particular bevvy is described by the brewery as a traditional dark, full-bodied Scotch Ale.
Tasting Notes
An attractive amber beer with a little fruit, a touch of chocolate and plenty of malt in the aroma. The taste is malty and citrous, and the finish is very dry, mostly bitter and smoky.

TALL SHIPS

ABV 5%   **Bottle size** 330 ml   **Serve** cool
Ingredients Pale malt; crystal malt; chocolate malt; Target and Hersbrucker hops

This beer was first produced in August 1991 to welcome competitors in the Tall Ships Race on their arrival into Aberdeen. A case or two of this hearty brew aboard may well have trimmed their speed but would have worked wonders for their spirit on the high seas, as it is brewed in the style of a real India Pale Ale, which traditionally boasted a robust body and a sackful of hops to keep it fresh on the way to the subcontinent.
Tasting Notes
A golden beer with an unusual smoky aroma of hops and malt. Malty and fruity to taste, it is also a little smoky and tart, with hops leading in the bittersweet, smoky, malty finish.

BORVE ALE (Extra Strong)

ABV 10%   **Bottle size** 330 ml   **Serve** cool
Ingredients Pale malt; crystal malt; Target and Hersbrucker hops

Like the 4% beer, this is also labelled 'Borve Ale', although it is commonly known as 'Extra Strong'. At 10%, it seems rather an understatement for this unusual 'wee heavy', which is presented with a foil cover over the cap. What adds to its headiness is the use of

American oak Bourbon casks which were previously
used to mature Scotch whisky, and this oak-whisky
combination imparts an unusual character. The brew
first appeared in 1984, before the Bourbon casks were
installed. In those days, ordinary casks filled with oak
chips acted as maturation vessels. All this comes after a
traditional brewing process beginning with a wort at
1085 OG. When this is fermented out, the resultant
ABV, though declared here at 10%, may in fact fluctuate
between 9.5 and 11%.

Tasting Notes
An amber beer with a smoky, lightly lemony aroma.
The taste is vinous and strong, with loads of malt but
also a dominant smokiness and whisky notes
throughout. Mouth-warming, bittersweet, smoky and
malt whisky-like finish.

BRAGDY CEREDIGION

**Bragdy Ceredigion, Brynhawk, New Road,
Newquay, Ceredigion SA45 9SB.
Tel./Fax (01545) 561417 Brewery tel. (01239) 654888**
Mail order service

This brewery was constructed in a converted barn on a
working West Wales farm in 1997. The address above is
the office address: the brewery itself is in the village of
Pentregat. The beers are targeted at the local tourist
trade and have bilingual Welsh/English labels, hand-
drawn by Julia Tilby, wife of brewer Brian Tilby. Each
beer is siphoned into bottles direct from the fermenter,
or from a cask, and is primed with raw demerara sugar.
Best before dates are 12–18 months after bottling. All the
beers are declared suitable for vegetarians.

GWRACH DDU

ABV 4%   **Bottle size** 500 ml   **Serve** cool
Ingredients Maris Otter pale malt; crystal malt; amber
malt; First Gold hops

Translated as 'Black Witch', Gwrach Ddu was first
brewed for Halloween, in 1998. The cask version is dry
hopped and sold as a 'dark porter', whereas this bottled
equivalent – a touch of 'cyfareddol du' (black magic), as
the label used to claim – is labelled a 'stout'. Try it with
a selection of strong Welsh cheeses, suggests Brian.

Tasting Notes
A ruby-coloured beer with a creamy aroma of dark malt.

On the palate it is dry and immediately moreish, with flavours like fruit, bitterness and roasted malt well restrained, before a gently bitter, toasty, dry finish that is also lightly fruity.

DRAIG AUR

ABV 4.2%   **Bottle size** 500 ml   **Serve** cool
Ingredients Maris Otter pale malt; crystal malt; amber malt; Challenger and Fuggle hops

Launched in cask at CAMRA's Cardiff Beer Festival in 1998, and in bottle soon after, 'Gold Dragon' is another brew to try with rich cheeses. The strength, originally set at 5%, has now been reduced to a more quaffable 4.2%.
Tasting Notes
An orange-gold ale with a fruit salad aroma. The taste is hoppy and bitter, with blackcurrant and other fruitiness. Dry, bitter finish.

BARCUD COCH

ABV 4.3%   **Bottle size** 500 ml   **Serve** cool
Ingredients Maris Otter pale malt; crystal malt; amber malt; Challenger and Golding hops

The name of this bitter, introduced in summer 1998, means 'Red Kite'. Challenger hops provide the main bitterness in the copper, with Goldings supplying some late variation and also dry hopping the brew in the fermenting vessel. The beer was once described on the label as being 'coch', 'prin' and 'prydferth'– red, rare and beautiful, just like the bird it is named after.
Tasting Notes
A reddish-bronze beer with a fruity hop aroma. The taste is smooth and quite bitter, and features fruity flavours. Dry, gently bitter, fruity-hop finish.

BLODEUWEDD

ABV 4.5%   **Bottle size** 500 ml   **Serve** cool
Ingredients Pale malt; Hallertau hops

Brewed from organic malt and organic hops, and primed with organic sugar, this beer, launched in 2000 and now officially accredited as organic by the Soil Association, takes its name from Welsh legend. Blodeuwedd, it is said, was a beautiful maiden created from flowers by two powerful magicians. Tragedy befell the girl when she plotted with her lover to kill her husband and, for her punishment, was transformed into an owl, 'a creature of the night'. 'Blodeuwedd' is Welsh for owl and literally translates as 'flower face'.

Tasting Notes
A golden ale with a fruity nose. The taste features spicy, peppery hops, bitterness and underlying light fruit, before a very hoppy, bitter finish.

CWRW 2000

ABV 5%   **Bottle size** 500 ml   **Serve** cool
Ingredients Maris Otter pale malt; crystal malt; amber malt; pale chocolate malt; Challenger and Fuggle hops

Brewed originally for the new millennium celebrations, Cwrw 2000 ('Ale 2000') owes its longevity to the picture of seaside Llangranog on the label, which makes it a good seller among summer visitors to the area.

Tasting Notes
A ruby ale with a full, biscuity malt aroma. The taste is soft and malty with suggestions of dark fruit and a light citrus edge. Bitter, malty finish with a touch of roasted malt and a lingering hint of fruit.

NADOLIG

ABV 6.2%   **Bottle size** 500 ml   **Serve** cool
Ingredients Maris Otter pale malt; crystal malt; amber malt; pale chocolate malt; Challenger, Fuggle and Golding hops; spices

Laced with spices – including cinnamon and nutmeg – for a festive feel, Nadolig (literally 'Christmas') is only available from October to January.

Tasting Notes
A red beer with mixed spices in the aroma and a well-rounded combination of malt and perfumed spice in the taste. Bittersweet, scented, increasingly bitter finish.

YR HEN DARW DU

ABV 6.2%   **Bottle size** 500 ml   **Serve** cool
Ingredients Maris Otter pale malt; crystal malt; amber malt; dark chocolate malt; black malt; Challenger hops

'The Old Black Bull', for those not versed in the language of Heaven. This complex winter warmer takes its name from the brewery's bovine neighbours on the Pentregat farm. It also recalls a Welsh legend of the

Green Lady of the Lake, who, it is said, provided the Welsh Black cattle as a gift for saving her magical white cow from slaughter.
Tasting Notes
A deep ruby beer with a slightly leathery, fruit cocktail aroma. The taste is smooth, bitter, fruity and a touch warming. Dry, bitter, lightly roasted, fruity finish.

BRAGDY YNYS MÔN

**Bragdy Ynys Môn (Isle of Anglesey Brewery),
Cae Cwta Mawr, Lôn Cae Cwta, Talwrn, Llangefni,
Anglesey LL77 7SD. Tel. (01248) 723801
E-mail: martyn@angleseyale.co.uk
Web site: www.angleseyale.co.uk**
Mail order service

Martyn Lewis founded this brewery in June 1999, installing a five-barrel plant in a former cow shed. The beers listed below were initially bottled by Hanby Ales, but are now filled on site (unfiltered and straight from the cask).

MEDRA

ABV 4%   **Bottle size** 500 ml   **Serve** cool
Ingredients Maris Otter pale malt; crystal malt; Fuggle and Cascade hops

Literally translating as 'I can', Medra seems a peculiar name for a beer. Its origins lie in the days of slate quarrying in North Wales, when men seeking employment were asked what jobs they could do. The men of Anglesey were always able to turn their hands to anything, simply replying 'Medra' when asked if they could handle a suggested task. Anglesey, henceforward, became known as 'Gwlad y Medra', the Land of I Can.

WENNOL

ABV 4.1%   **Bottle size** 500 ml   **Serve** cool
Ingredients Maris Otter pale malt; crystal malt; Cascade hops

Introduced in spring 2000, Wennol ('swallow' in Welsh) was inspired by the nesting of the said bird in a stable opposite the brewery.
Tasting Notes
An amber ale with malt and grassy hops in the aroma.

The taste is spicy, lightly fruity and mostly bitter, with some toasted malt flavour. Hoppy, bitter finish.

SOSPAN FACH

ABV 4.3%   **Bottle size** 500 ml   **Serve** cool
Ingredients Pale malt; crystal malt; First Gold hops

The Little Sospan, more associated with South Wales rugby, and Llanelli RFC in particular, than North Wales, is the name Martyn has bestowed on his organic beer.

TARW DU

ABV 4.5%   **Bottle size** 500 ml   **Serve** cool
Ingredients Maris Otter pale malt; crystal malt; chocolate malt; black malt; roasted barley; Cascade and Fuggle hops

The first of the brewery's bottled ales, launched in November 1999, Tarw Du ('Black Bull') recalls the former use of the premises in its name. Bottled beer is now stored in the area where the bull used to be kept.
Tasting Notes
A near-black stout with a slightly leathery aroma of dark malt and roasted barley. Silky malt features on the palate, with roasted grain, a little fruit and a touch of sourness. Strong roasted grain finish.

AMNESIA

ABV 4.9%   **Bottle size** 500 ml   **Serve** cool
Ingredients Maris Otter pale malt; crystal malt; Cascade and Fuggle hops

A stronger version of Medra, Amnesia was trialled at Christmas 2000 and is now brewed monthly.
Tasting Notes
An amber beer with a flowery, spicy nose. The taste is also spicy and fruity, with good, crisp bitterness and a persistent malty sweetness. Spicy, hoppy, bitter finish.

BRANSCOMBE VALE

**Branscombe Vale Brewery, Great Seaside Farm, Branscombe, Devon EX12 3DP.
Tel./Fax (01297) 680511**

It was in 1992 that Branscombe Vale set up home in an old farm that is now owned by the National Trust. It has dabbled in bottled beers in the past but only in 2002 did it make the move into regular bottle-conditioned beer production, with beer brewed at Branscombe and bottled by Devon neighbour O'Hanlon's, without filtration or re-seeding of yeast. The best before dates are set at nine months.

DRAYMAN'S BEST BITTER

ABV 4.2%   **Bottle size** 500 ml   **Serve** cool
Ingredients Pipkin pale malt; crystal malt; Phoenix hops

Drayman's Best is a single-varietal hop beer brewed with Branscombe's own spring water. Also sold in cask form.
Tasting Notes
An amber ale with a pinch of chocolate throughout, from the maltiness in the nose to the bitter, hoppy taste and the dry finish.

BREWSTER'S

Brewster's Brewery, Penn Lane, Stathern, Leicestershire LE14 4JA.
Tel. (01949) 861868 Fax (01949) 861901
E-mail: sara@brewsters.co.uk
Web site: www.brewsters.co.uk

In centuries past, brewsters were female brewers and their work was prolific, many brewing beer for consumption at home at a time when water supplies were less than reliable. There is a small core of professional women brewers employed today in breweries across Britain, but the brewster in the name of this Leicestershire business is Sara Barton. Sara used to work for Courage, brewing some of the biggest names in world beer. Leaving it all behind, she returned to her native Vale of Belvoir, setting up this microbrewery in 1998. In addition to the Vale Pale Ale listed below, Sara plans to bottle her Claudia Wheat Beer (4.5%).

VALE PALE ALE

ABV 4.5%   **Bottle size** 500 ml   **Serve** cool
Ingredients Maris Otter pale malt; caramalt; Northdown, Golding and Cascade hops

Belvoir Castle features on the label of this beer inspired by the vale in which the brewery sits. It was one of Sara's first beers, launched in cask in 1998 but only released in bottle in summer 2003. Drink with white meat and fish dishes is her dining recommendation.

Tasting Notes

A light copper bitter showcasing its Cascade hops right from the juicy, grapefruit aroma, through the zesty, bitter, citrous taste to the tangy grapefruit finish.

BRIDGE OF ALLAN

Bridge of Allan Brewery, The Brew House, Queens Lane, Bridge of Allan, Stirlingshire FK9 4NY.
Tel. (01786) 834555 Fax (01786) 833426
E-mail: brewery@bridgeofallan.co.uk
Web site: www.bridgeofallan.co.uk
Mail order service

Founded in 1997, this Victorian spa town brewery now serves around 75 pubs. It produces quite a range of bottled beers, but only one is bottle conditioned.

BRIG O'ALLAN

ABV 4.1%   **Bottle size** 500 ml   **Serve** cool
Ingredients Maris Otter pale malt; crystal malt; chocolate malt; wheat malt; Hallertau and Golding hops

This traditional 80/- style beer was introduced in 2001. The beer is allowed two weeks in conditioning tanks after fermentation, so that it drops bright. No finings are used, making it appealing to vegetarians. The beer is then primed with sugar and re-seeded with fresh yeast.

Tasting Notes

A dark amber ale with a malty nose. The taste is surprisingly crisp and bitter with a toasted malt flavour. Bitter, toasted malt finish.

Availability of Beers

Beers in this book are mostly sold locally, through farmers' markets, small grocers, craft shops and delicatessens. Some breweries also sell direct to the public, but this may be by the case only, and some offer a mail order service, which is mentioned if relevant. Otherwise beers can be obtained through specialist off-licences or mail order companies, many of which are listed in the Beer Shops section at the back of the book. If a beer has a listing with a major retailer (supermarket or off-licence chain), this is indicated at the end of the entry.

BROADSTONE

**The Broadstone Brewing Company Ltd.,
The Rum Runner, Wharf Road, Retford,
Nottinghamshire DN22 6EN. Tel. (01777) 719797
Web site: www.broadstonebrewery.com**
Mail order service

Alan Gill, founder of Springhead Brewery, moved on to
establish The Broadstone Brewing Company in 1999.
Since spring 2001, the brewery has been based at The
Rum Runner pub in Retford. Alan brews five regular
cask beers, plus seasonals, as well as the three bottled
beers mentioned below, which are conditioned in casks,
fined and primed, allowed to stand for 24 hours and
then bottled. Best before dates are fixed at 12 months.

TWO WATER GROG

ABV 4%   **Bottle size** 500 ml   **Serve** cool
Ingredients Pearl pale malt; crystal malt; crystal rye;
roasted barley; Northdown and Bramling Cross hops

This bottled version of The Rum Runner's own house
bitter (it's not sold in its cask version anywhere else)
draws on the naval grog tradition for its name (the
daily ration aboard ship was often made up of two parts
water to one part rum).

BLACK ABBOT

ABV 5%   **Bottle size** 500 ml   **Serve** cool
Ingredients Pearl pale malt; crystal malt; crystal rye;
roasted barley; Northdown hops

A dark and mysterious name for a dark and mysterious
beer, according to Alan. The label provides a warning
not to mess with the Black Abbot or 'oblivion and
chaos will be the outcome'.

BROADSTONE GOLD

ABV 5%   **Bottle size** 500 ml   **Serve** cool
Ingredients Pearl pale malt; Northdown hops

Alan's very first beer at Broadstone, this beer festival
award-winner is described as a 'golden pale ale in the
Belgian style', which will come as no surprise to readers
who sampled the adventurous beers he created when he
was brewing at Springhead.

BURTON BRIDGE

**Burton Bridge Brewery, 24 Bridge Street,
Burton upon Trent, Staffordshire DE14 1SY.
Tel. (01283) 510573 Fax (01283) 515594**

Burton Bridge Brewery, a microbrewery in the pale ale
capital, was established in 1982 by former Allied
Breweries employees Bruce Wilkinson and Geoff
Mumford. They began bottle conditioning beers in the
same year, making them one of the first small breweries
to expand into bottling.

BURTON PORTER

ABV 4.5%   **Bottle size** 500 ml   **Serve** cool
Ingredients Pale malt; crystal malt; chocolate malt;
Challenger and Target hops

The simple yellow paint and rubber stamp label that
used to adorn bottles of this popular porter has long
given way to a more sophisticated paper badge.
However, inside the bottle the beer is just the same as
before, following the same recipe as draught Burton
Porter. Bottles are filled from one-week-old casks, and
the beer is said to be on form at any stage from one- to
six-months-old (the period indicated by the best before
date). This and all Burton Bridge's bottled beers are
warm-conditioned at the brewery for around ten days
before dispatch to ensure a good secondary
fermentation is underway.
Tasting Notes
A dark red, almost black, porter with an aroma of fruit
and chocolate. Dry roast malt in the taste is backed by
gentle, sweet malt, with dryness, roast malt and
bitterness coming through to dominate the finish.

BRAMBLE STOUT

ABV 5%   **Bottle size** 500 ml   **Serve** cool
Ingredients Pale malt; chocolate malt; Challenger hops;
blackberry juice

Introduced in 1999, Bramble Stout is an unusual
creation, consisting of the brewery's Top Dog Stout with
blackberry juice added to the cask before bottling.
Tasting Notes
An almost black beer, with a smoky, biscuity, fruity
aroma. In the mouth it is bitter, blackberry-fruity and
roasty. Bitter, fruity, strong roast finish.

DERBYSHIRE ESTATE ALE

ABV 5%   **Bottle size** 500 ml   **Serve** cool
Ingredients Maris Otter pale malt; Northdown, Fuggle and
Golding hops

A special bottling for the National Trust, and launched
in March 2002 for sale in the organisation's outlets in
Derbyshire, Derbyshire Estate Ale is actually one of the
brewery's regular cask beers, Stairway to Heaven, under
a new name.

EMPIRE PALE ALE

ABV 7.5%   **Bottle size** 500 ml   **Serve** cool
Ingredients Pipkin pale malt; invert sugar; Challenger and
Styrian Golding hops

The Guardian newspaper's *Best Bottle-Conditioned Beer*
1997, and runner-up in the joint *Guardian*/CAMRA
competition a year later. As its name suggests, this brew
is a re-creation of the classic IPAs which once sailed out
to the far corners of the Empire from Burton upon
Trent. Being very strong, bitter and hoppy, it fits the bill
admirably. The days of the Raj are recalled on the label,
too, which depicts an army officer in full regalia
alongside a Victorian cricketer, both patriotically
embraced by a Union flag. The first brew arrived in
1996 and now the ale is brewed twice a year. After
primary fermentation, it is conditioned in cask for six
months and is dry-hopped with Styrian Goldings two
weeks before being primed and bottled. The yeast
carried over from the cask takes care of the bottle
fermentation. B United distributes this beer in the USA.
Tasting Notes
Bitter oranges are the main characteristic of this heady,
copper-coloured IPA. They feature, with hops, in the nose;
they figure highly in the malty taste, again with powerful
hops on the side; and carry right through to the warming,
mouth-tingling finish.

TICKLE BRAIN

ABV 8%   **Bottle size** 500 ml   **Serve** cool
Ingredients Pale malt; crystal malt; invert sugar;
Northdown hops

At 8%, this beer – first brewed in 1996, as the intended
first of a series of beer style re-creations – more than
tickles the brain. However, the brewery gives credit for

this euphemism to William Shakespeare, from whose writings the name is derived. The ale is an interpretation of an early (16th-century) hopped beer, as might have been produced by brewer monks. To emphasise the era it comes from (at least in spirit), Henry VIII, the king who ordered the dissolution of the monasteries, dominates the label. The result is an Abbey-style beer which keeps for a year after bottling (according to the best before date), but is best drunk about two months into its shelf life.

Tasting Notes

A dark red beer with a sweet, malty, lightly fruity aroma. The taste is sweetish, malty and very fruity (hints of raspberries), with good bitterness to ensure it does not become cloying. Mouth-numbing, fruity and bitter finish.

BUTTS

Butts Brewery Ltd., Northfield Farm, Great Shefford, Hungerford, Berkshire RG17 7BY.
Tel. (01488) 648133

Butts Brewery was established in 1994 in converted farm buildings by Chris Butt. His draught beers now find their way into around 80 outlets in West Berkshire and surrounding counties, and two bottled beers, Barbus Barbus and Blackguard, were introduced in 1999. Two more beers have since followed. Each beer is primed, filtered and then re-seeded with Butts own yeast prior to bottling. Beers are then conditioned in the bottle for at least a month before they are released for sale. Since the last edition of this book, the brewery has gone organic and received accreditation from the Soil Association for its beers.

BLACKGUARD

ABV 4.5%   **Bottle size** 500 ml   **Serve** cool
Ingredients Not declared

Blackguard (pronounced 'blaggard') is Butts's popular porter, introduced as a winter brew but now likely to be found on the bar all year round. The label features a variation on the brewery's playing card joker logo, showing a 'jester with attitude', as Chris describes it. Ingredients-wise, the only information the ever-secretive Mr Butt will supply is that he uses British malt and British hops.

Tasting Notes
A ruby-coloured beer with a contrasting white head.
The appetising aroma features orange hop fruit and a
peppery roastiness, while the soft, bittersweet, roasted
malt taste has a touch of liquorice and more fruit. Long,
dry, bitter, charcoal-like roast finish.
Major stockists local Waitrose and Somerfield

BARBUS BARBUS

ABV 4.6%   **Bottle size** 500 ml   **Serve** cool
Ingredients Not declared

Barbus Barbus is the Latin name for the barbel fish and
this beer celebrates the sport of coarse fishing. In cask
form, it has quickly become the brewery's most popular
ale, and the bottled version has also gained itself a fan
club. Three hop strains contribute to the flavour,
although, yet again, the brewery refuses to say which.
Tasting Notes
An attractive bronze beer with a full hoppy nose backed
with juicy orange fruit notes. The orange-citrus theme
continues on the palate, but with hop bitterness quickly
taking over. Very hoppy, dry fruity finish.
Major stockists Safeway, local Waitrose and Somerfield

GOLDEN BROWN

ABV 5%   **Bottle size** 500 ml   **Serve** cool
Ingredients Not declared

Chris Butt confesses to being a Stranglers fan, hence the
use of one of their song titles for this beer's name. In
the lyrics there is reference to 'tied to a mast', which
explains the girl tied to a mast of a ship on the label.
The beer contains three different malts and just one
hop strain.
Tasting Notes
A light ruby ale with a toasted malt aroma and a rich,
nutty, toasted malt taste. Silky smooth, it also has a
pleasant tang of hop before a long, nutty, bitter finish.
Major stockist local Somerfield

LE BUTTS

ABV 5%   **Bottle size** 500 ml   **Serve** cold
Ingredients Pale malt; wheat malt; hops not declared

Why bother with cross-Channel booze runs when you
can buy a French lager brewed in Berkshire? Le Butts is

produced with lager yeast and a lager hop to parody the efforts of the booze cruisers and, through its name, has a little fun at the expense of the Canadian lager giant Labatt in the process.

Tasting Notes
A golden beer with a spicy, fruity, almost sherbety aroma. Light, tart fruit features in the taste over delicate malt and soft, peppery hops, with the same peppery bitterness and fruit in the finish.

Major stockist local Somerfield

CHILTERN

The Chiltern Brewery, Nash Lee Road, Terrick, Aylesbury, Buckinghamshire HP17 0TQ.
Tel. (01296) 613647 Fax (01296) 612419
E-mail: info@chilternbrewery.co.uk
Web site: www.chilternbrewery.co.uk
Mail order service

Chiltern Brewery was set up in 1980 on a small farm and specialises in beer-related foods (cheeses, sausages, mustards, etc.), as well as traditional ales. On site is a very well-stocked visitors' centre-cum-shop and a small but interesting collection of Buckinghamshire breweriana. Chiltern produces a range of bottled beers but only one is bottle conditioned.

BODGERS BARLEY WINE

ABV 8.5%   **Bottle size** 500 ml   **Serve** cool
Ingredients Maris Otter pale malt; Fuggle, Golding and Challenger hops

Brewed first in 1990, to commemorate the tenth anniversary of the founding of the brewery, Bodgers recalls the tradition of the Chiltern Bodger (a local craftsman-chairmaker) in its name, and the year of the brewery's birth in its original gravity (1080). It is occasionally made available on draught but otherwise is bottled as a fine accompaniment to the Chiltern range of beer-related foods. The brewery particularly recommends it with powerful cheeses, full-flavoured sausages and strong meats. Bottled in house, the beer is fined rather than filtered and is not primed with new yeast or sugar. The bottles are kept at the brewery to mature for four weeks and are then released for consumption – if you follow the best before date – sometime within the next 12 months. The brewery's own literature describes it as 'a thunderbolt of a barley wine'.

Tasting Notes

An unusual, light amber beer, tasting fruity, dry and yet with a very sweet maltiness. The nose combines sweet malt with a light, resin-like hop aroma. Sweet malt and hop bitterness merge in the warming finish. Sweetness fades as the beer ages in the bottle.

CHURCH END

**Church End Brewery Ltd., 109 Ridge Lane,
Ridge Lane, Warwickshire CV10 0RD.
Tel. (01827) 713080 Fax (01827) 717328**

Church End Brewery was founded in 1994, in an old coffin workshop next to The Griffin Inn in Shustoke, Warwickshire. In 2001 it moved to new premises, five miles away in Ridge Lane. Church End had already experimented with bottle-conditioned beers on a few occasions before making a major commitment when launching Rugby Ale in the spring of 1998. Since then two further bottles have been added to the range. All are bottled by Wessex Craft Brewers and carry a nine–12-month best before date.

NUNS ALE

ABV 4.5%   **Bottle size** 500 ml   **Serve** cool
Ingredients Pale malt; crystal malt; Green Bullet, Cascade and Amarillo hops

Brewed to raise money for St Mary Abbey in Nuneaton (which once had its own brewery and was responsible in part for the town's name), Nuns Ale first appeared in 2002 and is now produced several times a year. The choice of hops is interesting to say the least, with Green Bullet from New Zealand teamed up with Cascade and the rare Amarillo from America.

Tasting Notes

A yellow-gold ale with an aroma of spicy, fruity hops. The taste is crisp, bitter and fruity, with lemon notes to the fore, building to a dry, bitter, lemony finish.

RUGBY ALE

ABV 5%   **Bottle size** 500 ml   **Serve** cool
Ingredients Pale malt; crystal malt; amber malt; chocolate malt; Northdown hops

Church End's Warwickshire home is not far from the town of Rugby, the birthplace of the sport of the same name back in 1823. The brewery, therefore, sought to capitalise on the 1999 Rugby World Cup with the launch of this dark beer – a joint venture with Rugby Tourist Board. However, the recipe has now changed, with Hallertau hops giving way to Northdown.

Tasting Notes
A ruby ale with tropical fruit notes, dark malt and a slight smokiness in the nose. Dark malt figures in the mouth, but with a lightening sweet fruitiness. Coffee and chocolate feature in the bitter finish.

ARTHUR'S WIT

ABV 6%   **Bottle size** 500 ml   **Serve** cool
Ingredients Pale malt; torrefied wheat; Mount Hood and Cascade hops

Introduced as a cask beer five years ago, Arthur's Wit was bottled for the first time in 2002. Despite its Belgian sounding name, this is not a spiced wheat beer, but a strong golden ale – and a good bread and cheese accompaniment, according to the brewery.

Tasting Notes
A big malty aroma heralds this powerful, bittersweet mix of malt and orangey hops, the hops taking over, along with bitterness, in the finish.

CITY OF CAMBRIDGE

City of Cambridge Brewery Co Ltd, Ely Road, Chittering, Cambridge CB5 9PH. Tel. (01223) 864864
E-mail: sales@cambridge-brewery.co.uk
Web site: www.cambridge-brewery.co.uk

City of Cambridge Brewery was opened by Steve Draper in May 1997 and moved to new premises, on the Ely road (A10), just north of the city, in 2002. All available cask beers are bottled regularly to maintain stocks, and are kräusened with fresh Hobson's Choice wort first.

JET BLACK

ABV 3.7%   **Bottle size** 500 ml   **Serve** cool
Ingredients Maris Otter pale malt; crystal malt; caramalt; roasted malt; First Gold hops

Not much explanation needed for the name of this

beer: the colour says it all. A Cambridge Beer Festival champion from 1998.

Tasting Notes
Subtle chocolate features in the aroma of this softly malty, light-bodied beer which has a gentle fruit edge and some roasted malt in the easy finish.

BOATHOUSE BITTER

ABV 3.8%   **Bottle size** 500 ml   **Serve** cool
Ingredients Maris Otter pale malt; crystal malt; First Gold and Cascade hops

Most of the brewery's bottled beers reflect the life and culture of the university city of Cambridge in their names, this one majoring on the rowing heritage.

Tasting Notes
A deep amber beer with a rich, chocolatey nose, supported by a little citrus hoppiness. The taste is malty and fruity (tell-tale pineapple notes from the Cascade hops), with hints of chocolate, but quite dry. Very dry, mostly bitter, malt and fruit aftertaste. Plenty of depth for its modest strength.

Major stockist local Asda

HOBSON'S CHOICE

ABV 4.1%   **Bottle size** 500 ml   **Serve** cool
Ingredients Maris Otter pale malt; caramalt; First Gold hops

This brew, launched in 1997, takes its name from the story of Mr Hobson, a Cambridge horse-merchant who, as legend has it, allowed only the particular horse he specified to be hired – hence 'Hobson's Choice'.

Tasting Notes
A bronze beer with a fresh, fruity, spritzy nose, backed by malt. On the palate, it is crisp and generally bitter but delicately fruity, too, although it is clearly less malty to taste than some of the brewery's other ales. Very dry, bitter finish with lingering fruit.

Major stockists local Asda and Waitrose

BLEND '42'

ABV 4.4%   **Bottle size** 500 ml   **Serve** cool
Ingredients Maris Otter pale malt; crystal malt; caramalt; roasted malt; First Gold hops

As its name suggests, this beer is actually a mix of two

of City of Cambridge's other brews – Hobson's Choice and Atomsplitter. The '42' refers to the answer to the Ultimate Question to Life, the Universe and Everything, as posed by the late Douglas Adams in his *Hitch-Hiker's Guide to the Galaxy* (Adams was born in Cambridge).

Tasting Notes

An amber ale with a juicy, citrous nose. Juicy, fruity and peppery hops dominate the taste and also bring a crisp, firm bitterness. Long, dry, bitter and hoppy aftertaste.

SUNSET SQUARE

ABV 4.4%   **Bottle size** 500 ml   **Serve** cool
Ingredients Maris Otter pale malt; crystal malt; caramalt; roasted malt; First Gold hops

A new beer named after a square in Cambridge that is renowned as a suntrap on late summer evenings.

DRUMMER STREET STOUT

ABV 4.5%   **Bottle size** 500 ml   **Serve** cool
Ingredients Maris Otter pale malt; crystal malt; roasted malt; torrefied wheat; sea salt; Challenger and Golding hops

The newest bottled beer, introduced in 2003: a stout named after a street in the city where buses congregate!

Tasting Notes

A near-black stout with fruity notes over dark malt in its aroma. The moderate body makes for easy drinking as the bitter coffee notes of the malt are balanced and sweetened by fruit. Hints of charcoal in the bitter finish.

MICH'AELMAS

ABV 4.6%   **Bottle size** 500 ml   **Serve** cool
Ingredients Maris Otter pale malt; crystal malt; caramalt; roasted malt; First Gold and Cascade hops

This is the brewery's Christmas beer, a Cambridge Winter Beer Festival cask ale award-winner.

ATOMSPLITTER

ABV 4.7%   **Bottle size** 500 ml   **Serve** cool
Ingredients Maris Otter pale malt; crystal malt; caramalt; roasted malt; First Gold hops

It was in Cambridge that scientist Ernest Rutherford did much of his research into splitting the atom and this beer, introduced in bottle in 1998, recalls those days. (The working title for the beer was Rutherford's IPA.)

Tasting Notes
An amber beer with a rich, malty, chocolatey nose, backed by a hint of orange. Mouthfilling malt and lemon/orange fruitiness feature in the well-rounded taste which leans towards sweetness but never quite gets there as hop bitterness blends in. Clean, dry, pleasantly bitter finish, with lingering malt and orange notes.

Major stockist local Asda

DARWIN'S DOWNFALL

ABV 5%　　　**Bottle size** 500 ml　　**Serve** cool
Ingredients Maris Otter pale malt; crystal malt; caramalt; roasted malt; First Gold hops

Darwin's Downfall is another of City of Cambridge's blends, this time successfully combining Atomsplitter and Parkers Porter. Its name recalls Charles Darwin's links with the university city and the label shows the various stages of human/ape evolution.

Tasting Notes
A flavoursome, ruby-coloured beer with luscious tropical fruit in the aroma. The taste is bitter and fruity, with some roasted grain behind, and a dry, roasted, bitter finish.

PARKERS PORTER

ABV 5.3%　　**Bottle size** 500 ml　　**Serve** cool
Ingredients Maris Otter pale malt; crystal malt; caramalt; roasted malt; First Gold hops

The central area of greenbelt in Cambridge is a meadow known as Parkers Piece, as recalled in the name of this porter.

Tasting Notes
A dark ruby beer featuring nutty, roasted malt in the aroma. The taste is malty, nodding towards sweetness through the dark malt, rather than roastiness. It is fairly fruity and has a good bitter balance. Dry, fruity, gently bitter finish, with a suggestion of liquorice.

BRAMLING TRADITIONAL

ABV 5.5%　　**Bottle size** 500 ml　　**Serve** cool
Ingredients Maris Otter pale malt; crystal malt; caramalt; roasted malt; First Gold and Bramling Cross hops

Distinctive Bramling Cross hops make their presence known in the both the title and the taste.
Tasting Notes
Strong blackcurrant notes fill the aroma of this reddish-amber bitter and emerge again in the fruity taste. Not as sweet as many beers of this strength, it has good balancing bitterness, and a dry, bitter, fruity finish.

CLEARWATER

Clearwater Brewery, 2 Devon Units, Great Torrington, Devon EX38 7HP. Tel./Fax (01805) 625242

A brewery founded in 1999, Clearwater acknowledges the impact of the English Civil War on Devon in its beer names. Its bottled beers are all filled on site from casks conditioned at the brewery for seven–ten days. A new small bottling plant was installed in summer 2003.

CAVALIER ALE

ABV 4%   **Bottle size** 500 ml   **Serve** cool
Ingredients Pipkin pale malt; crystal malt; chocolate malt; Challenger and Golding hops

Remembering the Royalists who supported King Charles I in the Civil War, this beer also marks the defeat of those Cavaliers at the local battle of Torrington in 1646.
Tasting Notes
Malt and figgy hop fruit stand out in the nose of this amber ale. Figgy-orangey fruit continues in the taste, which is mostly malty but bitter, with roasted notes. The bitter finish features the same fruit.

1646

ABV 4.8%   **Bottle size** 500 ml   **Serve** cool
Ingredients Pipkin pale malt; crystal malt; Golding hops

1646 was the year when Sir Thomas Fairfax took the town of Torrington for the Parliamentarian side, bringing to an end Royalist resistance in the West Country. A re-enacted scene fronts the bottle's label.
Tasting Notes
There's a surprise in the nose of this golden ale, as an Ovaltine maltiness is the main feature and not hops. Malt continues up front in the taste but there's also a light, citrous edge from the hops. The finish is bittersweet and malty, with some hop lingering.

OLIVER'S NECTAR

ABV 5.2%   **Bottle size** 500 ml   **Serve** cool
Ingredients Pipkin pale malt; crystal malt; roasted barley;
Challenger and Golding hops

Another re-enactment features on the label of Oliver's
Nectar – obviously a reference to Cromwell, who, after
the battle of Torrington, went on to become Protector
of England.
Tasting Notes
A dark copper beer with spicy hop overlaying malt in
the nose. The taste is tangy and nutty with a lemon
fruitiness and a dark malt backdrop. Hops and toasted
malt figure in the finish as bitterness takes over.

CONISTON

**Coniston Brewing Co. Ltd., Coppermines Road,
Coniston, Cumbria LA21 8HL.
Tel. (01539 4) 41133 Fax (01539 4) 41177
E-mail: coniston-brewery@kencomp.net
Web site: www.conistonbrewery.com**

This brewery was set up in 1994 behind Coniston's
Black Bull pub. The ten-barrel plant achieved a minor
miracle in turning out CAMRA's supreme *Champion Beer
of Britain* in 1998, in the shape of Bluebird Bitter. With
orders flooding in, and capacity way surpassed by
demand, Coniston contracted out the brewing of this
bottled version to Brakspear, who also produced the
bottles of Old Man Ale that were introduced in 2000.
Since the demise of the Henley brewery, the contract to
brew Coniston beers for the bottle has remained with
former Brakspear head brewer Peter Scholey. Through
his new business, he now produces the beers himself,
using equipment at Hepworth & Co in Horsham, and
the ingredients he ordered in advance for Brakspear.

BLUEBIRD BITTER

ABV 4.2%   **Bottle size** 500 ml   **Serve** cool
Ingredients Maris Otter pale malt; crystal malt;
Challenger hops

Hot on the heels of the success of cask Bluebird (3.6%),
this stronger version soon began to win accolades of its
own. A gold medal at London's International Food
Exhibition in 1999 was soon followed by first prize in

the *Beauty of Hops* competition. In 2001, the beer picked up yet another *Beauty of Hops* gold, this time judged by a panel of female experts as *The Ultimate Fem'ale in a Bottle*, and in 2003 it earned a silver in the *International Beer Competition*. Before bottling, the beer is filtered and re-seeded with the same primary yeast. The best before date is set at 12 months after bottling. The beer takes its name from the famous *Bluebird* land and water speed machines used by Donald Campbell, who was tragically killed on Coniston Water in 1967. The beer is imported into the US by Shelton Brothers.

Tasting Notes
A copper-coloured beer with a peppery, spicy, fruity hop nose. Pepper, spice and the zest of citrus continue in the clean, crisp taste and the dry, bitter finish.

Major stockists Safeway, Sainsbury, Waitrose, Co-op, Morrisons, Booths, local Asda

OLD MAN ALE

ABV 5%   **Bottle size** 500 ml   **Serve** cool
Ingredients Maris Otter pale malt; crystal malt; roasted barley; Challenger hops

Named after the mountain overlooking Coniston, Old Man – described as 'an old style bitter' – was first produced in cask in 1995, although at a lower ABV (4.4%) than this bottled version.

Tasting Notes
A ruby-coloured strong ale with a malty aroma featuring a little orange fruit. The crisp taste also features dark malt and spicy, orangey hops, with a suggestion of creamy toffee behind. Dry, bitter, malty finish with roasted barley notes.

COORS

**Coors Brewers Ltd., PO Box 217, High Street, Burton upon Trent, Staffordshire DE14 1BG.
Tel. (01283) 511000 Fax (01283) 513873**

**Museum Brewing Company, Horninglow Street, Burton upon Trent, Staffordshire DE14 1YQ.
Tel. (01283) 513565 Fax (01283) 513509
E-mail: steve.wellington@coorsbrewers.com
Web site: www.bass-museum.com**

Proof that large-scale brewing is now an international affair was provided by the sale of Bass. The historic brewing company was purchased in 2000 by Interbrew, which, because it also owned Whitbread, was then forced to sell off part of its new acquisition. In stepped Coors, one of America's major brewers, to purchase most of the Bass breweries and some of its brands, including the Worthington's range. Thus a high-tech Colorado company became owners of the Bass Museum, a shrine to the halcyon days of traditional ale production, and with it its vibrant Museum Brewing Company.

The Museum Brewery began life as a static display. It is housed in a former engine room, in a corner of what used to be the Bass tradesmen's yard, amidst former cobblers', coppersmiths' and tailors' units. The equipment was recovered from M&B's Cape Hill brewery in Birmingham, with parts of the kit dating from 1850 and 1920. Although pieced together in 1976, the equipment only became fully operational again in 1994 and, with long-term Bass employee Steve Wellington installed as brewer, began to specialise in reviving lost beer brands from the company's archives.

A new bottling line, capable of filling 900 bottles per hour, was introduced to cope with demand for Worthington's White Shield, which was acquired following the closure of King & Barnes in Horsham. The beer had suffered a chequered recent past. At the end of 1997 Bass had announced that the beer, one of the world's classic bottle-conditioned ales, was to be discontinued, with sales down to a mere 1,000 barrels a year. After a wave of protest, Bass relented and sold the brewing and marketing rights to King & Barnes, who made a success of the beer, even taking gold in the 2000 *Champion Beer of Britain* competition. Regrettably, the Horsham brewery was closed shortly after, leaving White Shield looking for another new home. Steve Wellington was only too keen to accept the challenge. However, similarity to White Shield has meant that production of the Museum's own Masterpiece IPA (sold mainly under personalised labels) has been suspended. Under Coors, a major rebranding of the Worthington's range has taken place, including for White Shield, which Coors has added to its general portfolio.

WORTHINGTON'S WHITE SHIELD

ABV 5.6%   **Bottle size** 275/500 ml **Serve** cool
Ingredients Pearl pale malt; crystal malt; Fuggle, Golding and Northdown hops

For years Worthington's White Shield, along with

Guinness Extra Stout, was the welcome standby for serious drinkers who found themselves tragically marooned in a keg-only pub. In many ways, it's the archetypal Burton pale ale, so it's wonderful news that it has now returned home, after short stopovers at Bass plants in Sheffield and Birmingham, and most recently at King & Barnes. The beer is now brewed every week and, following primary fermentation, it is filtered and re-seeded with new 'sticky' yeast (a different strain to that used earlier in the brewing process). Once in your possession, bottles should improve with keeping up to the best before date of 12 months after filling. White Shield enthusiasts would consider that equivalent to drinking green beer: some happily tuck crates away for a rainy day long into the future. The beer is imported into the US by B United.

Tasting Notes
An amber beer with a malty, fruity nose, including a hint of tropical fruit. The full taste features silky, nutty malt sweetness, solid hop bitterness and a light undercurrent of tropical fruit and almond. Bitter hops dominate the finish.

Major stockists Safeway, Asda, Sainsbury, Booths, Unwins

BULLION

ABV 6.5%   **Bottle size** 500 ml   **Serve** cool
Ingredients Pearl pale malt; Fuggle, Golding and Northdown hops.

A *Tesco Beer Challenge* winner (the second for Museum, after the spiced Wulfric in 2001), this pale golden beer was exclusive to Tesco until July 2003. Recommended with 'spicy foods, roasts, cold meats and cheeses'.

Tasting Notes
Luscious tropical fruits, with pineapple prominent, fill the aroma of this powerful ale. The taste is similarly estery, with juicy fruit notes and hints of almond. Quite syrupy, but not too sweet. Dry, bitter, hoppy finish.

Major stockist Tesco

P2

ABV 8%   **Bottle size** 275 ml   **Serve** cool
Ingredients Halcyon pale malt; crystal malt; black malt; Fuggle and Golding hops.

P2 is a dark, very strong, Russian-style stout, of the sort once shipped to the imperial court of Russia during the

19th century. Unearthed in the Bass archives, the beer is allowed eight or nine days' primary fermentation, then cooled to 10° C in tanks for two weeks. The temperature is then lowered further for another couple of weeks of conditioning before the beer is primed with sucrose (if the residual fermentibles are not sufficient) and bottled. Although a six-month best before date is applied, the strength of the beer ensures it survives and matures well beyond this period.

Tasting Notes

A very dark brown, almost black, beer with a honey-coloured head and a powerful aroma which combines fruit with the scent of polished leather. In the mouth, the beer is not as aggressive as expected, but instead smooth and sweetish with good roast malt and fruit flavours. The dry finish features mellow, sweetish roast malt with pleasant hop bitterness to balance.

NO. 1 BARLEY WINE

ABV 10.5%   **Bottle size** 275 ml   **Serve** cool
Ingredients Halcyon pale malt; Fuggle and Golding hops

No. 1 is a re-creation of the famous Bass barley wine of the same name which was consigned to the archives a number of years ago. In its latter days, that beer was pasteurised but it had been enjoyed by many drinkers in its natural, bottle-conditioned form for decades. No. 1 is an intriguing beer. Its hue is dark red yet the colour is only derived from pale malt that caramelises during the extra-long, 12-hour boil. This evaporates the wort down from an initial five barrels to three. With three separate hop charges at various stages, however, this is no sweet, cloying mixture. The beer is matured in cask for more than 12 months before bottling.

Tasting Notes

This well-rounded, dark ruby beer has a powerful, sherry-like nose. The taste is mouth-filling, warming and exceptionally fruity with some liquorice character and bitterness. Ultra-long, creamy, bitter fruit finish.

CORVEDALE

Corvedale Brewery, The Sun Inn, Corfton, Craven Arms, Shropshire SY7 9DF. Tel. (01584) 861503
Web site: www.suninncorfton.co.uk

Publican Norman Pearce is the brewer in the tiny brewery housed behind The Sun Inn in rural

Shropshire. His beers are bottled for him by Hanby Ales
and special/commemorative brews are also bottled up
when available. Small runs of 'own label' beers are often
sold to local restaurants.

TERESA'S BIRTHDAY

ABV 4.2%   **Bottle size** 500 ml   **Serve** cool
Ingredients Maris Otter pale malt; crystal malt; wheat
malt; Northdown and Susan hops

A tawny beer devised by Norman for his wife's birthday:
the strength is raised by 0.1% every January.

NORMAN'S PRIDE

ABV 4.3%   **Bottle size** 500 ml   **Serve** cool
Ingredients Maris Otter pale malt; crystal malt; wheat
malt; Northdown hops

Norman's own beer, his first commercial brew,
introduced in autumn 1999.
Tasting Notes
An amber ale with a soft, fruity, bubblegum-like aroma.
The taste is bitter and fruity with a lingering trace of
bubblegum, while the finish is bitter.

SECRET HOP

ABV 4.5%   **Bottle size** 500 ml   **Serve** cool
Ingredients Maris Otter pale malt; crystal malt; wheat
malt; Susan hops

As its name suggests, this beer began life using an
unknown hop strain. Initially given only a number
(93/50), the hop – grown near Ledbury – is now in
general circulation under the name of Susan.
Tasting Notes
A crisp, amber bitter with a strong blackcurrant nose.
Juicy blackcurrants and bitterness fill the mouth before
a slightly toasted, bitter, blackcurrant finish.

DARK AND DELICIOUS

ABV 4.6%   **Bottle size** 500 ml   **Serve** cool
Ingredients Maris Otter pale malt; crystal malt; chocolate
malt; wheat malt; Northdown and Susan hops

Described by Norman as a 'black bitter', this beer was
introduced as a one-off for Christmas 2000 but has

CORVEDALE

proved popular enough to take its place as a regular on
the bar of The Sun.
Tasting Notes
A ruby beer with an aroma that is hop-fruity rather
than deeply malty, as expected, but with a little
chocolate all the same. The taste is fairly bitter and hop-
fruity, with roasted malt and another hint of chocolate.
Dry, bitter, roasted finish.

COUNTRYLIFE

**Countrylife Brewery, The Big Sheep, Abbotsham,
Devon EX39 5AP. Tel. (01237) 420808
E-mail: simon@countrylife.freeserve.co.uk
Web site: www.countrylifebrewery.co.uk**

This small brewery was acquired from Lundy Island in
1999 and set up at the Pig on the Hill pub, near
Westward Ho! The plant was then moved in 2002 to
The Big Sheep farm attraction, where the beers are
offered in daily tastings to visitors and brewery tours are
available in summer. The beers are filtered prior to
bottling and re-injected with fresh yeast. A 12-month
shelf life is predicted.

OLD APPLEDORE

ABV 4.2%   **Bottle size** 500 ml   **Serve** cool
Ingredients Maris Otter pale malt; crystal malt; roasted
malt; wheat malt; Fuggle and Golding hops

A stronger version of Countrylife's cask beer of the same
name (3.7%). A fish and chips or pie and mash sort of
beer, suggests brewer Simon Lacey.

WALLOP

ABV 4.4%   **Bottle size** 500 ml   **Serve** cool
Ingredients Maris Otter pale malt; wheat malt; Fuggle and
Golding hops

A golden ale that Simon thinks goes well with Chinese
or Indian food.

GOLDEN PIG

ABV 4.7%   **Bottle size** 500 ml   **Serve** cool
Ingredients Maris Otter pale malt; Challenger and
Golding hops

Golden Pig was the first of Countrylife's bottled beers (the same beer as its cask equivalent). Good with fish, according to Simon.

Tasting Notes
A golden bitter with malt and fruit in the nose, strong hop-fruit and bitterness in the taste and a long, tangy hop finish.

COUNTRY BUMPKIN

ABV 6%   **Bottle size** 500 ml   **Serve** cool
Ingredients Maris Otter pale malt; chocolate malt; Challenger and Golding hops

Country Bumpkin is, again, the bottled equivalent of a draught ale, which Simon reckons makes a good match for steak meals.

Tasting Notes
An amber ale, with an aroma that is spicy, malty and a little fruity. A tasty, powerful mix of strong hops, fruit and sweet malt follows on the palate, rounded off by a hoppy, bitter, fruity finish.

COX & HOLBROOK

Cox & Holbrook, Manor Farm, Brettenham Road, Buxhall, Suffolk IP14 3DY. Tel. (01449) 736323

Accountant David Cox set up his five-barrel brewery in Great Finborough in 1997 and moved it a few miles to the outskirts of the village of Buxhall in 2001. He resumed production in summer 2003 but, while the brewery was in transit and the new premises were being made ready, bottling was carried out by Iceni Brewery.

GOODCOCK'S WINNER

ABV 5%   **Bottle size** 500 ml   **Serve** cool
Ingredients Maris Otter pale malt; caramalt; chocolate malt; Fuggle hops

There's more than an echo of Roy of the Rovers about this notably hoppy brown ale. Apparently, its name commemorates the winning goal scored by Archie Goodcock in the final game of the North Eastern Alliance's 1933–4 season, which gave Billingham North End victory over Stockton United and clinched the championship! A footballer in period kit gives the thumbs-up on the label.

Tasting Notes
A russet-coloured ale with a tropical-fruity, malty nose.
Deliciously fruity, the taste has sweetness to the fore but
plenty of crisp hop balance. Dry, bittersweet finish.

IRON OAK SINGLE STOUT

ABV 5%   **Bottle size** 500 ml   **Serve** cool
Ingredients Maris Otter pale malt; crystal malt; roasted
barley; flaked barley; Northdown hops; oak

Iron Oak is the name of the forge belonging to local
artistic blacksmith Graham Chaplin and his logo
appears on the label. The unusual ingredient – as
suggested in the name – is a little toasted oak wood.
The brewery has plans to add a double and a triple
stout to the range alongside this 'single' version.
Tasting Notes
A near-black stout, with an aroma of creamy malt and
roasted grain. Roasted malt and bitterness lead in the
mouth, but with malty sweetness behind. Dry, slightly
creamy, bitter, liquorice-and-roast finish.

REMUS

ABV 5%   **Bottle size** 500 ml   **Serve** cool
Ingredients Maris Otter pale malt; crystal malt; caramalt;
Cascade hops

Remus is named after an old Suffolk Punch horse which
is a major attraction at nearby Stowmarket's Museum of
East Anglian Life. His picture adorns the label.
Tasting Notes
A dark red beer with an unusual herbal, slightly fruity
aroma, backed by a hint of chocolate. The taste is also
herbal, as well as malty and bittersweet, with some
apple notes. Dry, herbal, dark malt finish. A novel brew.

STORMWATCH

ABV 5%   **Bottle size** 500 ml   **Serve** cool
Ingredients Maris Otter pale malt; chocolate malt; roasted
barley; wheat malt; Fuggle and Golding hops

Though the label includes a stunning picture of
lightning forking over the village of Wrabness, on the
Stour Estuary, taken by the aforementioned Graham
Chaplin, the inspiration for this premium ale was
actually Jethro Tull's 1979 album of the same name
(David admits to being a long-time fan).

Tasting Notes
A reddish-brown beer with a lasting white head. The aroma is lightly chocolatey, malty and fruity, while the taste is clean and fruity, with a crisp, bitter (almost liquorice-like) balance. Dry, fruity, bittersweet finish.

STOWMARKET PORTER

ABV 5%   **Bottle size** 500 ml   **Serve** cool
Ingredients Maris Otter pale malt; chocolate malt; wheat malt; roasted barley; flaked barley; Fuggle hops

A visit to Cox & Holbrook may mean dodging the dozens of game birds that take their life in their claws by criss-crossing the surrounding country lanes. Not surprisingly, a brace of pheasants has been adopted as the brewery's main emblem and the same birds are depicted on the label of this beer.
Tasting Notes
A very dark brown, easy-drinking beer with a soft coffee nose. The fruity taste is well rounded and not too sweet, with subtle roast grain notes. Lightish body. Dry, pleasantly bitter, roasted grain finish.

UNCLE STAN

ABV 5%   **Bottle size** 500 ml   **Serve** cool
Ingredients Maris Otter pale malt; crystal malt; chocolate malt; Fuggle hops

Named after the brewer's own Uncle Stan, this is a rare example of a single brown, 19th-century-style stout.
Tasting Notes
A ruby beer with fruit, liquorice and a trace of chocolate in the aroma. Hop fruit features on the palate, with some bitterness. Malt is evident throughout the sweetish taste. Dry, fruity, bittersweet finish, with subtle roasted grain and a suggestion of liquorice.

CROPTON

Cropton Brewery Co., The New Inn, Cropton, near Pickering, North Yorkshire YO18 8HH.
Tel. (01751) 417330 Fax (01751) 417310
Web site: www.croptonbrewery.co.uk
Mail order service

Cropton Brewery was set up in 1984 in the cellar of the New Inn, just to supply that pub. By 1994 it had outgrown the cellar and a purpose-built brewery was installed behind the pub, which also now has a visitor's centre for brewery tours. The beers all now bear logos claiming they are suitable for both vegetarians and vegans. They are matured in conditioning tanks, filtered and then re-seeded with fresh yeast before bottling, and all carry a 12-months best before stamp. The US importer is Shelton Brothers.

KING BILLY BITTER

ABV 3.6%   **Bottle size** 500 ml   **Serve** cool
Ingredients Pale malt; Challenger and East Kent Golding hops

King Billy is a rare, bottle-conditioned session ale. Its name was derived from the statue of King William III outside the King William pub in Hull, which Cropton has long supplied with cask beer. In 1993, the landlord of the pub asked for a brew which his regulars could 'drink all day and not become excitable', hence this popular quaffing brew.
Tasting Notes
A golden beer with a surprisingly strong aroma of malt, hops and creamy fruit. Reasonably thin in body, it tastes malty and dry before an even drier, increasingly bitter finish.
Major stockist (all beers) local Tesco

ENDEAVOUR

ABV 3.8%   **Bottle size** 500 ml   **Serve** cool
Ingredients Pale malt; Challenger and Golding hops

Named after Captain Cook's famous ship, that originally sailed from nearby Whitby, Endeavour is a new bitter aimed at the tourist market in the seaside resort (a replica of *Endeavour* sails into Whitby every year and draws in the crowds).
Tasting Notes
A dark golden ale with hop fruit and malt in the nose and taste, and a light, bittersweet finish.

TWO PINTS BITTER

ABV 4%   **Bottle size** 500 ml   **Serve** cool
Ingredients Pale malt; crystal malt; Challenger and East Kent Golding hops

A pint of Two Pints was first served at the New Inn back

in 1984, the brewery's first year of operation, but the beer did not find its way into a bottle until 1996. It's now the brewery's biggest selling beer, taking its name from the idea that one pint of Two Pints 'is worth two of any other'. The label shows a landlord handing over two foaming tankards of ale.

Tasting Notes
A dry, amber-coloured bitter with citrous fruitiness, malt and bitterness the key elements in the taste, preceded by a hoppy, malty nose. The dry finish is bitter and hoppy.

HONEY FARM BITTER

ABV 4.2%   **Bottle size** 500 ml   **Serve** cool
Ingredients Pale malt; honey; First Gold hops

This beer (for a time known as Honey Gold) was introduced in cask-conditioned form for Cropton's own first beer festival, held in March 1998, and is now a summer supplement to the brewery's standard draught range. It is a single-varietal hop brew, using only the popular dwarf hop, First Gold, plus a dose of Yorkshire honey.

Tasting Notes
A golden beer with a honeyed nose. The crisp, bitter taste has a light hop edge, with soft honey evident particularly on the swallow. Bitter, hoppy finish with more than a hint of honey.

SCORESBY STOUT

ABV 4.2%   **Bottle size** 500 ml   **Serve** cool
Ingredients Pale malt; crystal malt; roasted barley; Challenger and Golding hops

This rich, dark stout takes its name from the late William Scoresby, a whaling captain who hailed from Cropton – which explains the presence of a whaling ship being tossed on the high seas on the label. Among his various achievements, Scoresby is said to have invented the crow's nest. He is now commemorated with a plaque at Whitby harbour. The cask equivalent of this beer made its debut in 1988 and this bottled option was first produced in 1996.

Tasting Notes
This almost black beer (with just a hint of red) has a strong coffee aroma. The taste is soft, malty and coffeeish, enhanced by some burnt grain notes. Bitter coffee features in the finish.

UNCLE SAMS BITTER

ABV 4.4%   **Bottle size** 500 ml   **Serve** cool
Ingredients Pale malt; crystal malt; Cascade hops

Certainly the most distinctive of Cropton's bottled ales, Uncle Sams is a homage to the American microbrewer revolution and is chock-full of the perfumed aroma and taste of American Cascade hops. Lest there be any doubt about its inspiration, the label has a Wild West image, with a gun-toting Annie Oakley (or some other girl sharp-shooter) as the focal point. Both this and the original cask version were introduced in 1997.

Tasting Notes
A golden beer with an aroma rich in tangy Cascade hops. These spill over into the taste, bringing strong bitter lemon notes. The aftertaste is dry and full of scented hops.

RUDOLPH'S REVENGE

ABV 4.6%   **Bottle size** 500 ml   **Serve** cool
Ingredients Pale malt; crystal malt; roasted barley; Cascade, Styrian Golding and Challenger hops

This is Cropton's Christmas beer and shares with Uncle Sams an American nuance, thanks to the use of Cascade hops. At 4.6%, it is one of the UK's less potent Christmas ales, and is also sold in cask.

Tasting Notes
A red ale with a malty, lightly citrous aroma. Citrous fruit continues in the malty taste, as the aromatic hops take hold and roasted barley drifts well into the background. The long aftertaste is hoppy, tangy and roasty.

YORKSHIRE MOORS

ABV 4.6%   **Bottle size** 500 ml   **Serve** cool
Ingredients Pale malt; crystal malt; roasted malt; Challenger and Styrian Golding hops

Created to help commemorate 50 years of the National Park service in 2002, Yorkshire Moors has now become a permanent part of the Cropton range, replacing Backwoods Bitter (the recipe is basically the same, but this is more quaffable than the 5.1% Backwoods).

Tasting Notes
A light ruby ale with a citrous, malty nose that is also a little peppery. The soft, dark malt taste is balanced by a

peppery, fruity bitterness that smacks of cherries. The finish is dry and malty, yet also bitter and hoppy, with some roast character.

MONKMAN'S SLAUGHTER

ABV 6%   **Bottle size** 500 ml   **Serve** cool
Ingredients Pale malt; crystal malt; roasted malt; Challenger and East Kent Golding hops

Originally known by the name 'Special Strong', this powerful beer takes its unusual, and rather macabre, title from two quite innocent sources. These are Messrs Colin Monkman and Colin Slaughter, the brewery's barley farmer and head brewer, respectively.
Tasting Notes
A ruby-coloured ale with vinous fruit and dark malts dominant in the nose. The taste is initially sweetish, fruity and malty, with roast grain gradually taking over. Roasty, bitter aftertaste, with hints of liquorice.

DARWIN

**Darwin Brewery Ltd., 63 Back Tatham Street, Sunderland, Tyne & Wear SR1 3SD.
Tel. (0191) 515 2535 Fax (0191) 515 2531
E-mail: info@darwinbrewery.com
Web site: www.darwinbrewery.com**

Darwin Brewery was founded in 1994 as a research facility for students at the University of Sunderland's Brewlab. In 1997, its directors took over the nearby Hodge's Brewery and the whole business was relocated to a new site in Sunderland in 2002. One of the brewery's specialities is the re-creation of historic beer styles, such as some of the bottled brews below. A new range of specialist beers (novel and traditional) is planned and these will be bottled in small quantities (150-bottle batches). Darwin also brews beers for High Force Brewery (see separate entry).

RICHMOND ALE

ABV 4.5%   **Bottle size** 500 ml   **Serve** cool
Ingredients Pale malt; crystal malt; brown malt; black malt; Fuggle and Golding hops

Showing Richmond Castle on its 'stained-glass'-style label, Richmond Ale is described as a 'double brown ale' and is brewed using North Yorkshire malt and a northern yeast strain. A recipe from a Ripon brewery gave Brewlab director Dr Keith Thomas a feeling for the malt character of a beer that might have been available in the late 1800s and records from a maltings near Richmond showed what brewers were ordering at the time. For the yeast, Keith turned to local fruit. He felt that the brewers of the time would have thrown their yeast around without much thought and he considered that yeast living wild on fruit in the area today would have been related to the brewers' yeast of the time. Richmond Ale is also available in cask form and as a filtered bottle, so look carefully for the tastier bottle-conditioned version, which is kräusened prior to filling.

Tasting Notes
A ruby-red/brown beer with an aroma of malt and toffee. The taste is deeply malty, nutty and fruity, with balancing hop bitterness. Dry, bitter, malty finish.

HAMMOND'S PORTER

ABV 4.7%   **Bottle size** 500 ml   **Serve** cool
Ingredients Pale malt; crystal malt; black malt; maize; glucose sugar; Fuggle hops

Once again Darwin proves that there is life after death. This time the brewers have resurrected the taste of Hammond's Bradford brewery, using 1903 brewery records and authentic yeast from the brewery that became a victim of Bass Charrington consolidation. Small runs mean that the beer is only likely to be found in the North-East.

Tasting Notes
Virtually black in colour, with a beige foam, this porter has a mix of chocolate, coffee and treacly malt in the nose, a smooth, bittersweet, roasted malt taste, with a light hop balance, and a finish of sweet coffee, with hops gradually building.

EXTINCTION ALE

ABV 8.2%   **Bottle size** 500 ml   **Serve** cool
Ingredients Pale malt; crystal malt; Fuggle and Golding hops

Extinction Ale is based on a bottled beer discovered in a cellar on the North York Moors in 1998. Dating from 1927, the beer – a barley wine bottled from the remains of a cask – was thought to have come from the now defunct Scarborough and Whitby brewery. Thanks to close analysis at Brewlab – which sought to identify hops from the bitterness of the beer and the malt from its colour – plus a trawl through brewing archives, a comparable recipe was produced. Extinction Ale is now brewed using yeast isolated from that original bottle. A cask version has also been sold. One to try with a rich dessert perhaps.

Tasting Notes

A red-brown, powerful ale with a vinous malty and fruity (strawberries) aroma. Clean and well-rounded on the palate, it tastes sweet, malty and fruity (prune?). Mouth-numbing, mostly sweet, fruity finish.

HAMMOND'S STINGO

ABV 10%   **Bottle size** 500 ml   **Serve** cool
Ingredients Pale malt; black malt; maize; glucose sugar; Fuggle hops

Like the aforementioned Hammond's Porter, this powerful barley wine was re-created at Brewlab with the help of the County and Durden Park groups of amateur brewing enthusiasts.

Tasting Notes

A ruby beer with a heady nose of vinous fruit and malt. The gum-tingling taste has lots of malt and bitter orange fruit, with a red berry fruitiness emerging on the swallow. Bitterness fights back in the finish, but sweet fruit lingers.

DOGHOUSE

Doghouse Brewery, Scorrier, Redruth, Cornwall TR16 5BN. Tel./Fax (01209) 822022

Why end up in the doghouse by slinking off to the pub when you can now get into the same trouble at home? Doghouse Brewery was set up in 2001 in a former canine rescue centre. Its three bottled ales are all treated with priming sugars and filled directly from the cask, with six months allowed in the best before dates.

STAFFI STOUT

ABV 4.8%   **Bottle size** 500 ml   **Serve** cool
Ingredients Pale malt; crystal malt; black malt; roasted barley; Fuggle and Golding hops

'A Staffordshire bull terrier has a strong bite and so does

this stout', says brewer Steve Willmott. He also reckons it's a good partner for a steak and ale pie.
Tasting Notes
A ruby beer with light fruit and creamy malt in the nose. Nutty, roasted malt in the taste is rounded off by a malty, roasted finish.

BOW WOW

ABV 5%   **Bottle size** 500 ml   **Serve** cool
Ingredients Pale malt; crystal malt; chocolate malt; roasted barley; Challenger hops

A strong ale continuing the 'doggie' theme.
Tasting Notes
A tawny ale with an estery, pear drop and treacly malt nose. Malty to taste, with a tart fruitiness, it finishes malty and bittersweet.

DINGO LAGER

ABV 5%   **Bottle size** 500 ml   **Serve** cold
Ingredients Lager malt; Hallertau hops

Brewed with a lager yeast, this is the brewery's wild dog response to ubiquitous Aussie beer brands.
Tasting Notes
A pale golden beer with a light, malty aroma. Light, sweet malt in the taste is offset by sharp, fruity hops. Bittersweet finish.

DUNN PLOWMAN

Dunn Plowman Brewery, The Brewhouse, Bridge Street, Kington, Herefordshire HR5 3DW.
Tel. (01544) 231993 Fax (01544) 231985
Mail order service

Dunn Plowman was set up in 1987 and moved to its present site, behind the Queen's Head pub in Kington, which is run as a separate concern, in 1994. It is a family business, with Steve and Gaye Dunn as proprietors. As well as the long-standing two beers mentioned opposite, other beers from the Dunn Plowman range may also be bottled from time to time, including the wheat beer, Golden Haze (5%). The beers are filtered, then re-seeded with fresh yeast of the same strain and primed with sugar before bottling. Best before dates are fixed at nine months.

OLD JAKE

ABV 4.8%   **Bottle size** 500 ml   **Serve** cool
Ingredients Maris Otter pale malt; wheat malt; flaked barley; roasted barley; Fuggle and Golding hops

A stout, first bottled in 2000, and now brewed all year. As the label explains, the name commemorates the passing of the family's beloved black and tan crossbreed dog.

CROOKED FURROW

ABV 6.5%   **Bottle size** 330/500 ml **Serve** cool
Ingredients Maris Otter pale malt; crystal malt; black malt; Fuggle and Golding hops

Strong enough to tempt a ploughman off the straight and narrow, this powerful ale was first produced in draught form in 1997 and was channelled into bottle for the first time in 1999.
Tasting Notes
An amber-coloured strong ale with a fruity, malty, spicy aroma. Although it is fruity, with cherry notes, in the mouth, it is not too sweet, but the alcohol is obvious. Dry, bitter fruit finish.

DURHAM

The Durham Brewery, Unit 5A, Bowburn North Industrial Estate, Bowburn, Co. Durham DH6 5PF.
Tel. (0191) 377 1991 Fax (0191) 377 0768
E-mail: gibbs@durham-brewery.co.uk
Web site: www.durham-brewery.co.uk
Mail order service

Durham Brewery was set up by music teachers Steve and Christine Gibbs who foresaw redundancy heading their way as cuts in their local education budget loomed. That was back in 1994 and the brewery now produces a wide range of cask beers and seven highly-regarded bottle-conditioned beers. All are brewed and bottled on site, with beers passing from fermenters into conditioning tanks, where they are chilled and fined with non-animal finings. This ensures that all the bottled beers – as their labels declare – are perfectly acceptable to vegetarians and vegans. The yeast count is then adjusted before bottling takes place. One month's conditioning is allowed before the beers go on sale.

CLOISTER

ABV 4.5%   **Bottle size** 500 ml   **Serve** cool
Ingredients Pale malt; crystal malt; Challenger, Target,
Columbus and Saaz hops

Like this golden ale, all the brewery's beer names have
connections with the spiritual roots of the city of
Durham and in particular the spellbinding cathedral.
Tasting Notes
A dark golden bitter with a citrus hop aroma backed
by light malt. The taste is crisp, pleasantly bitter,
citrously fruity and hoppy, with a very dry bitter and
hoppy aftertaste.

GRADUATION

ABV 4.5%   **Bottle size** 500 ml   **Serve** cool
Ingredients Pale malt; lager malt; wheat malt; Target,
Cascade, Saaz, Golding and Styrian Golding hops

Reflecting the town's university connections in its title,
Graduation is a complex beer seasoned with no less
than five different hops, which are added at various
stages of the brew.
Tasting Notes
A pale golden ale with a lemon/citrous nose and a crisp,
bitter taste filled with lemon notes and sweet malt for
balance. Bitter, lemony finish.

EVENSONG

ABV 5%   **Bottle size** 500 ml   **Serve** cool
Ingredients Pale malt; crystal malt; Golding hops

Evensong, introduced in 2001, is based on a recipe
dating from 1937.
Tasting Notes
A rich ruby ale with a white head and a soft aroma of
citrus and berry fruits along with gentle dark malt. The
soft taste features a restrained fruitiness, gentle malt and
a rounded bitterness, with toasted malt emerging in the
lightly fruity malt finish.

BLACK ABBOT

ABV 5.6%   **Bottle size** 500 ml   **Serve** cool
Ingredients Pale malt; lager malt; Munich malt; pale
chocolate malt; black malt; wheat malt; crystal rye; Saaz
and Northdown hops

Durham used to bottle a beer with the similar name of Black Bishop, but, despite being close in strength and title, Black Abbot is quite a different beer. It's actually a dark lager.

Tasting Notes

A rich ruby beer with a white foam. The aroma is complex: gentle, nutty, roasted malt, mellow coffee and a hint of fruit. The taste is well balanced and clean, with dark malt and a persistent fruity edge continuing into the moreish finish.

ST CUTHBERT

ABV 6.5%   **Bottle size** 500 ml   **Serve** cool
Ingredients Pale malt; crystal malt; Challenger, Target, Columbus, Golding and Saaz hops

St Cuthbert was Durham's first bottle-conditioned beer and was initially called Millennium City – a reference to the fact that Durham was celebrating its 1,000th year as a city at the turn of the millennium. However, with interest in matters millennial fading after the start of 2000, Durham re-christened the beer in honour of the saint whose relics were brought to Durham from Lindisfarne by monks. Inspired by a vision, the monks' decision to settle here heralded the foundation of the city and St Cuthbert still lies in the magnificent cathedral.

Tasting Notes

This strong amber ale has an orange aroma and a smooth, toffeeish malt taste, with a perfect balance of citrus fruits. Hints of pear drops expose the strength, but the beer falls on the bitter side of bittersweet. Soft, lingering, bitter finish of malt and fruit.

BENEDICTUS

ABV 8.4%   **Bottle size** 500 ml   **Serve** cool
Ingredients Pale malt; crystal malt; Golding, Target, Saaz and Styrian Golding hops

Based on St Cuthbert, but with a deeper golden colour, Benedictus was added to the range in 2001.

Tasting Notes

An orange/copper barley wine with orange and pineapple fruits sharing the aroma. Lots of malty body follows in the mouth, but with fruity, spicy hops taking the lead. The bitter, hoppy finish leaves a warming glow. Somewhat reminiscent of Chimay White in its strength and hoppiness.

TEMPTATION

ABV 10%   **Bottle size** 500 ml   **Serve** cool
Ingredients Pale malt; lager malt; black malt; roasted
barley; wheat malt; Target and Golding hops

We all know the Biblical perils of succumbing to
temptation, but Durham thinks it's worth making an
exception for this brew. The name it was first sold
under reveals the style: it was simply called Imperial
Russian Stout.

Tasting Notes
A beer as black as sin with a beige clerical collar. Traces
of mellow coffee, fruit and treacly malt enhance the
lightly winey aroma. In the mouth, the beer is light and
easy drinking, making a mockery of the declared
strength, with sweet malt well to the fore ahead of
coffee and fruity hop notes. Soft liquorice emerges in
the gum-numbing, sweet coffee finish

EARL SOHAM

**Earl Soham Brewery, The Street, Earl Soham,
Suffolk IP13 7RT. Tel. (01728) 684097
E-mail: fram.station@btinternet.com
Web site: www.earlsohambrewery.co.uk**

Founded behind The Victoria pub in the village of Earl
Soham in 1984, this brewery moved along the road to
larger premises in a converted garage in 2001. Next
door stands Tastebuds, a well-stocked post-
office/delicatessen that sells Earl Soham's beers on
draught and in bottle. In addition to the one beer
mentioned below, other Earl Soham cask beers – such as
Sir Roger's Porter (4%), Albert Ale (4.4%), Empress of
India (4.7%) and Jolabrugg (5%) – may find their way
into bottle from time to time.

VICTORIA BITTER

ABV 3.6%   **Bottle size** 500/750 ml **Serve** cool
Ingredients Maris Otter pale malt; Golding, Fuggle and
Styrian Golding hops

Given a best before date of six months, this beer – first
brewed in 1985 – is bottled straight from the cask.
'Drink within weeks and come back for more' is the
advice of brewery owner John Bjornson. He also
suggests trying Victoria Bitter with salads.

ENVILLE

**Enville Brewery, Cox Green, Hollies Lane,
Enville, Stourbridge, W. Midlands DY7 5LG.
Tel. (01384) 873728 Fax (01384) 873770
Web site: www.envilleales.com**

Established on a derelict Victorian farm, reviving
brewing in the village of Enville, which had ceased in
1919, due to the loss of manpower during the Great
War, Enville is known for its honey beers. The owner,
Wil Constantine-Cort, is a beekeeper and a former
brewer at Premier Ales, which closed in the early 1990s.
Both the following beers are bottled off-site under
contract having been fined first at the brewery.

ENVILLE ALE

ABV 4.5%   **Bottle size** 500 ml   **Serve** cool
Ingredients Maris Otter pale malt; Challenger and East
Kent Golding hops; honey

Allegedly based on a recipe handed down from the
proprietor's great-great aunt in Cumbria, Enville Ale was
the brewery's first beer, when it was established in 1993.
The honey is added in conditioning tanks after primary
fermentation has finished.
Tasting Notes
A golden beer with a honey and lemon aroma. The
bittersweet taste is crisp and lemon-fruity, characteristics
carried forward to the finish, where the honey flavour
emerges once more.

GOTHIC ALE

ABV 5.2%   **Bottle size** 500 ml   **Serve** cool
Ingredients Maris Otter pale malt; crystal malt; black
wheat malt; Challenger and Fuggle hops; honey

As dark as the night, Gothic Ale was Enville's second
brew. Its label depicts bats swooping around a Gothic
church tower at nightfall and describes the contents as
'a black dinner ale'. Honey is added in the same way as
for Enville Ale. The beer was not in production at the
time of writing this book, but it may well return.
Tasting Notes
A black beer with an intriguing honey-chocolate aroma.
There is more honey and chocolate in the taste, along
with a gentle roasted bitterness. The bittersweet finish is
pleasantly roasty.

EXE VALLEY

Exe Valley Brewery, Silverton, Exeter, Devon EX5 4HF.
Tel. (01372) 860406 Fax (01372) 861001
E-mail: guysheppard@supanet.com
Web site: www.siba-southwest.co.uk/breweries/exevalley

Former publican Richard Barron established this
brewery as Barron Brewery in 1984 but was joined in an
expanded enterprise, re-named Exe Valley, by former
brewers' agent Guy Sheppard in 1991. The brewery
moved into bottled beer production in 2001, using
Keltek Brewery for bottling (direct from casks). Best
before dates are fixed at seven months post-bottling.

HOPE

ABV 4.3%   **Bottle size** 500 ml   **Serve** cool
Ingredients Optic pale malt; Golding and Challenger hops

This charity beer was launched in 2003 to help provide
funds for a local hospice which was celebrating its 21st
anniversary. £21 per barrel sold is donated to the cause.
Tasting Notes
A fruity-tasting golden bitter, with a fruity aroma and a
bitter, dry, hoppy finish.

DEVON GLORY

ABV 4.7%   **Bottle size** 500 ml   **Serve** cool
Ingredients Optic pale malt; crystal malt; chocolate malt;
Fuggle, Golding and Challenger hops

A draught beer for many years, Devon Glory was the
first of Exe Valley's beers to be regularly bottled.
Tasting Notes
A copper-coloured, bittersweet, malty beer with hints of
chocolate and spice among the estery fruit notes of the
aroma. Roasted malt leads in the finish.

FELSTAR

The Felstar Brewery, Felsted Vineyard, Crix Green,
Felsted, Essex CM6 3JT. Tel./Fax (01245) 361504
E-mail: felstarbrewery@supanet.com
Mail order service

Felstar Brewery was built in 2001 in the old bonded
stores of Felsted Vineyard, the first commercial vineyard

in East Anglia. Production of its own beers neatly filled a space on the site's own shop, between English wines and ciders. The brewery is run by former graphic designer Marcello Davanzo, who has chosen the rooster as his brewery logo. If you ever call into Marcello's shop, you'll know why. Try driving out again without running over one of his free-ranging poultry stock! His beers are bottled on site, being racked bright after conditioning in the cask and primed with the same yeast as used in primary fermentation. Marcello is one of the most inventive brewers around, cheerfully tearing up the rulebooks and mixing and matching ale recipes with lager production methods. His bottom-fermented beers are kräusened and/or primed with unrefined molasses.

CRIX GOLD

ABV 4%   **Bottle size** 500 ml   **Serve** cool
Ingredients Lager malt; caramalt; wheat malt; First Gold, Jenny and Brewer's Gold hops

The sprawling settlement of Felsted is actually made up of several smaller villages, most ending in 'Green'. Crix Green is where the brewery is located (follow the brown vineyard signs) – hence the name of this and other beers. An unusual selection of hops includes the new dwarf hop named Jenny.
Tasting Notes
A golden ale with a fresh, citrous hop nose backed by biscuity malt. Tart lemon notes dominate the crisp taste before a dry, bitter finish.

HOPS & GLORY

ABV 4%   **Bottle size** 500 ml   **Serve** cool
Ingredients Maris Otter pale malt; crystal malt; chocolate malt; wheat malt; Brewer's Gold and Fuggle hops

'Fruity when young, complex when mature', is how Marcello describes this best bitter which is brewed a couple of times a year.

GRAND CRIX

ABV 4.1%   **Bottle size** 500 ml   **Serve** cool
Ingredients Maris Otter pale malt; caramalt; crystal malt; unmalted barley; Bramling Cross and Ruth hops

The use of the new dwarf hop named Ruth is but one

idiosyncrasy of this bitter which Marcello suggests will go very well with seafood dishes. Maturity is the name of the game here, with the beer given a long conditioning in oak casks that have been seasoned with fresh root ginger and coriander. The beer is brewed just once a year.

Tasting Notes
A light-bodied, copper beer with a perfumed aroma of ginger and other spices. Tangy spice also leads in the bitter taste and continues to feature in the dry, bitter aftertaste.

LORD KULMBACH

ABV 4.4%   **Bottle size** 500 ml   **Serve** cold
Ingredients Maris Otter pale malt; lager malt; crystal malt; black malt; wheat malt; Brewer's Gold and Fuggle hops

Marcello describes this as a bottom-fermented stout, in other words a stout that has been brewed like a lager. Primary cold fermentation takes ten days, five more days are permitted to allow diacetyl (unwanted butterscotch notes) to round out and then the beer is cold-matured for eight weeks. It makes a perfect accompaniment for roast beef or meaty sausages, the brewer claims.

Tasting Notes
A near-black beer with light roasted malt and a blackberry fruitiness in the nose. The same fruit emerges in the crisp, clean taste before being passed by roasted malt. The dry aftertaste is also bitter and roasted.

HOPPIN' HEN

ABV 4.5%   **Bottle size** 500 ml   **Serve** cool
Ingredients Maris Otter and Pearl pale malt; crystal malt; wheat malt; roasted barley; First Gold, Jenny and Hersbrucker hops

A beer that is best drunk young, according to Marcello. This premium ale features dwarf and German hops and is primed with maple syrup.

Tasting Notes
A copper beer with a fruity, malt and hops aroma, underscored by soft melon and pineapple notes. The taste is a crisp mix of malt and fruity hops, with the same tropical fruit notes in evidence. Dry, hoppy, lightly fruity finish.

OLD CRIX

ABV 4.5%   **Bottle size** 500 ml   **Serve** cool
Ingredients Maris Otter pale malt; crystal malt; chocolate malt; wheat malt; First Gold and Perle hops

When Marcello remarks that Old Crix is just perfect with a truffle omelette, he reveals his continental roots once again. Truffles may be even rarer in the UK than in Italy, so how about a game pie or a mature cheese instead? Again Marcello has pulled out all the stops to produce a beer that is different. This time he takes an ale recipe and brews it in the continental fashion, using a double-decoction system (the wort is pumped from vessel to vessel and exposed to varying temperatures to extract the brewing sugars). He then dry hops the beer with more Perle hops.

Tasting Notes
Rich orange notes emerge in the otherwise malty aroma of this robust amber ale. The taste is nutty and malty with a good hop overlay and hints of fruit. The 'mature oak' signposted on the label also comes through. Bitter fruit and hops fill the aftertaste.

GOOD KNIGHT

ABV 5%   **Bottle size** 500 ml   **Serve** cool
Ingredients Maris Otter pale malt; crystal malt; caramalt; chocolate malt; roasted barley; Bramling Cross, First Gold and Perle hops

Another double-decoction beer, Good Knight is a strong mild/porter with lager connections. A beer that matures well in the bottle, declares the brewer.

PECKIN' ORDER

ABV 5%   **Bottle size** 500 ml   **Serve** cold
Ingredients Lager malt; crystal malt; wheat malt; Brewer's Gold and Perle hops

Taking three months from brewing to bottling, Peckin' Order enjoys a primary fermentation with a gradually-reduced temperature and ten days' rest before long cold conditioning. One to try with oriental food, perhaps.

Tasting Notes
Malt, fruit and floral hop notes mark out the aroma of this dark golden brew. Its taste is lightly fruity, with a buttery maltiness plus lemon notes on the swallow. Creamy malt finish with bitterness and hop emerging.

ROOSTERS REST

ABV 5%　　　**Bottle size** 500 ml　　**Serve** cool
Ingredients Maris Otter pale malt; caramalt; torrefied
wheat and barley; Bramling Cross, Jenny and Hersbrucker
hops

Roosters Rest is a strong bitter. It is the bottled version
of a cask beer that was cheekily called Betty's Best,
introduced to commemorate The Queen's Golden
Jubilee in 2002.

HAUNTED HEN

ABV 6%　　　**Bottle size** 500 ml　　**Serve** cool
Ingredients Maris Otter pale malt; caramalt; chocolate
malt; chocolate wheat malt; torrefied wheat; Golding, Jenny
and Hersbrucker hops

Brewed every October and ripened in heavily toasted
oak rum casks, Haunted Hen is a stout brewed for
maturity and is claimed to be at its best when over a
year old. A Chelmsford Winter Beer Festival award-
winner in 2003 in its cask form.
Tasting Notes
A virtually black beer with a rich, biscuity, malt and
coffee nose. Liquorice notes feature in the bittersweet,
nutty, roasted taste, with a nagging suggestion of fruit
throughout, though perhaps not as much body as
expected. Bittersweet, roasted malt finish.

FREEMINER

**Freeminer Brewery Ltd., Whimsey Road, Steam Mills,
Cinderford, Gloucestershire GL14 3JA.
Tel. (01594) 827989 Fax (01594) 829464
Web site: www.freeminer.com**

Established in 1992, and the only brewery in the Royal
Forest of Dean, Freeminer suffered from a fire in a
neighbouring industrial unit in 2000, which forced a
two-month suspension of production. Up and running
again, it eventually moved to new, larger premises in
December that year. The brewery proudly recalls the
area's mining heritage in many of its beer names. (For
the record, a 'freeminer' is a male born within the
hundred of St Briavels who has claimed his birthright to
mine the area without charge by reaching the age of 21
and working a year and a day in a local mine.)

Freeminer's bottled beers (with the exception of the new Gold Miner) were out of production at the time of writing this book but were due to return in the near future.

FREEMINER BITTER

ABV 4%   **Bottle size** 500 ml   **Serve** cool
Ingredients Optic pale malt; crystal malt; Golding and Fuggle hops

Freeminer boss Don Burgess is bullish about his beers and, judging from the acclaim they have received in the media, rightly so. This one he describes as a 'no-nonsense beer for drinkers who appreciate beer with taste', a pointer to the distinctively heavy hopping in the Northern style.
Tasting Notes
A dark golden beer with a hoppy, biscuity malt nose, followed by a nicely balanced taste of soft, malty fruit and an increasingly aggressive, spicy hop bitterness. The dry, hoppy and bitter finish lasts well.

SPECULATION ALE

ABV 4.7%   **Bottle size** 500 ml   **Serve** cool
Ingredients Optic pale malt; crystal malt; chocolate malt; Fuggle and Golding hops

Well-appreciated by *Decanter* magazine, which awarded it five stars in 1997, Speculation Ale is a premium strength bitter with a smoky character. Its name is derived from a long-closed mine which is now a popular picnic area. Don recommends it with roast beef.
Tasting Notes
A full-flavoured, orange-brown beer with fruit and malt in the aroma. The same characteristics continue immediately in the taste but are soon overwhelmed by powerful hop bitterness that continues into the finish.

GOLD MINER

ABV 5%   **Bottle size** 500 ml   **Serve** cool
Ingredients Optic pale malt; pale crystal malt; First Gold hops

Exclusive to Co-op supermarkets for 12 months, Gold Miner was launched in summer 2003, although the beer had previously enjoyed considerable success as a

cask beer called Gold Standard, winner of a *Beauty of Hops* award for its use of First Gold hops. Bottling is handled for Freeminer by Marston's.
Major stockist Co-op

SHAKEMANTLE GINGER ALE

ABV 5%   **Bottle size** 500 ml   **Serve** cool
Ingredients Optic pale malt; wheat malt; ginger; Golding hops

CAMRA's *Champion Speciality Beer* in 1998 (in its cask form), cloudy Shakemantle resembles a Belgian wheat beer. From a conventional cask beer base, Freeminer develops this ale by stealing methods from traditional ginger beer production, flavouring the drink only with real ginger (a blend of four dried gingers and fresh root ginger) and forgoing artificial additives and extracts. Don Burgess suggests adding a little fresh lemon to the glass, and readily admits that this beer will not suit every drinker. However, it may appeal to vegans, as the beer is not fined. One to drink with Chinese foods perhaps. Shakemantle was one of the Forest of Dean's iron mines.
Tasting Notes
A cloudy, yellow/gold beer with a pronounced ginger beer and lemon aroma. The ginger is more subtle on the palate, just lurking warmly in the background behind a dry, lemony, refreshing taste. The finish, too, is dry and lemony with the ginger coming through quite softly, alongside a cracker-like wheatiness.

TRAFALGAR IPA

ABV 6%   **Bottle size** 500 ml   **Serve** cool
Ingredients Optic pale malt; crystal malt; Golding hops

The heavy hop character of this potent brew recalls the days of the British Empire when strong, hoppy IPAs were stashed aboard sailing ships for the long journey to the Indian subcontinent. Trafalgar IPA is reputedly based on a formula for a 9% beer but the restraints of excise duties prohibit the recipe from being followed to the letter. As if there weren't enough hops in the brew to start with, Freeminer also dry hops to embellish the nose and finish. This clearly impressed judges at the 1997 *Beauty of Hops* awards who accorded the beer the title of *Best Bottled Single Varietal*. The beer's name has two connections: the naval battle is recalled on the label, but Trafalgar was also a Forest of Dean mine, the first in the world to be electrically lit. It makes an excellent accompaniment for a cheese like Stilton, according to Don.

Tasting Notes

A copper beer with a full floral hop nose. The full-bodied taste is fairly sweet and malty before an explosion of fruity hops takes over. The deep, dry and extremely hoppy finish leaves a lingering smack of bitter oranges.

DEEP SHAFT STOUT

ABV 6.2%   **Bottle size** 500 ml   **Serve** cool
Ingredients Optic pale malt; wheat malt; roasted barley; malted oats; Fuggle hops

'Not for wimps', says Don Burgess. Deep Shaft is a powerful, flavoursome stout with a very dark hue, recommended to foodies in particular as an accompaniment to a sweet pudding. However, its best recommendation to date is the award of *Bottle-Conditioned Beer* of 1996 by *The Guardian* newspaper.

Tasting Notes

A powerful beer with the colour of black coffee. Coffee also features (with malt) in the aroma and dominates the long, dry finish, with bitterness and some liquorice. In-between, the taste mixes a little dark fruit with coffee and bitter roast grain.

FROG & PARROT

Frog & Parrot, 64 Division Street, Sheffield, South Yorkshire S1 4SG. Tel. (0114) 272 1280

This brew pub began production in 1982 and uses malt extract rather than whole malt to make its single beer, Roger & Out, which is generally only on sale at the pub itself.

ROGER & OUT

ABV 12.5%   **Bottle size** 330 ml
Serve at room temperature
Ingredients Malt extract; Challenger, Styrian Golding and Golding hops

This beer once had the privilege of being described in the *Guinness Book of Records* as Britain's strongest ale. That honour has since been claimed by other ridiculously strong brews but Roger & Out will always be known as the original mind-blower. It was first produced in cask form in 1982 and this bottled version followed soon after. It took its name from the brew pub's former manager, Roger Nowill. Today it is brewed about once a month. The cask beer is allowed two months to condition, before being fined. The bottles are then simply hand-filled from the cask. A rather timid six-week best before date is placed on the labels but the pub is in no doubt about the beer's longevity. Special certificates and T-shirts have been issued with purchases, proclaiming the beer's reputation for potency.

Tasting Notes
A dark brown beer with a heady, alcoholic aroma. To taste, it is very sweet and malty but with some hop bitterness and fruit (strawberries) to balance. Sweet fruit and malt feature in the warming finish.

FROG ISLAND

Frog Island Brewery, The Maltings, Westbridge, St James Road, Northampton NN4 8DU.
Tel. (01604) 587772
Web site: www.frogislandbrewery.co.uk
Mail order service

Taking its name from an area of Northampton that is prone to flooding, Frog Island hopped into the brewing world in 1994. It set up shop in an old malthouse once owned by the defunct Thomas Manning brewery. The bottle-conditioned beers listed are available under 'own labels' for celebrations, fund-raising events and other occasions. They are bottled on site, unprimed, direct from the conditioning tank, without the use of isinglass finings (making all three acceptable to vegetarians).

NATTERJACK

ABV 4.8% **Bottle size** 500 ml **Serve** cool
Ingredients Maris Otter pale malt; wheat malt; Target and Golding hops

Natterjack – extending the amphibian theme – was only introduced in bottle in 2000, but the cask equivalent had already been around for about five years.

Tasting Notes
A copper ale with a rich, orangey, hoppy aroma. The bittersweet taste is powerfully fruity and hoppy (smoky

orange notes), while the finish is bitter and fruity with a strong, lingering hoppiness.

FIRE-BELLIED TOAD

ABV 5%   **Bottle size** 500 ml   **Serve** cool
Ingredients Pale malt; crystal malt; wheat malt; Phoenix hops

This single-varietal hop beer was introduced in 1998 and comes wrapped in a dramatic label showing a mythical bird-creature attacking the eponymous toad. The best before date is set at around six months.
Tasting Notes
A dark golden, hoppy ale. The aroma features orangey citrous notes from the hops, whilst the taste is fruity but bitter, again with citrous notes and tangy hop. Long-lasting, dry, bitter, tangy hop-fruit finish.

CROAK & STAGGER

ABV 5.6%   **Bottle size** 500 ml   **Serve** cool
Ingredients Pale malt; crystal malt; chocolate malt; wheat malt; Target and Cascade hops

Croak & Stagger was Frog Island's first foray into the bottled beer world. It is a variation of a cask winter ale of the same name that was first brewed in 1995. Brewers Bruce Littler and Graham Cherry toned down the ABV (to provide a little less Croak and a smaller chance of a Stagger) and began bottling in 1996. Though a dark winter ale by definition, it is now sold all year. The best before date is set at eight months.
Tasting Notes
Dark amber in colour, this robust ale has an aroma of dark, chocolatey malt and hop fruit. The very full, sweet taste is packed with orange and pineapple hop flavours on a smooth, chocolatey malt base, before a dry, bittersweet, chocolatey finish, with tangy hops.

FULLER'S

Fuller, Smith and Turner PLC, Griffin Brewery, Chiswick Lane South, Chiswick, London W4 2QB. Tel. (020) 8996 2000 Fax (020) 8995 0230 Web site: www.fullers.co.uk

One of the capital's two major brewers, Fuller's operates on a site linked to beer production for over 325 years.

FULLER'S

Messrs Fuller, Smith and Turner came together in 1845 and descendants of the founders are still on the board today, running a highly successful and much acclaimed business. Its beers are imported into the US by Paulaner.

1845

ABV 6.3%   **Bottle size** 500 ml   **Serve** cool
Ingredients Pale malt; crystal malt; amber malt; Golding hops

1845 was first brewed in February 1995, with the Prince of Wales doing the honours and adding the hops to the copper. It was a new ale to commemorate the 150th anniversary of the founding of the Fuller, Smith and Turner company and its conception was precise: it was designed as beer to reflect the type of brew available during the 1840s, hence the use of only Golding hops, the inclusion of amber malt for some biscuity character and the decision to bottle-condition it. Its success (twice CAMRA's champion bottle-conditioned beer) has meant that it is now a permanent member of the award-winning Fuller's range of traditional ales, with brews taking place monthly. In winter, the brew is sometimes available in cask form. After primary fermentation, 1845 enjoys two weeks in conditioning tanks and is then filtered, re-seeded with fresh primary fermentation yeast and bottled, with no primings. Two weeks of conditioning follow before the bottles are released. Once this two-week period has been observed, Fuller's reckons that the beer is at its best and will remain so at least up to the 12-month best before date. The bottle is of Fuller's own individual, award-winning design.
Tasting Notes
A rich, dark amber beer with a glorious, fruity, malty nose, balanced by hints of sherry and Golding hop. The very full, smooth, malty and fruity taste is quickly tempered by hop bitterness. Hops and bitter fruit feature in the lingering finish.
Major stockists Safeway, Sainsbury, Asda, Waitrose, Morrisons, Co-op, Budgens, Booths, Unwins

VINTAGE ALE

ABV 8.5%   **Bottle size** 550 ml   **Serve** cool
Ingredients (2002 vintage) Golden Promise pale malt; Golding hops

Fuller's Vintage Ale is usually brewed in a one-off batch of 85,000 bottles in September each year. The packaging is high quality, allowing the brewery to charge around £3.50 per bottle. For that, you get an individually numbered item in a presentation box, with a best before date set three years on. More importantly, you get a rather special beer. Fuller's aficionados will probably gather that the ale is in fact a version of the brewery's excellent Golden Pride, a rich barley wine which is parti-gyled (brewed from the same mash) with ESB and London Pride. But, by giving this beer the bottle conditioning treatment (including four weeks in conditioning tanks before filtering and re-seeding with fresh Fuller's yeast), the result is a noticeably lighter, fresher beer, quite different to the original Golden Pride, which is supplied in pasteurised bottles. Some brews have used annual champion strains of barley and hops, although now there has been a return to standard floor-malted barley and regular hops. The 2002 edition, timed to coincide with The Queen's Golden Jubilee, had a golden theme, using only Golden Promise pale malt and Golding hops. Only 50,000 bottles of this brew were released. In March 2003, Fuller's organised a fascinating 'vertical tasting' of all six Vintage Ales produced to date, showcasing how the beers have matured and the flavours ripened over the years.

Tasting Notes

Vintage Ale 1997 (tasted after six years): Red in colour, with a raisin aroma and a silky, warming, fruity taste.

Vintage Ale 1998 (tasted young): Chestnut-coloured, with pronounced orangey, hop-resin notes in the aroma, alongside thick, treacly malt and a little sherry. Very full on the palate, it is rather sweet but also tangy and hop-fruity. Sugary sweet notes just win over fresh, fruity hops in the finish. Soft, creamy raisin notes emerge with time as the sugary notes fade.

Vintage Ale 1999 (tasted after 18 months): Amber, with a slightly savoury aroma of bitter, orangey hops. The taste is malty, sweet, fruity and warming, with a hint of almond. Malt, hops and bittersweet fruit fill the aftertaste. Becomes winey with maturity.

Vintage Ale 2000 (tasted young): Bright amber, with a luscious Seville orange aroma. The taste bursts with orange fruit and thick, malty sweetness, countered by zesty, orange peel bitterness. Bitter orange finish. Still sweetish when tasted two years on but with a Cointreau-like quality and a lipsmacking hop dryness in the aftertaste.

Vintage Ale 2001 (tasted young): Deep amber, with raspberryish fruit notes in the nose before a tangy, bittersweet, warming taste of orange fruit and a liquorice-like bitterness. Fruit, bitter hops and lingering

FULLER'S

sweetness run into the finish. Cherry and marzipan notes come through with age, along with more bitterness in the aftertaste.

Vintage Ale 2002 (tasted young): Dark copper, with an orangey, hoppy, tobacco-fragranced aroma and cherries and marzipan in the sweet, peppery taste.

Major stockists Safeway, Sainsbury, Waitrose

GALE'S

George Gale & Co. Ltd., The Hampshire Brewery, London Road, Horndean, Hampshire PO8 0DA. Tel. (023) 9257 1212 Fax (023) 9259 8641 Web site: www.gales.co.uk

Hampshire's major brewery, Gale's was founded in 1847 and is still family owned. Its commitment to bottle-conditioned beers, in evidence since the 1920s through its production of the classic Prize Old Ale, was reinforced in 1997 with the installation of a new bottling line. The line does not handle carbonated beer, but it allows Gale's to produce a wider range of naturally-conditioned bottled beers, including limited edition commemorative brews (such as Golden Century at 10% for the Queen Mother's 100th birthday in 2000) and 'own label' beers for companies. Gale's beers are distributed in the USA by B United, Regal Wines and Mannekin-Brussels.

FESTIVAL MILD ALE

ABV 4.8%   **Bottle size** 500 ml   **Serve** cool
Ingredients Maris Otter pale malt; crystal malt; black malt; Fuggle, Golding and Challenger hops

Gale's used to produce two milds – one light, one dark – both below 3% alcohol. They were phased out in the early 1990s but, in response to a request from the CAMRA Farnham Beer Festival in 1994, the brewery created this strong mild as a replacement. (Apart from the use of much more black malt, it is the same beer as HSB, mentioned below). Festival Mild proved so popular that it was added to the Gale's cask portfolio soon after and went on to collect the accolade of *The People's Pint* at CAMRA's Winter Beer Festival in 1997. It was also overall runner-up in CAMRA's *Champion Winter Beer of Britain* contest in 2003. This bottled version first appeared in 1999, but sales are largely confined to the export market, primarily the USA.

Tasting Notes
A very dark ruby beer with a roasted grain nose backed by malt and fruit. The mainly roasted taste has a delicate malty sweetness, some bitterness and a little fruit throughout. Bittersweet, malty finish.

HSB

ABV 4.8%   **Bottle size** 500 ml   **Serve** cool
Ingredients Maris Otter pale malt; crystal malt; black malt; Fuggle, Golding and Challenger hops

HSB (Horndean Special Bitter) was introduced in cask form in 1959 to expand a Gale's portfolio that was big on mild and had only one bitter, BBB. It was devised by the then head brewer, Ted Argylle, who pitched the beer at an OG of 1055, the average gravity of a standard bitter in the pre-war years. The OG is a little lower these days (1050) but the beer is still the brewery's major strong bitter. It has been available, pasteurised, in cans since the early 1980s, but only in 1999 did HSB finally receive the bottle conditioning treatment. The best before date is set much shorter than for Gale's stronger beers, at up to 24 weeks. Together with Festival Mild, it also differs in being crown capped, rather than corked.
Tasting Notes
A dark amber bitter with an aroma of estery fruit (bananas) and toffee-malt. Fruit continues in the taste, which has a trace of pear drops. Bitterness overcomes a little cloying sweetness and toffee-malt lurks in the background. Dry, hoppy, fruity, bitter finish.

CHRISTMAS ALE

ABV 8.5%   **Bottle size** 275 ml   **Serve** cool
Ingredients Maris Otter pale malt; crystal malt; Fuggle hops; raisins; cinnamon; mace

Largely brewed for export to countries like the USA, Sweden and Denmark, Christmas Ale is produced once a year for bottling in late September. The beer is conditioned in tank for a couple of months before being rough filtered. Fresh yeast is then added along with a raisin and spice mix which is introduced as an extract prepared at the brewery from the base ingredients. The spices ensure the beer never achieves perfect clarity but this shouldn't impair the enjoyment. Pour it gently into a wide-brimmed glass to appreciate the rich seasonal aroma. Gale's has produced various Christmas Ales over the years, but seems to have settled on this recipe (although don't rule out the addition of vanilla and/or cloves in the future!).

Tasting Notes
A ruby ale with a spicy, fruity, vinous aroma. The taste is mostly sweet but with a vinous edge, cake spices and tart fruit. This fruit mellows out in the finish as sweetness finally takes over.

CONQUEST ALE

ABV 9%   **Bottle size** 275 ml   **Serve** cool
Ingredients Maris Otter pale malt; Fuggle hops

This beer was created in 2001 for two markets: it is sold as Conquest Ale primarily in the USA and was also for a while available as Milestones Pale Ale at the Milestones museum in Basingstoke, which re-creates life in 19th- and 20th-century Hampshire. The beer is loosely based on the bottled brew Gale's produced to commemorate CAMRA's 25th birthday in 1996. The brewery considers it to be the most Champagne-like beer available in Britain today, as it is matured in the brewery for a minimum of two months and is given an injection of fresh yeast prior to bottling to promote a powerful secondary fermentation. The best before date is set at two years. Supplies may prove hard to find in the UK.

Tasting Notes
A dark golden ale with a full pear drop aroma. The same fruity notes emerge in the taste, which is slightly earthy but otherwise sweet, with a drying, lightly bitter hop balance. Dry, bittersweet, fruity finish.

PRIZE OLD ALE

ABV 9%   **Bottle size** 275 ml
Serve at room temperature
Ingredients Maris Otter pale malt; black malt; Fuggle and Golding hops

Famous for its corked bottle, Prize Old Ale is fundamental to the traditional, family image of Gale's. It was introduced in the 1920s, when a new head brewer brought the recipe with him from Yorkshire. The recipe has remained largely unchanged in the subsequent 80 years, except for the use of pelletised hops instead of whole and the loss of wooden hogsheads which were used for conditioning the beer. The replacement metal tanks may not be as charming or quaint but, according to head brewer Derek Lowe, they produce more reliable beer, and it is in these containers that the beer is aged for six–12 months. The beer is fined in the tanks after about six months and, before being bottled, more of the same original yeast may be added. Being corked, the beer should be stored lying down, to keep the cork moist. Prize Old Ale is aged for three months at the brewery. Once bottled, it will continue to improve for up to at least five years (although the best before date is set at two years). Some 20-year-old bottles have been known to be excellent, but this doesn't mean that all beers of such an age will prove as fulfilling. All bottles are now individually numbered. As an experiment, recently Gale's has been maturing some POA in Calvados casks, but these special, limited edition bottles are destined for sale in the USA (let's hope some are available in the UK, too).

Tasting Notes
(*based on young samples*) A dark ruby beer with a deep, vinous, fruity aroma with hints of vanilla. The taste is a powerful, mouth-filling combination of fruit (dates and raisins), bitterness and alcohol. The finish is dry, with bitter fruit and hops shading out sweetness.

Major stockist local Tesco

TRAFALGAR ALE

ABV 9%   **Bottle size** 275 ml
Serve at room temperature
Ingredients Maris Otter pale malt; crystal malt; Challenger and Fuggle hops

This powerful ale is brewed to celebrate Trafalgar Day (October 21), and production is likely to be stepped up as we approach the 200th anniversary of the Battle of Trafalgar in the year 2005. It proves particularly popular in the naval wardrooms of the nearby city of Portsmouth, home of Nelson's flagship, *HMS Victory*.

Tasting Notes
A ruby ale with a subdued fruity, malty, hoppy nose for its strength. To taste, it is sweetish, very malty and fairly sharp, but very well-balanced and easy to drink. Decent fruit character. Bitter, fruit and malt finish.

JUBILEE ALE

ABV 12%   **Bottle size** 275 ml
Serve at room temperature
Ingredients Maris Otter pale malt; Fuggle hops; sugar

Unless you live in the USA, this may be a redundant entry. Jubilee Ale was created for The Queen's golden celebrations in 2002 and that was intended to be that. However, America requested another batch and so, while the beer is, effectively, available, it is likely to be only on sale in the States. It might be worth trying the brewery shop, though, just in case. The beer has a long, 4–5 hours' boil and a ten-day fermentation. It is then matured for four or five months. There is no filtration before bottling, but extra yeast is added. Gale's thinks it could mature nicely over three or four years in the bottle and suggests it may go well with barbecue meats and salads.

Tasting Notes

A tawny brew with big, deep fruit in the nose, along with malt, molasses, a hint of sherry, spice, treacle and bitter oranges – complex, to say the least. The taste is predominantly sweet and fruity, with juicy oranges and darker fruit character. Malt fights back in the long finish alongside a little hop balance.

GLASTONBURY

Glastonbury Ales, Grovers Brewhouse, Unit 10, Wessex Park, Somerton Business Park, Somerton, Somerset TA11 6SB. Tel. (01458) 272244
E-mail: glastonburyales@aol.com
Web site: www.glastonburyales.co.uk
Mail order service

A new business, founded by brewer Greig Nicholls in 2002, selling 'Fine ales from the Vale of Avalon' and moving swiftly into bottling. Beers are matured in cask for three weeks prior to being racked bright, kräusened and bottled. Six-month best before dates are applied. The bottle labels merge legend and religion, incorporating an outline of the enigmatic Glastonbury Tor that dominates the local landscape, as well its St Michael's Tower, the 'Sword in the Stone' and the sign of the Cross (Glastonbury was an early Christian base).

MYSTERY TOR

ABV 3.8%   **Bottle size** 500 ml   **Serve** cool
Ingredients Maris Otter pale malt; crystal malt; wheat malt; Fuggle and Cascade hops

Roll up for the Mystery Tor! First brewed in July 2002, as a summer beer, this ale was maintained as part of the brewery's regular cask range after collecting a couple of major CAMRA beer festival honours.

Tasting Notes
A golden ale with a richly fruity, hop nose, a well-balanced bitter taste with a strong hop fruit accent, and more hops building in the fruity finish.

LADY OF THE LAKE

ABV 4.2%   **Bottle size** 500 ml   **Serve** cool
Ingredients Maris Otter pale malt; crystal malt; caramalt; wheat malt; Fuggle, Challenger and Mount Hood hops

A cask ale introduced in May 2002 and, like Mystery Tor, now a regular. In Arthurian legend, the Lady of the Lake lived in waters around Glastonbury and was keeper of the sword *Excalibur*.
Tasting Notes
A dark golden beer with malt and a little hop fruit in the aroma. Nicely balanced, the taste has an initial malt character, but tangy hops follow close behind to take over the aftertaste.

GOLDEN CHALICE

ABV 4.8%   **Bottle size** 500 ml   **Serve** cool
Ingredients Maris Otter pale malt; caramalt; wheat malt; Challenger and Mount Hood hops

Local legend has it that the Holy Grail was brought to Glastonbury after the Last Supper and is still buried under the Tor.
Tasting Notes
A pale golden, strong ale with fruity hops in the nose and a clean, hoppy, fruity taste. The moderate finish is similar, with hops developing.

FMB

ABV 5%   **Bottle size** 500 ml   **Serve** cool
Ingredients Maris Otter pale malt; crystal malt; amber malt; wheat malt; Challenger and Mount Hood hops

If you ask what the initials in the name of this strong ale stand for, you'll probably be told something anodyne like 'Fermented Malty Beer'. The truth is rather more vulgar, inspired by a local exclamation of surprise that ends with 'My Boots'.
Tasting Notes
Fruit and malt dominate the aroma of this light copper ale. The taste is bitter and malty, with a fruity background, and the finish is also bitter and malty.

GREEN TYE

**Green Tye Brewery, Green Tye, Much Hadham,
Hertfordshire SG10 6JP. Tel./Fax (01279) 841041
E-mail: bottled@gtbrewery.co.uk
Web site: www.gtbrewery.co.uk**
Mail order service

Established in 1999, Green Tye is a small brewery
housed behind The Prince of Wales pub (separate
business) in the village of Green Tye. Brewer William
Compton turns out a wide range of cask ales, many of
which find their way into bottle. He has bottled since
late 2002, allowing the beer to drop bright in the cask
and then kräusening. Twelve-month best before dates
are applied.

SHOT IN THE DARK

ABV 3.6%   **Bottle size** 500 ml   **Serve** cool
Ingredients Maris Otter pale malt; crystal malt; dark
chocolate malt; wheat malt; Challenger and Golding hops

This red-coloured quaffing ale was the first beer to be
brewed by Green Tye and was very much a trial – hence
the name. It is now regularly brewed in the winter
months.

UNION JACK

ABV 3.6%   **Bottle size** 500 ml   **Serve** cool
Ingredients Maris Otter pale malt; crystal malt; amber
malt; flaked maize; Challenger and Bramling Cross hops

In its cask form, Union Jack replaced Green Tye's IPA in
2002. This bottled version arrived later the same year
and is now a regular brew.
Tasting Notes
A dark golden session ale with plenty of hops and floral
notes in the aroma. The taste is mostly bitter and dry,
with hop character but also some background
sweetness. Light, dry and hoppy finish.

MUSTANG MILD

ABV 3.7%   **Bottle size** 500 ml   **Serve** cool
Ingredients Maris Otter pale malt; crystal malt; chocolate
malt; brown malt; flaked maize; Fuggle hops

First brewed in 2000, Mustang Mild takes its name from

the P-51 Mustang aircraft that flew, under British colours, from a World War II airfield not far from Green Tye Brewery. The beer is usually only brewed between April and June.

Tasting Notes
A light ruby ale with an aroma of fruit and toffeeish malt. The same flavours continue in the taste and the dry finish.

UNCLE JOHN'S FERRET

ABV 3.8%   **Bottle size** 500 ml   **Serve** cool
Ingredients Maris Otter pale malt; crystal malt; chocolate malt; flaked maize; Jenny hops

A ruby/brown mild seasoned with a new hedgerow hop called simply Jenny. It was first brewed in August 2002 to mark the re-opening of The Queen's Head at nearby Allen's Green, which had been closed for six years. One local related a story about his Uncle John, a landlord of the pub some 50 years before, whose pet ferret drowned in the natural spring that runs through the pub's cellar. Asked what his ferret was doing in the cellar, the answer apparently came back: 'backstroke ... for a while'.

SNOWDROP

ABV 3.9%   **Bottle size** 500 ml   **Serve** cool
Ingredients Maris Otter pale malt; crystal malt; Golding hops

A golden, winter beer, as its name implies, first bottled in 2002 after being introduced in its cask version in 2000.

SMILE FOR THE CAMERA!

ABV 4%   **Bottle size** 500/750 ml **Serve** cool
Ingredients Maris Otter pale malt; wheat malt; flaked maize; Susan hops; honey; elderflowers

This summer brew features another new hop, Susan, and was conceived as an entry for the *Beauty of Hops* competition to find the *Ultimate Wedding Beer* in 2002. It has since, reportedly, been drunk in place of Champagne at two weddings known to William, including one in France. To complete the sparkling wine concept, the larger, 750 ml bottles are stoppered with a cork and caged.

XBF

ABV 4%   **Bottle size** 500 ml   **Serve** cool
Ingredients Maris Otter pale malt; crystal malt; amber malt; flaked barley; Pilgrim hops

First brewed and bottled in April 2003 to celebrate the tenth annual beer festival (hence XBF) at the adjacent Prince of Wales pub (the brewery's cool room is used for stillaging some of the beer).
Tasting Notes
A copper-hued ale with blackcurrant and a little spice in the nose. The same spicy fruitiness runs into the taste and the dry, bitter aftertaste.

ST MARGARET'S

ABV 4.1%   **Bottle size** 500 ml   **Serve** cool/cold
Ingredients Maris Otter pale malt; Caragold malt; flaked maize; Willamette hops

St Margaret's, introduced in May 2003, was the first of a series of beers commemorating the local, now closed, Buntingford railway branch line. As well as American hops, the beer features Caragold malt, a creation of local maltsters French & Jupps.
Tasting Notes
A golden beer with a floral, fruity nose. The taste is moreishly malty with a balancing light hop note. Bittersweet, dry malt and hop finish.

AUTUMN ROSE

ABV 4.2%   **Bottle size** 500 ml   **Serve** cool
Ingredients Maris Otter pale malt; crystal malt; chocolate malt; wheat malt; flaked maize; Ros hops

Now showcasing another new hop, this time called Ros, this tawny/brown seasonal beer was added to the range in 2000 and is usually sold until November in cask.

GREEN TIGER

ABV 4.2%   **Bottle size** 500 ml   **Serve** cool
Ingredients Maris Otter pale malt; crystal malt; flaked maize; Golding hops; ginger

Designed as a summer quencher when created in 2000, this light amber ale includes fresh root ginger for a touch of subtle spice.

MAD MORRIS

ABV 4.2%   **Bottle size** 500 ml   **Serve** cool
Ingredients Maris Otter pale malt; wheat malt; Susan hops

A straw-coloured May Day beer (available usually for three months thereafter) to help the villagers of Green Tye with their morris dancing celebrations.

WHEELBARROW

ABV 4.3%   **Bottle size** 500 ml   **Serve** cool
Ingredients Maris Otter pale malt; crystal malt; wheat malt; Challenger hops

This amber beer takes its name from the brewery partners: 'Will' Compton and Gary 'Barra' Whelan.

COAL PORTER

ABV 4.5%   **Bottle size** 500 ml   **Serve** cool
Ingredients Maris Otter pale malt; dark chocolate malt; wheat malt; Bramling Cross hops

This porter – a winner of several beer festival awards since it arrived in cask in 2000 – is a treat with a hearty winter pie or a stew, according to William. Check the label closely to avoid confusion with Coal Ported, featured below.
Tasting Notes
Deep, deep ruby (almost black) in colour, this porter has a biscuity aroma of roasted malt and coffee, a nicely balanced taste of sweet malt, bitterness and mellow coffee, and a coffeeish finish.

MERRY MAKER

ABV 4.6%   **Bottle size** 500 ml   **Serve** cool
Ingredients Maris Otter pale malt; crystal malt; wheat malt; flaked maize; Challenger and Jenny hops

A Christmas ale first introduced in 2001.

COAL PORTED

ABV 4.7%   **Bottle size** 500 ml   **Serve** cool
Ingredients Maris Otter pale malt; dark chocolate malt; wheat malt; Bramling Cross hops; port

Brewed to the same recipe as Coal Porter, this brew is

given the added benefit of a whole bottle of port per firkin (nine gallons) and allowed to mature for two or three months before bottling. This obviously raises the strength slightly. Recommended with mature cheese and biscuits.

Tasting Notes
Near-black, this dark ruby-coloured brew has a soft fruitiness alongside roasted malt in the nose. The same fruit and roast features continue in the mouth and in the finish.

CONKERER

ABV 4.7%　　**Bottle size** 500 ml　　**Serve** cool
Ingredients Maris Otter pale malt; crystal malt; wheat malt; Hilary hops

The name of this robust autumn ale reflects the horse chestnut debris that covers the brewery car park at this time of year.

CITRUS SIN

ABV 4.8%　　**Bottle size** 500 ml　　**Serve** cool
Ingredients Maris Otter pale malt; crystal malt; wheat malt; Hilary hops; orange oil; cinnamon

Featuring, like Conkerer, the new Hilary hops, this dark copper-coloured winter ale also includes orange oil for extra citrus zest and cinnamon for a seasonal spice flavour (hence the contrived name). It was first brewed in 2001.

GREENE KING

Greene King PLC, Westgate Brewery,
Bury St Edmunds, Suffolk IP33 1QT.
Tel. (01284) 763222 Fax (01284) 706502
Web site: www.greeneking.co.uk

Founded in 1799, Greene King is now one of Britain's 'super-regional' breweries, having expanded by acquiring pub groups and Morland brewery in recent years. From Morland (now closed) Greene King acquired its only bottle-conditioned ale (although it does produce a range of pasteurised beers, including the notable Strong Suffolk, a complex blend of matured and young ales). Greene King has also been at the forefront of the movement to encourage beer drinking with food.

HEN'S TOOTH

ABV 6.5%   **Bottle size** 500 ml   **Serve** cool
Ingredients Pipkin pale malt; crystal malt; maltose syrup;
Challenger and Golding hops

Hen's Tooth was launched in 1998. The fact that this
name was chosen more than suggests that the beer
closely resembles the popular Old Speckled Hen in its
make up. The other relevance of the name is to convey
how rare it is to find a beer of this strength which is not
too heavy or chewy – as rare, as Morland put it at the
time, 'as a hen's tooth'. The beer is now brewed at Bury
St Edmunds to the same Morland recipe, and cool
conditioned for a week before being tankered down to
Hepworth & Co in Horsham for bottling. There the
yeast count and fermentability of the remaining sugars
are checked and, if required, these are corrected with
new yeast and primings. The yeast used throughout is
the Morland yeast, which is over 100 years old. The best
before date is set at 12 months.
Tasting Notes
A dark amber beer with a fruity, estery nose. Sweet and
a little nutty in the mouth, it features ripe malt and
plenty of hop, with just a hint of pear drops. Dry,
hoppy, bittersweet finish.
Major stockists Safeway, Tesco, Sainsbury, Waitrose,
Morrisons, Booths, Bottoms Up, Unwins

HAMPSHIRE

**Hampshire Brewery Ltd., 6–8 Romsey Industrial Estate,
Greatbridge Road, Romsey, Hampshire SO51 0HR.
Tel. (01794) 830529 Fax (01794) 830528
E-mail: online@hampshirebrewery.com
Web site: www.hampshirebrewery.com**

Founded in Andover in 1992, Hampshire moved to
Romsey in 1997, filling a void left in the town by the
closure of Strong's Brewery by Whitbread in 1981. The
brewery has now built up a core range of eight bottle-
conditioned beers, which are supplemented by short
runs in bottle of seasonal cask beers. These have
included (in monthly order): Grim Reaper (4.4%, an old
ale); Heaven Can Wait (4.8%, a dark wheat beer);
Temptation (4.2%, a best bitter); Not Tonight Josephine
(5%, a German helles); Desperate Dan (5%, an IPA);
Hampshire Hare (5%, a golden ale); T'ale of the Dragon
(4.2%, a lighter golden ale); Manneken (4.6%, a

Belgian-style ale); Uncle Sam (5%, an American-style pale ale); Luv'ly Jub'lee (4.2%, another golden ale); Ploughmans Punch (4.5%, a summer ale); Wild Thing (4.2%, another IPA); Porky & Best (4.5%, a best bitter); Bohemian Rhapsody (5%, a pilsner-style beer); Merlins Magic (5%, a ruby ale); Penny Black Porter (4.5%); Bonfire Bitter (4.2%, a best bitter); Good King Censlas (5%, a winter ale) and Californian Red (4.5%, an American-style beer with a hint of spruce). The beers are warm- and cold-conditioned after fermentation, then filtered and re-seeded with new bottling yeast. A nine-month best before date is stamped on each bottle.

KING ALFRED'S

ABV 3.8%   **Bottle size** 500 ml   **Serve** cool
Ingredients Maris Otter pale malt; crystal malt; Challenger, First Gold and Golding hops

Building on the county's association with King Alfred, this bitter was the brewery's first regular cask beer.
Tasting Notes
A copper ale with light fruit and malt in the nose. The taste is hoppy, but not without malt or sweetness, and gentle fruit persists throughout. Hoppy, dry finish.

STRONGS BEST BITTER

ABV 3.8%   **Bottle size** 500 ml   **Serve** cool
Ingredients Maris Otter pale malt; crystal malt; black malt; Challenger, Progress and Golding hops

Once, billboards advertising Strong's beers were commonplace in the South. Now Hampshire has revived the lost brewery's popular bitter and in doing so has underlined its own position and identity as the Romsey brewery of today.
Tasting Notes
A dark copper bitter with malt leading in the aroma but with plenty of hop fruitiness. On the palate, fruity spritziness lightens a rich, malty base. Hops take over in the initially bittersweet finish.

IRONSIDE BEST

ABV 4.2%   **Bottle size** 500 ml   **Serve** cool
Ingredients Maris Otter pale malt; crystal malt; Progress, Golding and Styrian Golding hops

A premium ale named after Edmund II, 11th-century

king of England. Part of Hampshire's ancient kings range.
Tasting Notes
A dark golden ale dominated by citrous hops in the nose – orange and grapefruit to the fore. Mouthfilling grapefruit and orange peel in the taste winds up with a dry, bitter, citrous finish.

LIONHEART

ABV 4.5%   **Bottle size** 500 ml   **Serve** cool
Ingredients Maris Otter pale malt; lager malt; Northdown, First Gold and Perle hops

A well-established golden ale with King Richard I connections.
Tasting Notes
Toffeeish malt and floral hop notes lead in the nose, while the same maltiness is crisped up by sharp hop in the mouth for an almost 'lemon toffee' taste. Dry, hoppy finish with lingering malt.

GOLD RESERVE

ABV 4.8%   **Bottle size** 500 ml   **Serve** cool
Ingredients Lager malt; caramalt; First Gold, Golding and Styrian Golding hops

A new addition to the bottled range, its name reflecting its brilliant colour.
Tasting Notes
Lemon fruitiness in the aroma is enhanced by a suggestion of tropical fruit. The crisp, fruity, slightly perfumed, hop-spicy taste has a clean, moreish, light malt base. Hop dryness emerges in the finish.

PENDRAGON

ABV 4.8%   **Bottle size** 500 ml   **Serve** cool
Ingredients Maris Otter pale malt; crystal malt; black malt; Challenger, Progress and Golding hops

Named after the father of King Arthur, this strong ale was first produced in cask form in 1993.
Tasting Notes
An appealing reddish beer with light banana notes in the malty aroma. On the palate, it is complex but well balanced, with light banana, malt and hops competing for attention. Dry, bitter, malt and hops finish, with still a little banana character.

PRIDE OF ROMSEY

ABV 5%   **Bottle size** 500 ml   **Serve** cool
Ingredients Maris Otter pale malt; crystal malt; Challenger, Golding and Cascade hops

Pride of Romsey – declared on the label to be an IPA – is a sort of 'thank you' beer, brewed in appreciation of the welcome the people of Romsey have given to the arrival of the brewery, and also to commemorate the revival of brewing in the town. It first appeared in cask form and instantly scooped a bronze medal at the 1998 *Brewing Industry International Awards*. This bottled version followed in the same year. The inclusion of Cascade hops was no doubt inspired by head brewer Dan Thomasson's earlier brewing experiences in the USA.
Tasting Notes
A copper-coloured beer with a slightly spicy, malty nose with hints of citrus fruits (grapefruit). The taste is a strong, bitter, mouth-filling combination of the same fruit, malt and hop, which carries on to dominate the dry finish.
Major stockists local Waitrose, Asda and Sainsbury

1066

ABV 6%   **Bottle size** 500 ml   **Serve** cool
Ingredients Maris Otter pale malt; lager malt; caramalt; Northdown, First Gold and Perle hops

1066 – William the Conqueror 1066, to give it the full name shown on the label – was first brewed as a cask beer in 1994. However, the beer has been modified since for bottle and cask.
Tasting Notes
A dark golden ale with lemon-citrus notes and a touch of pear drop in the malty aroma. Light-textured for its gravity, it is sweet and lemony to taste, with malt, hops and an alcoholic warmth in the background. Citrous hops feature in the dry, bittersweet finish.

HANBY

**Hanby Ales Ltd., New Brewery, Aston Park,
Soulton Road, Wem, Shropshire SY4 5SD.
Tel./Fax (01939) 232432
E-mail: jack@hanbyales.co.uk
Web site: www.hanbyales.co.uk**
Mail order service

Following the closure of Wem Brewery by Greenalls in 1988, its head brewer, Jack Hanby, set up his own business in the same Shropshire town. His base is a unit on an industrial park that, during World War II, was employed as a prisoner of war camp. The Nissen huts are still in evidence.

RAINBOW CHASER

ABV 4.3%   **Bottle size** 500 ml   **Serve** cool
Ingredients Maris Otter pale malt; Fuggle and Pioneer hops

Only introduced in bottle in 2001, Rainbow Chaser has been around in cask form for a number of years. Like the other beers, it is brewed and bottled on site, and matured in conditioning tanks. There is no filtration or re-seeding of yeast before bottling and no finings are used, which ensures that all beers are safe for vegans.

SHROPSHIRE STOUT

ABV 4.4%   **Bottle size** 500 ml   **Serve** cool
Ingredients Maris Otter pale malt; crystal malt; black malt; chocolate malt; Fuggle hops

New to bottle in 1999, Shropshire Stout had already won acclaim as a cask beer, first brewed in 1993.
Tasting Notes
A very dark brown beer with a full coffee/roast grain aroma. There is plenty of roast malt character in the mouth, along with citrous hop notes, good bitterness and just a touch of sourness. Dry, roasty, bitter finish.

GOLDEN HONEY

ABV 4.5%   **Bottle size** 500 ml   **Serve** cool
Ingredients Maris Otter pale malt; Fuggle, Golding and Cascade hops; honey

Australian honey is the leading feature of this premium ale, added late to the copper boil.

PREMIUM BITTER

ABV 4.6%   **Bottle size** 500 ml   **Serve** cool
Ingredients Maris Otter pale malt; crystal malt; Fuggle and Golding hops

Hanby's Premium was the brewery's first bottled beer, launched in 1997. It's also available as a cask ale and was formerly known as Treacleminer (the name was changed to ensure that buyers are not misled into thinking it is an overly sweet ale).

Tasting Notes

A copper-coloured ale with fruity hops in the nose. Clean and refreshing to taste, it has a nicely sharp, fruity hoppiness, with sweet malt behind. Hoppy and bitter, dry finish.

CHERRY BOMB

ABV 6%   **Bottle size** 500 ml   **Serve** cool
Ingredients Maris Otter pale malt; crystal malt; Fuggle and Golding hops; cherry essence

Winner of a couple of CAMRA's *Beer of the Festival* awards in its well-established cask version, this fruit-flavoured ale was introduced in bottled form in 1999. Cherry essence is added after fermentation.

Tasting Notes

An orange-gold beer with a clean white head. The aroma is very fruity, with estery pear drop notes and cherries. Cherry flavour leads on the palate, but this is a smooth, fairly sweet ale, not sour like many Belgian cherry beers. Dry, bitter cherry finish.

HARVEYS

**Harvey and Son (Lewes) Ltd., The Bridge Wharf Brewery, 6 Cliffe High Street, Lewes, East Sussex BN7 2AH.
Tel. (01273) 480209 Fax (01273) 483706
E-mail: maj@harveys.org.uk
Web site: www.harveys.org.uk**

This popular, family-run brewery, established in the 18th century, has an excellent reputation for its bottle-conditioned 1859 Porter (4.8%). The only problem is that the beer is now only bottle conditioned in small runs on special request (usually around March, when the cask version is available), and most bottles of the porter are pasteurised. However, Harveys did take the bold step of introducing the intriguing, award-winning bottled beer mentioned below in 1999.

IMPERIAL EXTRA DOUBLE STOUT

ABV 9%   **Bottle size** 330 ml   **Serve** cool
Ingredients Maris Otter pale malt; amber malt; brown malt; black malt; Fuggle and East Kent Golding hops

A tribute to Albert Le Coq, a Belgian who successfully marketed Courage's renowned Imperial Russian Stout to the Baltic region and particularly the Russian Empire in the early 1800s. This beer's label re-tells the Le Coq story, including how the brewery his company set up to brew his own powerful beer in Estonia was nationalised by the Bolsheviks in 1917. This beer is inspired by Le Coq's original recipe and the first vintage was sold exclusively in the USA – where such beers are widely revered – but later batches have also been made available in the UK. The beer is bottled with a cork stopper for Harveys by Gale's and is stored for 12 months before release. Full credit goes to Harveys for its faith in this fascinating beer style, when Scottish Courage, regrettably, has allowed the original Imperial Russian Stout to wither on the hop bine. B United are the US importers.

Tasting Notes
A near-black beer with a smoky, fruity, vinous aroma with hints of polished leather. This complex brew is vinously fruity, creamy, sweetish, spicy and roasty in the mouth, with a lingering, bitter, coffee-roast finish.

HIGH FORCE

High Force Hotel Brewery, Forest-in-Teesdale, Barnard Castle, Co. Durham DL12 0XH.
Tel. (01833) 622222 Fax (01833) 622264

The High Force Hotel is a whitewashed, 19th-century building situated by the 70-foot High Force waterfall in a designated area of outstanding natural beauty, close to the Pennine Way. A small brewery opened here in 1995 and claims to be the highest in Britain, at 1,060 feet above sea level. However, since April 2001, all beer production has been handled for High Force by Darwin Brewery.

FOREST XB

ABV 4.2%   **Bottle size** 500 ml   **Serve** cool
Ingredients Pale malt; crystal malt; chocolate malt; torrefied wheat; Willamette hops

The newer of the two High Force bottled beers, Forest XB was introduced in 1999 and reflects the brewery's setting at Forest-in-Teesdale in its name.

Tasting Notes
An interesting dark amber beer with a fruity, malty,

HIGH FORCE

lightly chocolatey aroma. A little salty on the palate, it has good bitterness and fruity hop notes over a rich malty base. Dry, bitter hop finish.

CAULDRON SNOUT

ABV 5.6%   **Bottle size** 500 ml   **Serve** cool
Ingredients Pale malt; crystal malt; black malt; Challenger hops

Cauldron Snout is named after a waterfall five miles from the hotel in Upper Teesdale. The label depicts a prehistoric water stone, used to indicate sources of water on the Pennine moors. If you make the effort to collect a bottle from the pub, you can also pay a visit to the local butcher's where they occasionally make Cauldron Snout sausages.
Tasting Notes
A very dark ruby beer with a clean, leathery aroma of dark malt. Full and bittersweet in the mouth, it has decent hop character, pruney fruit and smooth, mellow malt on the swallow. Bitter, dry, roasted malt finish.

HILDEN

Hilden Brewing Co., Hilden House, Grand Street, Lisburn, Co. Antrim BT27 4TY.
Tel. (028) 9266 3863 Fax (028) 9260 3511
E-mail: hilden.brewery@ukgateway.net
Mail order service

Hilden, founded in 1981, was, for some years, the only cask ale brewery in Northern Ireland, albeit a very small one with limited outlets. Access to the beers is still difficult, but the installation of a bottling line in 1999 now allows more people to sample Hilden's ales. Four-pack 'Hilden Ale Sacks' form part of the marketing exercise. The beers are bottled at the brewery, with a three-month best before date.

HILDEN ORIGINAL ALE

ABV 4.6%   **Bottle size** 500 ml   **Serve** cool
Ingredients Halcyon pale malt; crystal malt; chocolate malt; black malt; First Gold, Northdown and Golding hops

The big brother of the popular cask beer Hilden Ale (4%), Hilden Original was introduced in 1998. A filtered and pasteurised version of the same beer was sold at the same time as Scullion's Irish Ale. Now, to make the beers more individual, Hilden uses Golding hops in the bottle-conditioned beer and Hersbrucker in the pasteurised. The brewery reckons Hilden Original is worth trying with a stir fry or a pasta dish.

Tasting Notes
A copper beer with a fruity, malty nose. Smooth, slightly sweet and very fruity to taste, it has plenty of malt flavour and a light bitter edge. Bitterness builds to overshadow malt and fruit in the dry finish.

MOLLY MALONE SINGLE X

ABV 4.6%   **Bottle size** 500 ml   **Serve** cool
Ingredients Halcyon pale malt; chocolate malt; black malt; Northdown, Golding and Hallertau hops

A porter introduced in 2000 and now bottled in small quantities. It incorporates three strains of hops, including Hallertau from New Zealand.

Tasting Notes
A ruby porter with a slightly vinous, fruity aroma with roasted malt. The dry, vinous taste is mostly of gentle roasted malt which continues into the dry, bitter aftertaste.

HOBSONS

Hobsons Brewery & Co. Ltd., Newhouse Farm, Cleobury Mortimer, Kidderminster, Worcester DY14 8RD. Tel. (01299) 270837 Fax (01299) 270260 E-mail: beer@hobsons-brewery.co.uk Web site: www.hobsons-brewery.co.uk

This family-run brewery was set up in 1993 but moved to its current premises (an attractive old farm building) in 1996. An extension to the property in 2001 provided space for the addition of a bottling plant.

OLD HENRY

ABV 5.2%   **Bottle size** 500 ml   **Serve** cool
Ingredients Maris Otter pale malt; crystal malt; Challenger and Golding hops

The label says this is a beer 'best served with mature Shropshire Blue cheese'. Old Henry – described in the *Good Beer Guide* as 'an authentic winter ale' – is mostly available as a cask beer; this version is filtered and re-seeded with fresh yeast prior to bottling. Best before dates are fixed at 12 months.

Tasting Notes

A dark copper ale with a malty nose featuring a 'boiled sweet' fruitiness and a little burst of lemon. Estery flavours emerge in the mouth, with pear drop and almond to the fore against a backdrop of malt and bitterness. Bittersweet, slightly toasted finish, with a squeeze of lemon throughout.

HOGS BACK

Hogs Back Brewery Ltd., Manor Farm, The Street, Tongham, Surrey GU10 1DE.
Tel. (01252) 783000 Fax (01252) 782328
E-mail: info@hogsback.co.uk
Web site: www.hogsback.co.uk
Mail order service

This purpose-built brewery was set up in restored farm buildings (circa 1768) in 1992, providing a traditional rural setting for ale brewing. All the brewery's bottled beers are handled in house. The brews are filtered and then injected with fresh yeast prior to filling with, occasionally, priming sugars added to ensure a good fermentation in the bottle. Best before dates are set at 14 months. The elaborate, gold-embossed labels are the work of brewery partner Tony Stanton-Precious, a former draughtsman. Hogs Back also has a well-stocked shop/off-licence on site, offering a wide range of bottled beers from other breweries as well as their own. It is well worth a detour if you're in the area. Other Hogs Back beers may appear in bottle in the near future, including the pale Hop Garden Gold (4.6%) and the maltier Rip Snorter (5%). B United International imports the beers into the USA.

TEA (Traditional English Ale)

ABV 4.2%   **Bottle size** 500 ml   **Serve** cool
Ingredients Maris Otter pale malt; crystal malt; Fuggle and East Kent Golding hops

TEA is one of Hogs Back's longest established brews but was one of the last of the current crop to find its way into a bottle, when it was launched in October 1997. The beer is now brewed weekly. The cask version claimed the *Best Bitter* title at the 2000 *Champion Beer of Britain* contest.

Tasting Notes
An amber-coloured beer with a malty, citrous nose. Malt
and orange fruit feature in the dry, bitter taste, wrapped
up by a mostly bitter, citrous finish.
Major stockists Safeway, Sainsbury, Waitrose

BSA (Burma Star Ale)

ABV 4.5%   **Bottle size** 500 ml   **Serve** cool
Ingredients Maris Otter pale malt, crystal malt; chocolate
malt; Fuggle and East Kent Golding hops

Introduced in 1995 to commemorate the 50th
anniversary of VJ Day, and as a tribute to members of
the Burma Star Association and prisoners of war in the
Far East, BSA was re-labelled to mark the 50th
anniversary of the founding of the Association in 1951.
The beer is available in cask form as well as in this
bottle-conditioned version. It is now produced every
month. The label depicts servicemen of the day
(actually the partners' parents – one of whom served in
the Burma Star movement) and recalls the famous and
poignant quotation:
  'When you go home tell them of us and say –
    For your tomorrow we gave our today'.
The Imperial War Museum has taken stocks for sale to
its visitors and, for every bottle sold, Hogs Back pledges
a donation to the BSA's welfare fund.
Tasting Notes
A red ale with a malty aroma, supported by fruity hop.
The taste is hoppy and dry, with plenty of dark malt
behind, and the finish is dry, lightly roasted and
notably hoppy, with hints of orange.
Major stockist local Sainsbury

OTT (Old Tongham Tasty or Over The Top)

ABV 6%   **Bottle size** 500 ml   **Serve** cool
Ingredients Maris Otter pale malt; crystal malt; chocolate
malt; Fuggle and East Kent Golding hops

A cask beer introduced in bottle in 2000. The label
features pigs flying 'over the top' of the brewery.
Tasting Notes
A very dark ruby beer with gentle roasted malt and
subtle pear fruit in the nose. The taste is sweet, lightly
estery and filled with dark malt, but with roasted
bitterness in the background. Thick, sweet finish with a
little roasted bitterness.
Major stockist local Sainsbury

VINTAGE ALE

ABV 6.5%   **Bottle size** 500 ml   **Serve** cool
Ingredients Maris Otter pale malt; crystal malt; chocolate malt; Fuggle and East Kent Golding hops

First brewed for Christmas 2000 and now a regular in the range, Vintage Ale is matured at the brewery before bottling and is good to drink with red meat and game dishes, it is claimed. The screen-printed bottle is topped with a swing stopper and packed into a straw-lined wooden box.
Tasting Notes
Vintage Ale 2000: A ruby ale with a gently fruity, lightly vinous, malty nose with hints of roast malt and a yeasty, savoury note. Rich dark malt flavours fill the mouth, with more yeast savouriness and some winey fruit. Fruity, increasingly bitter, alcoholic finish.

BREWSTER'S BUNDLE

ABV 7.4%   **Bottle size** 275 ml   **Serve** cool
Ingredients Maris Otter pale malt; crystal malt; Fuggle and East Kent Golding hops

Another commemorative brew, this ale was initially produced each February, but is now bottled every two months. The 'Bundle' in question is Charley, the first baby daughter of Hogs Back's lady brewster, Maureen Rolfe. Charley was born in February 1994 at the weight of 7lb 4oz (hence the 7.4% ABV). The beer is good with white meats and fish dishes, claim the brewers.
Tasting Notes
A deep amber-coloured beer with a malty, fruity aroma. The taste is smooth, sweet, malty and fruity (with some tropical notes), before a mellow finish of bittersweet fruit.

WOBBLE IN A BOTTLE/SANTA'S WOBBLE

ABV 7.5%   **Bottle size** 275 ml   **Serve** cool
Ingredients Maris Otter pale malt; crystal malt; chocolate malt; Fuggle and East Kent Golding hops

Wobble in a Bottle is the bottled version of Hogs Back's Christmas beer, Santa's Wobble (a Christmas edition is still released as Santa's Wobble, showing Santa on the label and topped with a white cap to represent snow). It was first produced in 1996 and is now brewed every three months or so. Serve, perhaps, instead of a port at the end of a dinner, but go easy or you might end up like the befuddled old chap on the label. The cask version is also made available in summer months, under the alternative name of 'Still Wobbling'.

Tasting Notes

An unusual, ruby-red beer with a rich, raspberry-ish aroma. The taste is full and fruity, with almond/ marzipan notes and a refreshingly sharp edge, but without much of the alcoholic heaviness or cloying sweetness you'd expect. Sharp bitterness dominates fruit in the gum-tingling finish.

A OVER T (Aromas Over Tongham)

ABV 9%   **Bottle size** 275 ml   **Serve** cool
Ingredients Maris Otter pale malt; crystal malt; chocolate malt; Fuggle and Golding hops

One of Hogs Back's earliest brews, A Over T (named after its unfortunate side-effect but diplomatically explained as standing for 'Aromas Over Tongham') first tempted drinkers back in 1993, when it appeared in cask form. The bottled version conforms to the same recipe, except for the nuances of the bottling procedure. Runner-up in 2003's *Beauty of Hops* contest to find the *Ultimate Beer for an After Dinner Cheese*.

Tasting Notes

Ruby-red in colour, this beer has a deep, malty aroma with background fruit. Full-flavoured, it is sweet and creamy to taste, featuring fruit and good bitterness before a warming finish that is fruity and bitter.

HOP BACK

Hop Back Brewery PLC, Units 22–24, Batten Road Industrial Estate, Downton, Salisbury, Wiltshire SP5 3HU. Tel. (01725) 510986 Fax (01725) 513116 E-mail: info@hopback.co.uk Web site: www.hopback.co.uk

Originally based at a Salisbury brew pub, The Wyndham Arms, Hop Back was set up in 1986. It moved to a unit on an industrial area at Downton in 1992 and continues to expand. It stepped up its bottled beer production in 1997 with the installation of a new bottling line. All bottled beers are cold-conditioned at 3° C, filtered and kräusened prior to bottling. Best before dates are set at 12–15 months after bottling. All beers are imported into the US by Shelton Brothers.

CROP CIRCLE

ABV 4.2%   **Bottle size** 500 ml   **Serve** cool
Ingredients Maris Otter pale malt; flaked maize; wheat
malt; East Kent Golding, Pioneer and Tettnang hops;
coriander

Winner of the small brewer category in the
Spring/Summer 2000 *Tesco Beer Challenge*, Crop Circle
was designed as an easy-drinking, light beer for the
warmer months, with bitterness playing second fiddle
to aroma when it came to the choice of hops. Goldings
and Pioneer do most of the hop work, with German
Tettnangs added late in the copper. Coriander is added
at this stage, too, to enhance the summery fruitiness.
This Crop Circle is quite a different beer to a previous
Crop Circle produced by Hop Back.
Tasting Notes
A light-bodied, pale golden beer with an aroma full of
zesty, lemon and orange notes and an earthy coriander
spiciness. The taste is rich in fresh, lightly perfumed,
summery flavours – orange, lemon juice and a growing
hoppy bitterness. Dry, hoppy, bitter and orangey finish.
Major stockist Tesco

TAIPHOON

ABV 4.2%   **Bottle size** 500 ml   **Serve** cool
Ingredients Maris Otter pale malt; East Kent Golding and
Pioneer hops; lemongrass; coriander

Introduced in spring 1999, Taiphoon is designed as a
perfect accompaniment for Oriental cuisine. The key
ingredient, lemongrass, imparts a distinctive exotic
spiciness.
Tasting Notes
A pale golden beer with a peppery, spicy, perfumed hop
nose. It is also peppery, scented and slightly ginger-like
in the mouth, with enough malt in the background for
balance. The finish is spicy, bitter and scented.
Major stockist Booths

ENTIRE STOUT

ABV 4.5%   **Bottle size** 500 ml   **Serve** cool
Ingredients Maris Otter and Optic pale malt; chocolate
malt; roasted barley; wheat crystal malt; Challenger and
Golding hops

A cask beer for over 10 years, Entire Stout finally made

it into bottle in December 2001 and went into regular production a year or so later. So much faith does Hop Back have in its stout, it has even withdrawn draught Guinness from its own Wyndham Arms pub in Salisbury, encouraging customers to give the cask version a go. Produced without isinglass finings, the beer is good news for vegetarians and vegans (the beer is simply transferred from the fermenting vessel to the tank from which it is bottled). Great to drink with a ploughman's, the brewers say.

Tasting Notes
A black beer with a coffee and caramel aroma preceding a crisp, bitter taste with a light, teasing sweetness and a dry, bitter, roasted finish.

Major stockists Safeway, Waitrose, Booths, Tesco, Somerfield, Morrisons, Sainsbury, Oddbins

SUMMER LIGHTNING

ABV 5%   **Bottle size** 500 ml   **Serve** cool
Ingredients Maris Otter pale malt; East Kent Golding hops

The story of Summer Lightning goes back to the late 1980s. Managing director and brewery founder John Gilbert came up with the recipe for this pale, crisp and hoppy, yet strong, beer to contrast with the other 5% beers of the time which were nearly all dark, sweet and sickly. In cask form it's been a trend-setter. Since winning the *Best New Brewery Beer* award at the *Champion Beer of Britain* contest in 1989, it has inspired brewers up and down the land to create strong but pale beers which have appeal beyond the traditional ale drinker. The bottle-conditioned version is now a single-varietal hop brew, dropping the Challenger hops it used to include in favour of East Kent Goldings only. The draught version is not single-varietal and differs in a number of other respects. Probably the most notable difference is in the carbonation level, with the bottled beer performing more briskly on the tongue. Interestingly, the brewery recommends serving this and the other bottled beers on the cold side of cool. In 1997, Summer Lightning was judged to be CAMRA's *Best Bottle-Conditioned Beer*.

Tasting Notes
A pale, easy-drinking, strong bitter, quenching but dry. The citrusy, hoppy and malty nose leads to a lightly fruity taste with crisp, clean hoppiness and a dry, hoppy, bitter finish.

Major stockists Safeway, Tesco, Waitrose, Somerfield, Booths, Oddbins

THUNDERSTORM

ABV 5%   **Bottle size** 500 ml   **Serve** cool
Ingredients Maris Otter pale malt; wheat malt; Progress
and Golding hops; coriander

In cask form, this pale gold, 'English wheat ale' picked
up the top honour at the 1996 *Beauty of Hops* contest,
in the category for beers made with only Progress hops
(although the beer now also includes Goldings). The
bottled version followed in spring 1997. Try it with fish,
suggest the brewers.
Tasting Notes
A dry, quenching beer that doesn't taste its strength.
Aromas of pears, bread and bubblegum precede a
citrus, dry, hoppy taste with fruit lurking in the
background. Very dry, bitter, hoppy, bready finish.
Major stockists Safeway, Tesco, Waitrose, Booths,
Oddbins

HOPDAEMON

**Hopdaemon Brewery Co. Ltd., 18A/B Canterbury Hill,
Canterbury, Kent CT2 9LS. Tel. (01227) 784962
E-mail: hopdaemon@supanet.com**

New Zealander Tonie Prins founded Hopdaemon in
2001 after working at Swale Brewery. The equipment is
housed in two outbuildings – a former plumbing
company and an ex-children's nursery – behind his
cottage on the fringe of Canterbury. He describes his
beers as 'traditional ales with a slight New World twist'
and, to market them, has combined the medieval
traditions of Canterbury and its cathedral with a
sprinkling of legend and a touch of home-spun folklore
based around the local hopgardens. He bottles the beers
by hand himself, chilling them for up to a week before
filling to allow proteins to drop out and then re-seeding
with dried bottling yeast. He also supplies 'own label'
beers for Southwark Cathedral and the British Museum.

SKRIMSHANDER IPA

ABV 4.5%   **Bottle size** 500 ml   **Serve** cool
Ingredients Pale malt; crystal malt; caramalt; Fuggle,
Golding and Bramling Cross hops

Taking as its inspiration the Herman Melville classic
Moby Dick and its references to skrimshander (the craft

of carving whale ivory), this beer, like the other bottled beers, is also sold in cask form.

Tasting Notes
Fruit salad and spicy hop aromas emerge from this copper ale. The taste is wonderfully fruity but delicate, with orange blossom fragrance alongside clean hops. The dry, hoppy finish has more lingering fruit as bitterness grows.

GREEN DAEMON

ABV 5%   **Bottle size** 330 ml   **Serve** cold
Ingredients Pale malt; lager malt; New Zealand hops

Tonie has yet to apply for official accreditation for this organic beer, so he has to settle for calling it 'Natural' instead. However, the ingredients are all organic, including hops flown in from back home which are not, Tonie is quick to point out, the organic Hallertau hops for which New Zealand has become known. Green Daemon is lagered for three weeks before bottling.

Tasting Notes
A golden beer with luscious tropical fruit in the nose. More juicy Caribbean fruits emerge in the mouth, with a whiff of perfume. Mildly bitter, fruity finish.

LEVIATHAN

ABV 6%   **Bottle size** 500 ml   **Serve** cool
Ingredients Pale malt; crystal malt; chocolate malt; caramalt; wheat malt; Fuggle and Bramling Cross hops

'A beast of beer', laughs Tonie, referring to the giant sea monster from the pages of the *Bible* that gives its name to his strong, but subtle, ale.

Tasting Notes
A red-brown beer with hints of pineapple and lemon in the hoppy nose. Easy-drinking for its strength, its taste is full of juicy, fruity hops plus a dash of pepper. The dry, fruity and hoppy finish lasts well.

HUGHES

Sarah Hughes Brewery, Beacon Hotel,
129 Bilston Street, Sedgley, Dudley,
West Midlands DY3 1JE. Tel. (01902) 883381

This old, Black Country brewhouse stands behind the gloriously unspoilt, multi-room Beacon Hotel, a

Victorian delight that flash brewery architects would give their eye-teeth to vandalise. The business was purchased by Sarah Hughes in 1920 and she took up the reins of brewing that had commenced back in the 1880s, or even earlier. She produced just one beer, the revered Dark Ruby, and continued to do so until her death in 1951. After lying idle for 30 years, the tower brewery was re-opened in 1987 by her grandson. With his brewer, Guy Perry, John Hughes has expanded the beer range a little, but only the classic strong mild is bottle conditioned.

DARK RUBY

ABV 6%   **Bottle size** 500 ml   **Serve** cool
Ingredients Maris Otter pale malt; crystal malt; Fuggle and Golding hops

Originally brewed by Sarah Hughes back in 1921, the bottled version of this beer was first made available in 1995. It is identical to the award-winning draught beer, and is simply filled from the cask by contract bottlers with no primings or finings, making it acceptable to vegans. The founder herself is depicted on the label. Sales in the US are handled by B United.
Tasting Notes
As expected, dark ruby in colour. The vinous aroma of fruit gives way to a smooth, fruity, rather sweet taste. Fruity, malty, sweetish finish with a little hop. Older samples become winey.

HUMPTY DUMPTY

**Humpty Dumpty Brewery, Church Road,
Reedham, Norfolk NR13 3TZ.
Tel. (01493) 701818 Fax (01493) 700727**
Mail order service

Opened by brewer Mick Cottrell in 1998 next to The Railway Tavern pub in Reedham, Humpty Dumpty moved in 2001 to a new site. Its new home is a large building handily situated alongside Pettitts Animal Park (a popular family attraction) in the same village. The new premises not only has allowed brewery expansion but also offers a spacious gift shop/off-licence, where Humpty Dumpty's bottled beers (in gift packs and individually), plus other local souvenirs, can be purchased. Reedham itself has an attractive riverside and an old chain ferry, connecting Norfolk to Suffolk.

NORD ATLANTIC

ABV 3.7%   **Bottle size** 500 ml   **Serve** cool
Ingredients Pearl pale malt; crystal malt; caramalt; wheat malt; Challenger and Fuggle hops

Humpty Dumpty's beer names either reflect its Broadland setting or recall the names of famous steam engines. Nord Atlantic obviously falls into the latter category.

LITTLE SHARPIE

ABV 3.8%   **Bottle size** 500 ml   **Serve** cool
Ingredients Pearl pale malt; caramalt; wheat malt; Fuggle and Cascade hops

Little Sharpie is another engine-driven beer. Like the other bottled beers, this is brewed and bottled on site after conditioning in cask. Each beer is kräusened to ensure a good secondary fermentation. Six months are allowed in the best before date.
Tasting Notes
A golden ale with fruity, spicy hops in the nose, a crisp, spicy, lemony, bitter taste, and a dry, bitter, lemon-hop finish.

HUMPTY DUMPTY

ABV 4.1%   **Bottle size** 500 ml   **Serve** cool
Ingredients Pearl pale malt; crystal malt; caramalt; wheat malt; Challenger and Fuggle hops

The beer that shares its name with the brewery is named after a locomotive from the 1920s.
Tasting Notes
A dark golden beer with spicy, light fruit in the nose. Bold flavours hog the palate – hops, bitterness and fruit primarily, over a sweet base – before a bitter, hoppy aftertaste.

CLAUD HAMILTON

ABV 4.3%   **Bottle size** 500 ml   **Serve** cool
Ingredients Pearl pale malt; chocolate malt; caramalt; roasted barley; Challenger hops

A famous locomotive-inspired, single-varietal hop ale that showcases dark malts and just the seasoning of Challenger hops.

GOLDEN GORSE

ABV 4.4%   **Bottle size** 500 ml   **Serve** cool
Ingredients Lager malt; wheat malt; Fuggle and First Gold hops

Although it seems to owe more to Broadland than Brunel, Golden Gorse is also named after a famous loco.
Tasting Notes
Pale gold in colour, this ale has fruit and hops in the aroma and a bittersweet, malt-and-lemon taste. Bitterness takes over in the finish, but fruit lingers.

CHELTENHAM FLYER

ABV 4.6%   **Bottle size** 500 ml   **Serve** cool
Ingredients Pearl pale malt; crystal malt; wheat malt; Challenger and Mount Hood hops

Another railway beer, this time incorporating some American Mount Hood hops.
Tasting Notes
A dark golden ale with orange among the fruit and malt in the nose. Orange fruitiness continues in the mouth, alongside bitterness and hops, before a long, hoppy, bitter finish. A robust, full-bodied beer.

RAILWAY SLEEPER

ABV 5%   **Bottle size** 500 ml   **Serve** cool
Ingredients Pearl pale malt; crystal malt; amber malt; wheat malt; First Gold hops

A single-varietal hop beer using the popular dwarf hop, First Gold.
Tasting Notes
Fruit leads in the aroma of this dark golden ale, with lots of malt overlaid by a surprisingly light, fruity hoppiness in the taste. Hop eventually wins through over malt in the finish, but lemon notes linger on.

BROADLAND GOLD

ABV 6%   **Bottle size** 500 ml   **Serve** cool
Ingredients Pearl pale malt; amber malt; wheat malt; Challenger hops

Unlike the other beers which are also sold in cask form, Broadland Gold is mostly brewed only for the bottle and is just available in winter months.

ICENI

**The Iceni Brewery, 3 Foulden Road, Ickburgh,
Mundford, Norfolk IP26 5BJ.
Tel. (01842) 878922 Fax (01842) 879216**

Iceni was founded by Ulsterman Brendan Moore in
1995 and some of his beers are named after Celtic
queens and/or the Iceni tribe, which once inhabited
this part of England. The beers, left to drop bright, are
kräusened with a wort and yeast mixture before bottling
from casks. Best before dates are set at one year.
Brendan – a driving force in the local microbrewing
movement – also bottles for other small producers.

HONEY MILD

ABV 3.6%   **Bottle size** 500 ml   **Serve** cool
Ingredients Halcyon pale malt; crystal malt; roasted barley;
flaked barley; Fuggle and Challenger hops; honey

This ruby beer is the same brew as Thetford Forest Mild
(see below), except for the addition of honey. It was
first produced in November 2000.
Tasting Notes
A complex beer for its strength, with a honey-caramel
nose with roasted bits – like liquid 'Crunchie' bars. The
taste begins malty sweet and honeyish but turns dry
and gently bitter. Dry, honeyed finish with dark malt.

THETFORD FOREST MILD

ABV 3.6%   **Bottle size** 500 ml   **Serve** cool
Ingredients Halcyon pale malt; torrefied wheat; roasted
barley; Fuggle and Challenger hops

Introduced in spring 2000, this mild is named after the
large tract of forest that runs up to the brewery's home.
Tasting Notes
A very dark ruby mild with a pleasant coffee and
biscuity malt aroma. On the palate, it is sweetish and
malty, but well balanced. Bittersweet, malty finish.

BOADICEA CHARIOT ALE

ABV 3.8%   **Bottle size** 500 ml   **Serve** cool
Ingredients Halcyon pale malt; Fuggle and Challenger
hops

Iceni's original beer, Boadicea first tempted Norfolk

drinkers back in 1995. It was re-introduced in 2000, replacing Boadicea Strong Ale (4.2%).

Tasting Notes

An amber ale with a slightly piney, nutty, fruity nose. Piney, spicy, perfumed hops lead in the mouth. The finish is bitter and increasingly hoppy.

ELVEDEN FOREST GOLD

ABV 3.9%   **Bottle size** 500 ml   **Serve** cool
Ingredients Halcyon pale malt; caramalt; Fuggle, Challenger and Brewer's Gold hops

Elveden Forest, close to the brewery's home, is probably best known these days as the site of one of the Centre Parks holiday villages.

Tasting Notes

A golden ale with floral hop nose. Easy-drinking, it tastes crisp, fruity, spicy and hoppy, with a light, hoppy finish and some lingering fruit.

CELTIC QUEEN

ABV 4%   **Bottle size** 500 ml   **Serve** cool
Ingredients Halcyon pale malt; caramalt; Fuggle and Challenger hops

Most of Iceni's labels are designed to look like the open pages of a book, displaying the name of the beer on the left side of the spread and a picture, plus a legend or quotation about the beer's name, on the right. This beer's image is of the Celtic Queen herself, pondering her duty 'to be a fierce warrior, leader of her people'.

Tasting Notes

An amber beer with a mixed fruit aroma. On the palate, there is full fruitiness and malt, but the beer is dry, not too sweet and nicely restrained, with a gentle, clean hop bitterness. Dry, fruity, moreish, bitter aftertaste.

FINE SOFT DAY

ABV 4%   **Bottle size** 500 ml   **Serve** cool
Ingredients Halcyon pale malt; caramalt; Fuggle and Challenger hops; maple syrup

Maple syrup is the unusual ingredient in this bitter. It is added when the beer is racked into casks after primary fermentation.

Tasting Notes

An attractive bronze beer with an aroma of ripe, sweet

malt and citrus fruit. The full, bittersweet taste is grainy, malty, dry and very fruity (citrus and melon), while the aftertaste is particularly dry and increasingly bitter.

SWAFFHAM PRIDE

ABV 4%   **Bottle size** 500 ml   **Serve** cool
Ingredients Halcyon pale malt; caramalt; fruit sugar; Fuggle and Challenger hops

Swaffham Pride was first brewed in autumn 1999 to commemorate the opening of the Ecotech Centre (shown on the label) in nearby Swaffham. Its fruity character makes it good with desserts, says Brendan.
Tasting Notes
A lovely fruit cocktail – tinned pears and peaches – aroma introduces this amber ale. Juicy fruit also dominates crisp bitterness and a light background sweetness in the taste, before a dry, bitter, nicely hoppy finish.

CRANBERRY WHEAT

ABV 4.1%   **Bottle size** 500 ml   **Serve** cool
Ingredients Lager malt; caramalt; wheat malt; Cascade hops; cranberries

Cranberries offer brewers a different angle when considering fruit beers. Being rather bitter, they provide fruit character without too much sweetness, as Fuller's discovered when introducing its Organic Honey Dew with Cranberry. Iceni's cranberry beer dates from 2000, arriving first in cask.
Tasting Notes
A peachey-golden beer with a fruity, hoppy nose. The taste is a mostly bitter mix of hop, malt and light cranberry, with bitterness gradually taking over. Dry, bitter cranberry finish.

SNOWDROP

ABV 4.1%   **Bottle size** 500 ml   **Serve** cool
Ingredients Lager malt; crushed wheat; Fuggle, Challenger and Cascade hops

An annual brew, Snowdrop appears in spring, and is another beer to try with puddings, according to Iceni.
Tasting Notes
A pale golden beer with a crisp, fruity (peaches and oranges) nose. The clean taste is a pleasant mix of

peachy fruit and crisp, lightly-scented hop bitterness.
The finish has a gentle smack of bitter, peachy fruit.

FEN TIGER

ABV 4.2%   **Bottle size** 500 ml   **Serve** cool
Ingredients Halcyon pale malt; caramalt; Fuggle and
Challenger hops; coriander

Coriander, one of the many herbs and spices used to
flavour beer before hops were imported into the UK, is
recalled in this novel bitter. The ancient practice was
revived initially by Nethergate Brewery in Suffolk, with
its Umbel Ale and Umbel Magna, in the early 1990s.
The label depicts a poacher.
Tasting Notes
A richly amber ale offering a well-balanced aroma of
light orange fruit and sweet malt. The taste is a crisp,
clean mix of lightly spicy, gently bitter fruits, while the
finish is dry, moreish and slightly perfumed, with bitter
fruit and emerging hop character.

ON TARGET

ABV 4.2%   **Bottle size** 500 ml   **Serve** cool
Ingredients Halcyon pale malt; caramalt; Target, Fuggle
and Challenger hops

Target hops provide the inspiration for the name of this
best bitter. It 'always hits the mark', if you believe the
label.
Tasting Notes
Amber in colour, this best bitter has toffeeish malt and
an earthy hop fruitiness in the aroma. The taste is
predominantly bitter and hoppy, but with good malt
support. Plenty of body for its strength. Very dry, bitter
and hoppy finish.

THOMAS PAINE PORTER

ABV 4.2%   **Bottle size** 500 ml   **Serve** cool
Ingredients Halcyon pale malt; crystal malt; flaked
wheat; torrefied wheat; roasted barley; Fuggle and
Challenger hops

Named after local hero Thomas Paine, a philosopher,
theologian and activist in the American War of
Independence – 'Born in Thetford in 1737: a noted
author, revolutionary and man of reason', according to
the label – this ruby porter was added in 1999.

HONEY STOUT

ABV 4.3%   **Bottle size** 500 ml   **Serve** cool
Ingredients Halcyon pale malt; crystal malt; caramalt; roasted barley; Fuggle and Challenger hops; honey

A near-black beer, based on the brewery's Celtic Stout, with Irish honey added for a new dimension.

PHOENIX

ABV 4.3%   **Bottle size** 500 ml   **Serve** cool
Ingredients Lager malt; crushed wheat; Phoenix hops

A single-varietal beer introduced in 2002, showcasing the not-widely-used Phoenix hops, with the fire-regenerated, mythological bird of the same name depicted on the label.
Tasting Notes
A golden ale with a sharp, hoppy, lemon juice aroma. Piney hops dominate the palate, leaving some light lemon in the hoppy, bitter finish.

DEIRDRE OF THE SORROWS

ABV 4.4%   **Bottle size** 500 ml   **Serve** cool
Ingredients Halcyon pale malt; roasted barley; Fuggle and Challenger hops

A beer dedicated to 'the fairest and most beautiful of all the daughters of Ulster'. The label says she was destined to 'bring sorrow and pain to all the heroes of Ulster'.
Tasting Notes
An orange-gold beer with a biscuity, malty nose. The well-balanced, gently bitter taste combines fruit, malt and hops. Dry, fruity, pleasantly bitter finish.

PORTED PORTER

ABV 4.4%   **Bottle size** 500 ml   **Serve** cool
Ingredients Halcyon pale malt; torrefied wheat; flaked barley; roasted barley; Fuggle and Challenger hops; port

Brendan Moore grew up with the Irish tradition of adding fortified wines to stout and in 2000 created his own all-in-one equivalent. A bottle of port is added to each firkin before bottling.
Tasting Notes
A dark ruby porter with soft roasted grain, a little fruit and some caramel in the aroma. The taste is also soft,

nutty, gently roasted and bittersweet, with a hint of winey fruit. Dry, bitter finish, with a little sweet fruit.

ROISIN DUBH

ABV 4.4%   **Bottle size** 500 ml   **Serve** cool
Ingredients Halcyon pale malt; torrefied wheat; roasted barley; Fuggle and Challenger hops

Inspired by a sweet, dark beer from the Midlands, Roísín Dubh is Gaelic for 'dark rose'. The beer first appeared back in 1996.
Tasting Notes
A deep red ale with a fruity, floral nose. Smooth, clean fruity flavours fill the mouth, with a solid balancing bitterness and a little nut. The aftertaste is dry, very moreish, soft and fruity, yet bitter, with a hint of toffee.

GOOD NIGHT OUT

ABV 4.5%   **Bottle size** 500 ml   **Serve** cool
Ingredients Halcyon pale malt; roasted barley; Fuggle and Challenger hops; port

First brewed for a brewers' get-together in 1998, this beer takes its name from the fact that the assembled throng considered the event a 'good night out'. The beer is based on Iceni's Deirdre of the Sorrows, but with a bottle of port added per firkin. 'Just the ticket', says the label.
Tasting Notes
Another amber beer with a mellow fruity nose, but this time the added port provides a 'crushed raspberry' aroma. The taste is remarkably fruity – raspberries and melons – but fairly dry and not sweet. Dry, bitter finish.

IT'S A GRAND DAY

ABV 4.5%   **Bottle size** 500 ml   **Serve** cool
Ingredients Halcyon pale malt; Fuggle and Challenger hops; ginger

Designed as a refreshing summer ale, It's a Grand Day ('for a great ale') is a stronger version of Iceni's Fen Tiger, but with the addition of stem ginger instead of coriander.
Tasting Notes
An amber beer with an aroma of fruit and ginger spice. The crisp, refreshing taste features plenty of ginger, but without the accustomed 'burn', and is well balanced to

allow malt and hop flavour through. Ginger and hops compete in the finish.

ICENI GOLD

ABV 5% **Bottle size** 500 ml **Serve** cool
Ingredients Halcyon pale malt; caramalt; Fuggle and Challenger hops

'Forge the metal of my enemies into gifts for the gods', reads the quotation reproduced on the label of this strong ale.
Tasting Notes
An orange-gold beer with a strong fruit cocktail aroma, laced with a little spice. It is not quite as sweet as other Iceni beers, but has the same fruitiness, as well as a touch of spice and a bitter edge. Very dry, bitter finish.

NORFOLK LAGER

ABV 5% **Bottle size** 500 ml **Serve** cold
Ingredients Lager malt; wheat malt; Hersbrucker hops

This lager was initially brewed in 1998 for a subsidiary company of Iceni Brewery called Lager UK Ltd. At the time, the beer was known as L.A.D. Lager. The first batch was a keg product (chilled and filtered but not pasteurised), the initials L.A.D. conveniently standing – apparently – for 'Lager Awareness Day'. Laddish marketing, complete with poses by a blonde model, helped the beer get off the ground and attracted the attentions of the tabloid press. The beer has since been sold in cask form and this bottle-conditioned version first arrived in 1999. The laddish image has been quietly dropped in recent years as the new name of Norfolk Lager has been adopted.
Tasting Notes
A pale golden beer with a floral hop nose. It is malty and sweet to taste, with clean, lightly perfumed hop notes. Dry, bittersweet, malt and hops finish. Tasty and well rounded.

NORFOLK GOLD

ABV 5% **Bottle size** 500 ml **Serve** cool
Ingredients Halcyon pale malt; caramalt; Fuggle and Challenger hops

Aimed at the tourist trade on the popular Norfolk coast, this beer is worth sampling with fish, according to

brewer Brendan. It was first bottled in 1998.
Tasting Notes
As its name implies, a golden beer with a slightly
toffeeish, spicy, fruity nose. There are distinct pineapple
notes in the taste, a little spice and a hint of tartness.
Dry, fruity, spicy finish.

RASPBERRY WHEAT

ABV 5%   **Bottle size** 500 ml   **Serve** cool
Ingredients Halcyon pale malt; lager malt; wheat malt;
Hersbrucker hops; raspberries

Although pulped raspberries are added after primary
fermentation in the Belgian style, this is not a sour
framboise-like fruit beer. It is more of a summer
quencher, brought to Norfolk from the USA by an
itinerant brewer who worked at Iceni for a while.
Tasting Notes
A pale golden beer with raspberries and bubblegum in
the aroma. Delicate and bittersweet on the palate, it is
refreshingly understated, with gentle raspberries edging
out light hops. Moreish, hop and raspberry finish.

SWAFFHAM GOLD

ABV 5%   **Bottle size** 500 ml   **Serve** cool
Ingredients Halcyon pale malt; caramalt; Fuggle and
Challenger hops; maple syrup

Another tourist-orientated beer, Swaffham Gold is the
brewery's Iceni Gold with added maple syrup, making it
popular with sweet dishes.
Tasting Notes
A smooth and tasty, dark golden beer with fruit, spice
and butterscotch in the nose. Butterscotch, malt and
fruit linger in the mouth, alongside a crisp, but mellow
bitterness. Dry malty, gently bitter aftertaste.

WINTER LIGHTNING

ABV 5%   **Bottle size** 500 ml   **Serve** cool
Ingredients Lager malt; wheat malt; Hersbrucker hops

Hersbrucker hops add a continental touch to this winter
beer which is surprisingly blonde in colour.
Tasting Notes
A pale golden ale with a fruit cocktail aroma. The very
fruity, bittersweet taste is full and well rounded. Nicely
bitter, very fruity, gently warming finish.

MEN OF NORFOLK

ABV 6.2%   **Bottle size** 500/750 ml **Serve** cool
Ingredients Halcyon pale malt; crystal malt; torrefied
wheat; flaked barley; roasted barley; Fuggle and Challenger
hops

Aimed at the hardy winter tourists to this lovely part of
the world, this strong, rich stout is only brewed for
bottling, with a sepia label to encourage gift purchases.
Tasting Notes
This near-black, very dark brown beer features dark malt
and little pineapple and pear drop in the aroma. The
taste is smooth, malty and sweetish, but nicely balanced
and not cloying. Liquorice notes, roasted grain and
estery fruit play in the background, before a lingering,
roasted, liquorice finish.

ITCHEN VALLEY

**Itchen Valley Brewery Ltd., Shelf House,
New Farm Road, Alresford, Hampshire SO24 9QE.
Tel. (01962) 735111 Fax (01962) 735678
E-mail: info@itchenvalley.com
Web site: www.itchenvalley.com**

Itchen Valley Brewery was founded in 1997 but
changed hands a year later. The new owners launched
into bottle-conditioned beers in a big way and bottling
now accounts for around 15% of the business. All the
beers are bottled on site, having been conditioned in
tanks for a week after fermentation, allowed to drop
bright without the use of finings (making the beers
acceptable to vegetarians), and then sterile filtered.
Fresh bottling yeast is re-pitched before filling. Two new
bottles are planned: Hambledon, a 4% elderflower and
honey ale named after the 'birthplace of cricket', and
Treacle Stout, at 4.4%. Itchen Valley's parent company
specialises in pub signage, hence the colourful bottle
labels. Many bottles are sold at farmers' markets.

GODFATHERS

ABV 3.8%   **Bottle size** 500 ml   **Serve** cool
Ingredients Maris Otter pale malt; crystal malt; Whitbread
Golding Variety, Progress, Golding and Fuggle hops

An original Itchen Valley beer, taking its name from the
fact that the founders of the brewery first discussed the

project while acting as godfathers at a christening. A *Champion Beer of Britain* bronze medallist in cask form.

Tasting Notes
A dark golden, easy-drinking beer with plenty of fruity hop character in the aroma, alongside a hint of toffee from the malt. The taste is also slightly toffeeish, balanced by a gentle, fruity hoppiness. Dry, nicely bitter, fruity and hoppy finish.

FAGINS

ABV 4.1%   **Bottle size** 500 ml   **Serve** cool
Ingredients Maris Otter pale malt; crystal malt; wheat malt; First Gold, Golding and Fuggle hops

Depicting the Dickensian villain on the label, Fagins is another early Itchen Valley brew that has been retained by the current ownership.

Tasting Notes
A dark amber ale with malt and grapefruit dominant in the nose. Grapefruit hoppiness and pleasant bitterness feature in the taste, on a silky malt bed. The aftertaste is dry, bitter and lightly fruity.

WYKEHAMS GLORY

ABV 4.3%   **Bottle size** 500 ml   **Serve** cool
Ingredients Maris Otter pale malt; crystal malt; chocolate malt; First Gold hops

Wykehams Glory, with its striking green label, is named after William of Wykeham, who founded nearby Winchester College in the 14th century.

Tasting Notes
Red-brown in colour, this best bitter has a fruity aroma (both tropical and citrous notes), a mostly bitter, fruity-hop taste, and a dry, bitter finish with lingering fruit.

PURE GOLD

ABV 4.8%   **Bottle size** 500 ml   **Serve** cool
Ingredients Maris Otter pale malt; lager malt; Saaz and Cascade hops

The most recent addition to the portfolio, and a very unusual beer to boot, Pure Gold is an ale/lager cross, bursting with hop flavour. The secret is the addition of American Cascade hops in the fermenter, to complement the gentler Saaz hops which make their presence known in the copper.

Tasting Notes
A bright golden beer with a stunning aroma of pineapple, grapefruit and resin-like hop. The hop flavours are full and juicy, with pineapple, grapefruit and a rounded bitterness drowning out an initial sweetish note. The finish is dry, strongly hoppy and fruity.

FATHER CHRISTMAS

ABV 5%   **Bottle size** 500 ml   **Serve** cool
Ingredients Maris Otter pale malt; crystal malt; Challenger hops

Despite its seasonal name, Father Christmas is sold all year round. The black and gold label declares, like all the other labels, that the beer is 'Brewed in the heart of Hampshire'.
Tasting Notes
A bright brown brew with a pleasantly fruity nose. The taste is well balanced and has a restrained sweetness, gentle fruit, a hint of spice and a mild bitterness. Moreish malt and hops linger in the dry finish.

WAT TYLER

ABV 5%   **Bottle size** 500 ml   **Serve** cool
Ingredients Maris Otter pale malt; crystal malt; Progress hops

Recalling, in its name, the famous leader of the Peasants' Revolt of 1381, Wat Tyler is described on the dark red label as 'a rebel of a beer' and 'a strong real ale winter warmer'.
Tasting Notes
This red-brown premium ale has a fruity, slightly estery, malty nose, a surprisingly bitter but well-balanced taste of smooth malt and hops, and a dry, bitter, hoppy finish.

JOLLYBOAT

The Jollyboat Brewery Ltd., The Coach House, Buttgarden Street, Bideford, Devon EX39 2AU. Tel. (01237) 424343

This North Devon brewery was established in 1995 and turned to bottling in summer 1998. Packaging is now handled by Keltek Brewery and the beers are filled direct from the cask, without filtration or re-seeding of yeast. All the brewery's beers have a nautical connection and the name 'Jollyboat' itself refers to the smaller vessel used by ships' crews in the days of sail, when they decided to pop over to dry land for a few beers.

PLUNDER

ABV 4.8%   **Bottle size** 500 ml   **Serve** cool
Ingredients Maris Otter pale malt; crystal malt; chocolate malt; black malt; wheat malt; Fuggle and two other hops

The more recent of Jollyboat's two beers into bottle. Like Privateer, below, Plunder is a version of the cask beer of the same name.
Tasting Notes
A red-brown ale with lemon notes and hints of chocolate in the malty nose. The taste is hoppy, with a light, chocolatey malt base and a persistent background fruitiness. Hoppy, bitter finish.

PRIVATEER

ABV 4.8%   **Bottle size** 500 ml   **Serve** cool
Ingredients Maris Otter pale malt; crystal malt; chocolate malt; wheat malt; Fuggle and Cascade hops

Under the name of Show of Strength, this beer is also labelled for sale at the Show of Strength Theatre Company in Bristol.
Tasting Notes
A dark amber beer with a malty, chocolatey aroma supported by citrus fruit. Dark malts lead in the nutty, bittersweet taste, with hints of orange and other citrus fruits emerging. Dry, bitter, fruit and nuts finish.

KELTEK

Keltek Brewery, Unit 3A, Restormel Industrial Estate, Lostwithiel, Cornwall PL22 0HG.
Tel/Fax. (01208) 871199
E-mail: keltekbrewery@aol.com

Founded in Tregony in 1997, to supply beers to the Roseland peninsula of Cornwall, Keltek was taken over by local wholesaler Andy White in 1998 and moved to Lostwithiel. Andy is very much a one-man band, brewing, bottling, selling and delivering the beers himself. All the beers are bottled (200–300 at a time) direct from the fermenter, without filtration or re-seeding of fresh yeast. A best before date of six months post-bottling is applied. Keltek also bottles for other small brewers in the South West.

KING

ABV 5.1%   **Bottle size** 500 ml   **Serve** cool
Ingredients Pale malt; crystal malt; Cascade and Hallertau hops

Featuring the mythical 'sword in the stone' on its colourful label, there's no difficulty guessing to which king this beer alludes. It was first produced in 1998 and is good to drink with curries, according to Andy. Twice winner of the Tucker's Maltings bottled beer competition, and winner of the SIBA (Society of Independent Brewers) *National Brewing Competition*'s bottled beer category in 2001.
Tasting Notes
A golden ale with a juicy, orange-fruit aroma. The taste is a delightfully balanced blend of powerful, zesty orange-hop flavour, ripe, sweetish malt and good bitterness. Dry, bitter fruit finish.

REVENGE/LOSTWITHIALE

ABV 7%   **Bottle size** 500 ml   **Serve** cool
Ingredients Pale malt; crystal malt; chocolate malt; Cascade and Hallertau hops

Revenge is a dark red strong ale to be enjoyed – suggests Andy – with a meat pie. Note the spooky skull-tankard on the label. The beer is sold as Lostwithiale in the town of Lostwithiel itself, with a label bearing the town's crest.
Tasting Notes
A strong, ruby ale with an aroma rich in roasted grain and toffee. A soft, sweet, malty, creamy, fruity taste follows, before a thick, creamy, sweet malt finish with a hint of roast. There's a clear alcoholic kick throughout.

KRIPPLE DICK

ABV 8.5%   **Bottle size** 275 ml   **Serve** cool
Ingredients Pale malt; crystal malt; chocolate malt; amber malt; First Gold and Hallertau hops

At 8.5%, there must be a warning in the title. There are

echoes of a beer once produced by St Austell Brewery in the name and style of this powerful ale, which was introduced by Andy in spring 2001.

Tasting Notes

A dark ruby barley wine with soft, creamy malt and pear drops in the nose. The taste is well balanced and surprisingly understated: fruit, malt sweetness and a liquorice-like bitterness are evident but are not overpowering. Pleasant, sweet, malty finish with a trace of the same liquorice bitterness.

KING

WJ King & Co (Brewers), 3–5 Jubilee Estate, Foundry Lane, Horsham, West Sussex RH13 5UE. Tel. (01403) 272102 Fax (01403) 754455 E-mail: sales@kingfamilybrewers.co.uk Web site: www.kingfamilybrewers.co.uk

Bill King, latterly managing director of King & Barnes, which was closed following its sale to fellow regional brewer Hall & Woodhouse, returned to brewing on a much smaller scale in 2001. Setting up this microbrewery in the same town of Horsham, Bill was swiftly brewing up to capacity and a bottled beer was soon added to the cask range. The beer is filled directly from the fermenter, without filtering or the use of isinglass finings. A second bottled brew, King's Old Ale (4.5%), is now planned.

RED RIVER ALE

ABV 5%   **Bottle size** 500 ml   **Serve** cool
Ingredients Pale malt; crystal malt; chocolate malt; Golding and two other (undeclared) hops

Flavoured with three Kent hops, Goldings and two others which Bill prefers to keep anonymous, this strong beer takes its name from a tributary that runs from a mill pond in Horsham and is one of a few such 'Red Rivers' coloured by rust from the region's old iron workings.

Tasting Notes

A light ruby beer with a white head. There is plenty of fruit on the malt in the nose, with a hint of chocolate behind. The smooth taste is nutty and has sweet, fruity notes, plus bits of roasted malt poking through, although it is generally bitter and robust. Nutty, roasty and bitter finish.

KING'S HEAD

**King's Head Brewing Company, 132 High Street,
Bildeston, Suffolk IP7 7ED. Tel./Fax (01449) 741434
E-mail: enquiries@bildestonkingshead.co.uk
Web site: www.bildestonkingshead.co.uk**

Bildeston is one of many attractive, small country
towns in Suffolk and The Kings Head is a big, high-
ceilinged old pub close to the main square. It's had its
own brewery since 1996 (originally known as Brettvale
Brewing Company), which is housed in an old stable
block to the rear. Jayne Tester does the brewing and
now produces four bottle-conditioned ales to
complement the draught selection. All the beers are
racked bright and then kräusened prior to bottling.

FIRST GOLD

ABV 4.3%   **Bottle size** 500 ml   **Serve** cool
Ingredients Maris Otter pale malt; crystal malt; First Gold
hops

A dark golden, single-varietal beer.
Tasting Notes
A spicy, lightly fruity nose with some soft orange notes
leads on to a bitter, lightly fruity taste.

APACHE

ABV 4.5%   **Bottle size** 500 ml   **Serve** cool
Ingredients Maris Otter pale malt; crystal malt; Fuggle and
Challenger hops

East Anglia is full of airfields and this beer is named to
commemorate the arrival of the Apache helicopter at
the Wattisham airbase near Bildeston.
Tasting Notes
An amber ale with a malty nose and a taste of soft
bitterness and gentle fruit. Bitter, toffeeish finish.

CROWDIE

ABV 5%   **Bottle size** 500 ml   **Serve** cool
Ingredients Maris Otter pale malt; crystal malt; black malt;
oats; First Gold and Fuggle hops

An oatmeal stout named after an old Scottish word for
oatmeal. The back label quotes the Robert Burns poem
Crowdie Evermair.

DARK VADER

ABV 5.4%   **Bottle size** 500 ml   **Serve** cool
Ingredients Maris Otter pale malt; crystal malt; chocolate malt; Golding and Fuggle hops

First produced for a local beer festival and named by its attendees, this porter has since picked up a couple of other awards at the Ipswich Beer Festival in its cask form.
Tasting Notes
A sweetish beer majoring on dark malt, from aroma through to the bittersweet finish.

LEATHERBRITCHES

Leatherbritches Brewery, The Bentley Brook Inn, Fenny Bentley, Ashbourne, Derbyshire DE6 1LF. Tel. (01335) 350278 Fax (01335) 350422 E-mail: all@bentleybrookinn.co.uk Web site: www.bentleybrookinn.co.uk

The Bentley Brook Inn is a successful country pub in the Derbyshire Peak District, run by the Allingham family since 1977. The small brewery at the rear has been experimenting with bottled beers for a number of years and now has a regular range of three, all bottled on site direct from a conditioning tank.

ALE CONNER'S TIPPLE

ABV 4.9%   **Bottle size** 500 ml   **Serve** cool
Ingredients Maris Otter pale malt; Progress and Styrian Golding hops

The name of the brewery is derived from the garments worn by ale conners in centuries past. The job of these erstwhile Customs and Excise men was to test the quality and strength of the beers in their patch. They did so by sitting on a small pool of beer and their assessment of it was based on how sticky their leather britches became. Now the ale conner is remembered in each of the bottled beers' names, starting with this strong ale.
Tasting Notes
A very pale, yellow-gold beer with a big grapefruit aroma. The taste is sweetish, with more grapefruit and scented floral notes. Floral hops persist in the finish, but bitterness just takes over.

ALE CONNER'S BESPOKE

ABV 5.2%   **Bottle size** 500 ml   **Serve** cool
Ingredients Maris Otter pale malt; crystal malt; Progress and Styrian Golding hops

Bespoke was Leatherbritches' first ever cask beer.
Tasting Notes
A dark golden ale with citrous hops in the nose. Floral, fruity notes lead in the mouth, including a hint of pear drop and a waft of orange blossom. Dry, floral-fruity, gently bitter aftertaste.

ALE CONNER'S PORTER

ABV 5.4%   **Bottle size** 500 ml   **Serve** cool
Ingredients Maris Otter pale malt; crystal malt; dark chocolate malt; Progress hops

The label of this and the other beers depicts two ale conners 'sitting down on the job', having lunch while their leather pants do their stuff. Only leather britches were able to stand the wear and tear of the profession.
Tasting Notes
A ruby beer with a dense, creamy head. A lightly roasted, biscuity malt aroma leads to a sweetish, biscuity taste, with a gentle creaminess and soft roasted malt. Bittersweet, malty finish with roasted flavours.

MALTON

Malton Brewery, rear of 12 Wheelgate, Malton, North Yorkshire YO17 7YL.
Tel. (01653) 697580 Fax (01653) 691812
E-mail: enquiries@suddabys.co.uk
Web site: www.maltonbrewery.com

Malton Brewery has been steaming away in an old stable block behind The Crown Hotel in Malton since 1984. Occasionally it produces the bottled beer below for sale at the hotel and to visitors to the brewery.

GOLDEN CHANCE

ABV 4.2%   **Bottle size** 500 ml   **Serve** cool
Ingredients Optic pale malt; dark crystal malt; torrefied wheat; Challenger and Styrian Golding hops

First brewed in March 2000 and now a regular cask

offering, this quaffable, golden best bitter is filtered and re-seeded with fresh yeast prior to bottling (at Cropton Brewery), with a six–eight-month best before date. Suitable for vegetarians and vegans.

MARSTON MOOR

Marston Moor Brewery, Crown House, Kirk Hammerton, York YO26 8DD. Tel./Fax (01423) 330341
E-mail: marston.moor.brewery@ic24.net

Marston Moor – taking its name from the famous Civil War battle of 1644 – was set up in 1983. It now makes such a good living providing a consultancy service to new microbreweries that its own beers are being brewed temporarily by Rudgate Brewery at Tockwith. The beers are bottled, however, at Marston Moor, straight from the cask, with six-month best before dates applied. Slight changes may be made to the beer recipes from time to time.

BREWERS DROOP

ABV 5%   **Bottle size** 500 ml   **Serve** cool
Ingredients Maris Otter pale malt; wheat malt; crystal malt; Challenger and Styrian Golding hops

One of the brewery's earliest and best-known cask ales, Brewers Droop was introduced to the bottle in 2000. The label carries a tongue-in-cheek warning about the consequences of drinking this strong ale on 'your most resolute anatomical appendages'.
Tasting Notes
An orange-golden ale with a lightly fruity nose (orange and pear notes). The taste is nicely balanced, mixing gentle fruit notes, malt smoothness and crisp bitterness. Bitter, lightly fruity finish.

BREWERS PRIDE

ABV 5%   **Bottle size** 500 ml   **Serve** cool
Ingredients Maris Otter pale malt; wheat malt; crystal malt; Challenger and Styrian Golding hops

If you try Brewers Pride on draught, you'll find it is notably less strong (only 4.2%) than this bottled version. 'It's a reet luvely sup', according to the label.
Tasting Notes
Copper in colour, this strong ale has a fruity, spicy

aroma with hints of banana toffee. The taste is also toffeeishly malty, with suggestions of banana and other fruit, although it is more bitter than sweet. Hops are more apparent in the bitter finish.

MAULDONS

**Mauldons Ltd., The Black Adder Brewery,
7 Addison Road, Chilton Industrial Estate,
Sudbury, Suffolk CO10 2YW.
Tel./Fax (01787) 311055
E-mail: sims@mauldons.co.uk
Web site: www.mauldons.co.uk**

Founded in 1982, Mauldons was set up by former Watney's brewer Peter Mauldon, who was keen to re-establish the family brewing name. Mauldons had brewed in Suffolk since the 1790s when the Sudbury premises was closed by its new owners, Greene King, at the turn of the 1960s. Peter's story is one of success, his most famous beer, Black Adder, winning CAMRA's *Champion Beer of Britain* contest in 1991. He retired in 2000, selling the business to former Adnams salesman Steve Sims. Steve has sought to capitalise on the fame of Black Adder, adding the subtitle 'The Black Adder Brewery' to the Mauldons name and launching the beer in bottle.

BLACK ADDER

ABV 5.3%   **Bottle size** 500 ml   **Serve** cool
Ingredients Maris Otter pale malt; crystal malt; black malt; Fuggle hops

First brewed in 1988, when the Rowan Atkinson *Blackadder* TV series was in its prime, this beer takes its name also from its dark appearance and its bite, according to Steve Sims. It makes an ideal partner for a ploughman's lunch, he adds. The beer is brewed at Mauldons but bottled, straight from the cask, by Iceni Brewery.
Tasting Notes
Near-black, with ruby tints, Black Adder has banana notes alongside coffeeish dark malt in the nose and follows this with a complex taste of banana, mellow dark malt and a pleasant bitterness that increases in the nutty, roasted malt aftertaste. Easy to drink for its strength.
Major stockist local Waitrose

MEADS OF MERCIA

**Meads of Mercia, c/o Orchard, Hive & Vine,
4 High Street, Leominster HR6 8LZ.
Tel. (01568) 611232 Fax (01568) 620224
E-mail: enquiries@ohv.wyenet.co.uk
Web site: www.orchard-hive-and-vine.co.uk**

Meads of Mercia is not a brewery, but, as its name
suggests, a mead- and other honey products-making
venture. The honey beer below is contract brewed, the
most recent batch at Teme Valley Brewery, with Wessex
Craft Brewers handling the bottling.

THE BEES KNEES

ABV 6.2%   **Bottle size** 500 ml   **Serve** cool
Ingredients Pale malt; chocolate malt; black malt; wheat
malt; Fuggle hops; honey

The Bees Knees is an accidental beer. Meads of Mercia
proprietor Geoff Morris misunderstood a request from a
customer who wanted a 'mead ale' to serve at a
historical re-enactment. A mead ale is apparently a half-
strength mead (around 7%), produced using beer yeast
rather than wine yeast, but Geoff instead commissioned
this ale brewed with Warwickshire honey. Pasteurised
honey is added – at a ratio of about 7 kg per brewers'
barrel – during the last 15 minutes of the copper boil
and becomes the first element to be fermented, leaving
honey flavour but not too much sweetness. As the beer
migrates from brewery to brewery, the recipe tends to
be tweaked.
Tasting Notes
A ruby beer with a thick honey aroma, also featuring
treacly dark malt and fruit. Dark malt flavours dominate
the sweet taste alongside plenty of winey fruit, on a
subdued honey base. Bitter fruit overshadows both
treacly dark malt and honey in the finish.

MEANTIME

**Meantime Brewing, 2 Penhall Road, London SE7 8RX.
Tel. (020) 8293 1111 Fax (020) 8293 4004
E-mail: alastair@meantimebrewing.co.uk
Web site: www.meantimebrewing.co.uk**

Meantime Brewing was set up by continental beer
specialist Alastair Hook, who re-creates classic European

beer styles (Belgian ales, kölsch, Viennese lagers, wheat beers, etc.) at his Greenwich base. Courtesy of Sainsbury's supermarkets, several of his bottled beers now grace the national stage, and two are bottle conditioned.

RASPBERRY WHEAT BEER

ABV 5%   **Bottle size** 330 ml   **Serve** cold
Ingredients Pale malt; wheat malt; raspberry fruit extract; hops may vary

Part of Sainsbury's *Taste the Difference* collection, Meantime's Raspberry Wheat Beer was launched in 2003, following the success of the brewery's other beers for the supermarket chain (most of these are filtered, but not pasteurised). The malt grist is split 50/50 between low-colour malt and wheat malt, and raspberry fruit extract is used for flavouring and to help the bottle fermentation. A treat with a bar of chocolate, claims Alastair.
Tasting Notes
A hazy red beer with raspberries and a hint of banana in the nose. A raspberry sharpness in the mouth is tempered by just enough sweetness to make this a tart, but quenching, drink, with a little banana lingering in the background. Dry, increasingly bitter, raspberry finish.
Major stockist (both beers) Sainsbury

BAVARIAN STYLE WHEAT BEER

ABV 5%   **Bottle size** 330/660 ml **Serve** cold
Ingredients Pale malt; wheat malt; hops may vary

Meantime's Wheat Beer – which includes a hefty 65% wheat malt in its grist – is traditionally decoction mashed (the wort is pumped between vessels and subjected to varying temperatures to extract the best brewing sugars), fermented with a German wheat beer yeast and kräusened with active wort before bottling. The hop content having little impact on the flavour, apart from adding balancing bitterness, Alastair may vary the strains used in both these bottled beers. Choose from a small bottle or one to share.
Tasting Notes
A cloudy yellow beer with banana, hints of pineapple, bubblegum and spice in the nose. Citrous notes, banana and gentle spice fill the bittersweet taste before a dry, bitter orange finish.

MOOR

**Moor Beer Company, Whitley Farm, Ashcott,
Somerset TA7 9QW. Tel./Fax (01458) 210050
E-mail: info@moorbeer.co.uk
Web site: www.moorbeer.co.uk**
Mail order service

Moor Beer Company was founded on a dairy farm (now
a pig farm) by Arthur Frampton in 1996. Some 40 pubs
currently take the cask beers locally. The two beers
listed below are bottled only in small quantities, by
hand from the cask, with best before dates set at three
months.

MERLINS MAGIC

ABV 4.3%   **Bottle size** 500 ml   **Serve** cool
Ingredients Maris Otter pale malt; crystal malt; lager malt;
Fuggle and Liberty hops

Conjuring up dreamy images of the myths and legends
of the South West, Merlins Magic, already an
established cask ale, was first bottle conditioned in
spring 1999.
Tasting Notes
An unusual, orange-gold beer with a fruity hop aroma.
Dry, fruity and malty to taste, it also has a citrous
hoppiness. Dry, bitter finish.

OLD FREDDY WALKER

ABV 7.3%   **Bottle size** 500 ml   **Serve** cool
Ingredients Maris Otter pale malt; crystal malt; black malt;
Nugget and Liberty hops

Old Freddy Walker, Moor's first bottled beer, appeared
in 1998 and is named after an old sailor living in the
brewery's village. It is also available in cask form. It is
one of the more unusual and novel beers in this book,
being brewed with Nugget hops, which are known for
their high alpha acid content. Alpha acids are
responsible for bitterness, so, generally speaking, you
don't need so many of them to make an impact.
Blended with Liberty hops into a mash produced from a
complex dark malt grist, they produce a dangerously
drinkable, deceptively strong brew with a full fruitiness.
These attributes helped Old Freddy collect the silver
medal at the Tucker's Maltings bottled beer competition
(for beers brewed in the South West) in 1999.

Tasting Notes

A very dark brown ale with a coffee-coloured head. The fruity, roasty aroma is followed by a full, complex taste in which sweetish stout flavours are topped with fruity, citrous notes and there is a good background bitterness throughout. The aftertaste is bittersweet, roasted and fruity.

MOULIN

**RTR Catering Ltd., Moulin Hotel & Brewery,
Kirkmichael Road, Moulin, by Pitlochry,
Perthshire & Kinross PH16 5EW.
Tel. (01796) 472196 Fax (01796) 474098
E-mail: hotel@moulin.u-net.com
Web site: www.moulin.u-net.com**
Mail order service

Moulin Brewery was opened in 1995 at the Moulin Hotel in Pitlochry, during celebrations for the hotel's 300th anniversary (the hotel housed a brewery when it opened in 1695, so it was deemed fitting to recommence brewing on the site). Brewing has been relocated since to the Old Coach House opposite the main building.

ALE OF ATHOLL

ABV 4.5%   **Bottle size** 500 ml   **Serve** cool
Ingredients Maris Otter pale malt; crystal malt; chocolate malt; roast malt; Fuggle hops

Ale of Atholl (taking its name from the brewery's location in the Vale of Atholl, an area in which it is more common to find whisky distilleries than breweries) was first bottle conditioned in late 1996. The cask is allowed to settle for three days, then the beer is racked off and re-seeded with the same yeast strain used in primary fermentation. Some sugar is added and the beer is immediately bottled in glassware neatly overprinted with the history of Moulin village. Brewer Chris Tomlinson suggests you try a glass with venison (Scottish, of course).

Tasting Notes

A ruby-coloured beer with a fruity, malty, lightly chocolatey nose with hop resin notes. Fruity, citrous hops and dark malt are well balanced in the dry taste. Dark malt and hops emerge again in the dry, gently bitter aftertaste.

NETHERGATE

Nethergate Brewery Co. Ltd., 11–13 High Street, Clare, Suffolk CO10 8NY.
Tel. (01787) 277244 Fax (01787) 277123
Mail order service

Established in 1986, Nethergate has produced some award-winning ales and has never been afraid to experiment. The coriander-flavoured beer mentioned below is normally only on sale in the USA, but bottles can be obtained from the brewery. Filtered and re-seeded with fresh yeast prior to filling, it is bottled under contract by Hepworth & Co in Horsham.

AUGUSTINIAN

ABV 5.2%   **Bottle size** 500 ml   **Serve** cool
Ingredients Maris Otter pale malt; crystal malt; Fuggle hops; coriander seeds

This Augustinian bears no similarity to Nethergate's cask beer of the same name, which weighs in at 4.8% and does not include coriander. This bottled beer is actually a bespoke beer for the American market, brewed to order for importers who liked the name but wanted a different sort of brew.
Tasting Notes
An amber ale with a piney, spicy, coriander aroma. The same piney spiciness continues through into the taste and aftertaste, overlaid at all times by perfumed orange notes.

NORTH YORKSHIRE

North Yorkshire Brewing Company Ltd., Pinchinthorpe Hall, Guisborough, North Yorkshire TS14 8HG. Tel./Fax (01287) 630200
E-mail: nyb@pinchinthorpe.freeserve.co.uk
Web site: www.pinchinthorpehall.co.uk
Mail order service

North Yorkshire was founded in Middlesbrough in 1989 and moved in 1998 to Pinchinthorpe Hall, a moated, listed house that was home to the noble Lee family and their descendants for centuries until 1957. The house now also includes a hotel and restaurant, and its own spring water is used for brewing. All the beers are now registered as organic.

BEST BITTER

ABV 3.6%   **Bottle size** 500 ml   **Serve** cool
Ingredients Pale malt; crystal malt; Hallertau hops

A pale bitter showcasing organic Hallertau hops from
New Zealand. Like the other beers, it is bottled on site.
Tasting Notes
A golden beer with a lightly hoppy, bubblegum aroma.
In the mouth it is clean, bittersweet and fruity, with a
crisp, but light, hop edge. Hops and bitterness grow, but
fruit lingers, in the drying finish.

PRIOR'S ALE

ABV 3.6%   **Bottle size** 500 ml   **Serve** cool
Ingredients Pale malt; Hallertau and First Gold hops

A beer that remembers in its name the fact that one of
the Lee family was once a prior of Guisborough, where
the hall stands.
Tasting Notes
Light malt and hop compete with bubblegum in the
nose of this golden session ale. The taste nicely balances
malt and tangy hop, giving a hint of tart fruit. Tangy
hop lingers in the aftertaste.

ARCHBISHOP LEE'S RUBY ALE

ABV 4%   **Bottle size** 500 ml   **Serve** cool
Ingredients Pale malt; crystal malt; chocolate malt;
Hallertau and First Gold hops

There was not only a prior in the family, but an
Archbishop of York, too. The beer is described on the
label as 'northern, rounded and full bodied'.
Tasting Notes
An amber ale with a spicy malt nose. Malt also leads in
the bittersweet taste, supported by citrous hop, before a
dry, bittersweet, hoppy finish.

BORO BEST

ABV 4%   **Bottle size** 500 ml   **Serve** cool
Ingredients Pale malt; crystal malt; Hallertau and First
Gold hops

The label calls it a 'traditional, dark Northern bitter',
and its name refers back to the brewery's first home
over on Teesside.

Tasting Notes
Amber in colour, this best bitter has a malt and
bubblegum nose and a sweetish, gentle taste of malt
and hops. More hop adds some bitterness to the
aftertaste.

FOOLS GOLD

ABV 4.6%   **Bottle size** 500 ml   **Serve** cool
Ingredients Pale malt; First Gold hops

The name of this premium ale combines the historic
setting of the brewery and the use of rare, organic First
Gold hops. A cross-eyed, medieval jester ('a fool')
features on the label.
Tasting Notes
Suggestions of bubblegum are once again found in the
aroma of this golden beer, which also has a light,
hoppy, melon-fruity fragrance. The taste is notably
hoppy and fruity, but well balanced. Hops dominate
the aftertaste.

GOLDEN ALE

ABV 4.6%   **Bottle size** 500 ml   **Serve** cool
Ingredients Pale malt; crystal malt; Hallertau and First
Gold hops

As for all the other beers, this strong pale ale carries a
certification stamp from the Organic Food Federation.
Tasting Notes
Light tart fruit features in the nose, while sweetish malt
is countered by fruity hop in the taste but retains the
upper hand. Bittersweet, fruity finish, with increasing
hop.

FLYING HERBERT

ABV 4.7%   **Bottle size** 500 ml   **Serve** cool
Ingredients Pale malt; crystal malt; chocolate malt;
Hallertau and First Gold hops

One of North Yorkshire's earliest brews, with a daft
name plucked out of the air by brewer George Tinsley's
sister. The airborn hero in the name is depicted –
complete with flying goggles – on the label.
Tasting Notes
Another amber beer with malt and hop in the aroma.
There's a good hop counterbalance to sweet malt in the
taste, and a hoppy, drying finish.

LORD LEE'S

ABV 4.7%   **Bottle size** 500 ml   **Serve** cool
Ingredients Pale malt; crystal malt; chocolate malt;
Hallertau and First Gold hops

Joint strongest of the bottled beers, named after Roger
Lee, a family member who became Lord Mayor of
London.

Tasting Notes
Amber, with a dense, creamy head, Lord Lee's is spicy
and malty to the nose, with a fine balance of malt and
hops in the mouth. Bitterness grows in the malty finish.

O'HANLON'S

**O'Hanlon's Brewing Company Ltd., Great Barton Farm,
Whimple, Devon EX5 2NY.
Tel. (01404) 822412 Fax (01404) 823700
Web site: www.ohanlons.co.uk**

O'Hanlon's was set up in 1996 to serve John O'Hanlon's
pub in Clerkenwell, London, but quickly expanded to
supply other outlets. In 2000, he sold the pub and
moved the brewery to Devon. The bottling operation
has expanded considerably and the brewery has now
secured the contract to brew and market the revered
Thomas Hardy's Ale (12%), a classic bottle-conditioned
beer discontinued by Eldridge Pope after the 1999
vintage. There are also plans to re-launch that former
brewery's Royal Oak, including in bottle-conditioned
form for the first time.

DOUBLE CHAMPION WHEAT BEER

ABV 4%   **Bottle size** 500 ml   **Serve** cool
Ingredients Optic pale malt; wheat malt; caramalt;
Challenger, First Gold and Cascade hops; coriander seeds

A wheat beer in the Belgian style, low on bitterness but
laced with aromatic hops (First Gold and Cascade are
the late hops) and spiced with coriander seeds. Prior to
bottling, the beer is filtered and re-seeded with dried
bottling yeast. Winner of SIBA's *Wheat Beer Challenge*
1999 and 2002, hence the addition of 'Double
Champion' to the beer's name.

Tasting Notes
A golden beer with a lightly spiced, lemon-orange peel
aroma. The taste is orange peel bitter, lightly perfumed

and dry, and the finish is dry, bitter and slightly bready, with lingering orange and perfume notes.
Major stockist Safeway

ORGANIC RYE BEER

ABV 4.5%   **Bottle size** 500 ml   **Serve** cool
Ingredients Pale malt; crystal malt; rye flakes; Hallertau hops

Despite being wholly organic, this beer is sold under the name of Original Rye in the US, because of difficulties in getting the Soil Association accreditation recognised in the States.
Tasting Notes
A copper ale with a nutty, malty, 'crispbread' nose that gives way to light fruit. The taste is also nutty, but with some citrus fruit in the hop balance. Nutty, bitter finish.
Major stockists local Sainsbury and Waitrose

RED ALE

ABV 4.5%   **Bottle size** 500 ml   **Serve** cool
Ingredients Optic pale malt; crystal malt; caramalt; roasted barley; Phoenix and Styrian Golding hops

A traditional Irish red ale, fairly new in bottle but dating back to 1997 in cask form.
Tasting Notes
A light ruby beer with citrous hops in the aroma and a bittersweet mix of slightly salty malt and restrained citrous hops in the taste. Bitterness grows in the dry finish as the hops subside but malt lingers.

YELLOWHAMMER

ABV 4.5%   **Bottle size** 500 ml   **Serve** cool
Ingredients Optic pale malt; caramalt; First Gold and Cascade hops

A golden beer with a complex hopping regime: First Gold hops are used for bitterness, Cascades are the late hop and then the beer is dry-hopped with more First Gold. Runner-up at the Tucker's Maltings bottled beer contest in 2003.
Tasting Notes
A soft, malty beer with a light 'sherbet lemons' fruitiness. Well-balanced and clean.
Major stockist Safeway

ORIGINAL PORT STOUT

ABV 4.8%   **Bottle size** 500 ml   **Serve** cool
Ingredients Optic pale malt; crystal malt; caramalt; roasted barley; flaked barley; Phoenix and Styrian Golding hops; Ferreira port

A 'corpse reviver', in the Irish tradition of hang-over cures, this dry stout is enhanced by the addition of Ferreira port prior to bottling, at a ratio of two bottles per brewer's barrel (36 gallons), which raises the strength from 4.6 to 4.8%. The cask version was one of O'Hanlon's early beers – the port was added to mark out the cask beer from a popular keg stout John's pub also sold – and this bottled equivalent was introduced in 2000. In 2001, it claimed the gold medal at Tucker's Maltings bottled beer competition. The draught version then took the top stout prize in CAMRA's *Champion Winter Beer of Britain* awards for 2002. Phoenix is the main bittering hop, with Styrian Goldings added late for aroma. The beer is lightly fined prior to bottling.
Tasting Notes
A near-black beer with a biscuity, roasted barley nose. This is a classic, dry, bitter stout in the mouth, with a trace of winey fruit. The dry, roasty, bitter finish has the same hint of fruit.
Major stockists Safeway, local Sainsbury

OAKLEAF

Oakleaf Brewing Company Ltd., 7 Clarence Wharf Industrial Estate, Mumby Road, Gosport, Hampshire PO12 1AJ. Tel. (023) 9251 3222 Fax (023) 9251 0148 E-mail: info@oakleafbrewing.co.uk Web site: www.oakleafbrewing.co.uk

Ed Anderson, a former Firkin brew pub brewer, set up Oakleaf with his father-in-law, Dave Pickersgill. They brew the bottled beers themselves, but they are packaged at Hop Back, where they are filtered and re-seeded with fresh yeast.

HOLE HEARTED

ABV 4.7%   **Bottle size** 500 ml   **Serve** cool
Ingredients Pale malt; caramalt; wheat malt; Cascade hops

This golden ale (good with spicy foods, it is claimed)

takes its name from the fact that it was originally
brewed for sale at the Hole in the Wall pub in Southsea.
The cask version was CAMRA's *Champion Beer of
Hampshire* in 2002.

Tasting Notes
An explosion of grapefruit notes awaits you in the
aroma and taste of this premium ale, with a light malty
sweetness in the background. The bitter, tangy Cascade
hops linger on in the finish.

BLAKE'S GOSPORT BITTER

ABV 5.2%   **Bottle size** 500 ml   **Serve** cool
Ingredients Pale malt; crystal malt; chocolate malt; flaked
barley; Fuggle and Golding hops

A mere glance at the ingredients listing tells you that
this is quite a different beer to Hole Hearted. The
addition of crystal and chocolate malt ensures that this
is much darker and the classic English ale hops Fuggle
and Goldings provide a more subdued fruitiness than
the American Cascades used in the first beer. A beer to
go with steaks and other red meats, the brewers suggest.

Tasting Notes
A ruby ale with a malty, chocolatey nose. Dark malt
leads in the bittersweet taste with persistent, fruity hops
in the background. Roasted malt takes over in the bitter
finish, but hop-fruit lingers.

OLD CHIMNEYS

**Old Chimneys Brewery, The Street, Market Weston, Diss,
Norfolk IP22 2NZ. Tel. (01359) 221411**

Suffolk brewery, despite the postal address, founded by
former Greene King and Broughton brewer Alan
Thomson in 1995. His first bottles came out in autumn
2000, majoring on strong beers for sipping, but more
quaffable brews have found their way into bottle in
recent years. All the beers are fined and kräusened
(sometimes primed) prior to bottling, and bottles are
then given three weeks' secondary fermentation at the
brewery before they go on sale. Best before dates are
generally 12 months after bottling (18 months for Good
King Henry). The beers are now also sold direct from
the brewery shop, which is open Friday, 2–7pm, and
Saturday, 10am–1pm. The range of railway-inspired
beers are also sold at Wetheringsett Station, Brockford,
during steam events.

VICTORIAN BROWN ALE

ABV 3.8%   **Bottle size** 500 ml   **Serve** cool
Ingredients Pale malt; crystal malt; amber malt; roasted barley; lactose; Challenger hops

First brewed in 2003 in aid of the Mid-Suffolk Light Railway, which receives a donation for every bottle sold, Victorian Brown Ale has allowed Alan to dig deep into the brewing history books and unearth some interesting ingredients. Amber malt, common in the 19th century, is rarely used these days, and the addition of lactose (milk sugar) is also intriguing. Lactose is not fermentible by standard brewers' yeast and so the sugars remain in the brew adding body and sweetness (the best known beer to include lactose is Mackeson, the classic milk stout). Victorian Brown, the label reveals, was the livery colour of the old railway's engines.
Tasting Notes
A light ruby ale with a nutty, chococolatey malt aroma. Soft and malty in the mouth, with chocolate notes and a slight hop sharpness, it finishes malty and bitter.

LEADING PORTER

ABV 4.2%   **Bottle size** 500 ml   **Serve** cool
Ingredients Pale malt; crystal malt; roasted barley; lactose; Fuggle and Challenger hops

Another historic re-creation for the Mid-Suffolk Light Railway, which used to run from Haughley to Laxfield and is now being restored. The label carries an old picture of Frank Hubbard, Leading Porter at Laxfield Station.
Tasting Notes
A near-black, dark ruby beer with an appealing aroma of coffee-cream chocolates. Creamy coffee notes fill the palate, with sweetness just edged out by rounded bitterness and a little background fruit. Light, moussey body; nicely bitter, roasted malt finish.

GREAT RAFT BITTER

ABV 4.3%   **Bottle size** 500 ml   **Serve** cool
Ingredients Pearl pale malt; crystal malt; caramalt; Fuggle, Challenger and Target hops

One of the brewery's three original draught beers, Great Raft has been available in bottle-conditioned form only since 2002. The beer takes its name from Britain's rarest

and largest spider, which inhabits a local fen.
Tasting Notes
A copper ale with a toffeeish malt aroma. Malt and
toffee lead again in the taste, but well balanced by clean
bitterness and light fruitiness. Bitter, malty finish with
spicy hops.

GOLDEN PHEASANT

ABV 4.9%   **Bottle size** 500 ml   **Serve** cool
Ingredients Pearl pale malt; caramalt; Challenger and
Target hops

Named after the oriental bird which lives in a nearby
forest, Golden Pheasant is also sold in cask form but has
been bottled since 2002.
Tasting Notes
A dark golden ale that pours with a white collar of
foam. Malt, fruit and a little spice feature in the nose,
while the taste offers malt, hops, fruit, nuts and estery
traces of almond. A complex, flavour-packed beer with
a nutty, bitter and dry finish.

NATTERJACK

ABV 5.4%   **Bottle size** 500 ml   **Serve** cool
Ingredients Pearl pale malt; crystal malt; caramalt; Fuggle
hops

Inspired by the heathland toad, Natterjack – a single-
varietal hop beer, based on the classic English bittering
hop, Fuggle – is another of Old Chimneys' original cask
brews. Bottling started in 2002.
Tasting Notes
Red-brown in colour, Natterjack has a nose of
chocolate, malt and a touch of spice. Fairly sweet, nutty
malt and spicy bitterness lead in the taste, with some
estery notes. Toasted malt, hops and bitterness combine
in the aftertaste.

LORD KITCHENER'S INDIA PALE ALE

ABV 5.7%   **Bottle size** 500 ml   **Serve** cool
Ingredients Pale malt; amber malt; caramalt; Target and
Challenger hops

The third beer brewed for the Mid-Suffolk Light
Railway, this authentic IPA is strong and well hopped,
as beers intended for the long sea journey to India
needed to be in the 19th century. Only Target hops are

boiled in the copper, but Alan allows Challenger hops to sit in the hop back as the wort is run off, infusing their own character into the brew and enhancing the aroma. Lord Kitchener (who opened the old railway line and was Commander-in-Chief in India, 1902–9) features on the label, in the famous 'Your country needs you' pose.

Tasting Notes
This tawny beer has lots of body: nutty, malty smoothness and sweetness emerge first in the taste, but hops arrive in force on the swallow. The aroma has light malt and lemony hops; the finish is long and hoppy.

BRIMSTONE

ABV 6.5%   **Bottle size** 275 ml   **Serve** cold
Ingredients Lager malt; sugar; Hallertau and Northern Brewer hops

This strong lager is named after a yellow butterfly and was first brewed in 2000.

Tasting Notes
A golden lager with a big fruity nose. The full-bodied taste has a piney hoppiness over smooth malt and a little fruit. Hoppy, bitter finish.

GREENSHANK

ABV 7%   **Bottle size** 275 ml   **Serve** cool
Ingredients Pale malt; caramalt; unrefined sugar; Hallertau hops

A strong, pale bitter brewed with organic ingredients. It was first produced in 2001 and is named after a bird.

Tasting Notes
A crisp but potent beer with a dark golden hue. Orange hop notes lead in the aroma, with a hint of tropical fruit, and the same orangey hops balance out the sweetness of the abundant malt in the taste. Bittersweet, fruity finish.

REDSHANK

ABV 8.7%   **Bottle size** 275 ml   **Serve** cool
Ingredients Halcyon pale malt; crystal malt; Fuggle and Challenger hops

Redshank is another strong ale to treat with respect. Like Greenshank, it shares its name with a wading bird.

Tasting Notes
A red beer with an estery aroma. Estery fruit flavours are tempered by hop, roasted bitterness and alcohol in the taste. The finish is hoppy, with lingering malt and winey fruit, but on the bitter side of bittersweet.

GOOD KING HENRY

ABV 9.6%   **Bottle size** 275 ml   **Serve** cool
Ingredients Halcyon pale malt; crystal malt; roasted barley; Fuggle and Challenger hops

Although this is an imperial Russian stout, with all its court connections, apparently this beer takes its name not from a ruler but from an unusual, rarely-grown vegetable. The re-creation of the style is very welcome and the beer should develop interestingly in the bottle.
Tasting Notes
A very dark ruby beer with a dark beige head. The aroma features a little estery fruit and some roasted malt, while the taste is clean and well balanced, with sweetness, alcohol, dark malt, estery fruit and almonds. Sweet, roasted barley and hop finish.

OLD LUXTERS

Old Luxters Vineyard, Winery & Brewery, Hambleden, Henley-on-Thames, Oxfordshire RG9 6JW.
Tel. (01491) 638330 Fax (01491) 638645
E-mail: sadie@chilternvalley.co.uk
Web site: www.chilternvalley.co.uk
Mail order service

Old Luxters was set up in 1990 in a 17th-century barn by David Ealand, owner of Chiltern Valley Wines. Apart from the brewery and vineyard, the site also houses a fine art gallery and a cellar shop. A new bottling line was installed in spring 1998 and the brewery has since expanded its contract brewing and bottling services for other producers. In total, conditioning and maturation for bottled beers at the brewery take five weeks, with beers filtered and re-seeded with primary fermentation yeast. Best before dates are one-year from bottling.

DARK ROAST

ABV 5%   **Bottle size** 500 ml   **Serve** cool
Ingredients Pale malt; crystal malt; chocolate malt; Fuggle and East Kent Golding hops

This cask and bottled brew arrived in 1997. The bottle is particularly attractive, with frosted glass, screen-printing in gold and a paper ribbon seal over the cap.

Tasting Notes
A dark chestnut beer with a malty aroma tinged with cocoa and citrous hops. Crisp, malty and gently roasty in the mouth, it is well balanced and has orangey citrous notes. Dry, bittersweet, mellow roast finish. Not as strong in roast flavour as its name implies.

LUXTERS GOLD

ABV 5% **Bottle size** 330 ml **Serve** cool
Ingredients Pale malt; Fuggle and Golding hops

In 1997, Old Luxters secured a contract with the Gilbey's wine importer/restaurateur company, to produce Gilbey's Gold (ABV 5%), a 'farmhouse ale' in dark green 330 ml bottles. The beer proved so successful that it was added to the permanent range, with the name changed accordingly. A good accompaniment for spicy foods, claims David Ealand.

Tasting Notes
A golden beer with spicy hops edging out malt in the aroma. The taste nicely balances malt and spicy hops, and there is a hint of grapefruit, too. Hoppy, dry finish.

FORTNUM'S ALE

ABV 5% **Bottle size** 330 ml **Serve** cool
Ingredients Pale malt; crystal malt; chocolate malt; Fuggle and Golding hops

A beer exclusively for Fortnum & Mason. The royal grocers approached Old Luxters for this special brew in 1999, having already sold Chiltern Valley's wines.

Tasting Notes
A copper-coloured beer with orange fruit and malt dominant in the aroma. Silky, nutty malt and fruity hops combine in the clean, bittersweet taste, while the aftertaste is hoppy, toasty, nutty and gently bitter.
Major stockist Fortnum & Mason, London

BARN ALE

ABV 5.4% **Bottle size** 500 ml **Serve** cool
Ingredients Pale malt; crystal malt; chocolate malt; Fuggle and Golding hops

Taking its name from the brewery's rustic location, Barn

Ale, first brewed in 1993, is considerably stronger than
the cask Barn Ale Special (4.5%) on which it is based.
The bottle is tall and slim, the lettering is screen-printed
in gold and a tamperproof paper seal covers the cap.
The brewery reckons it's a good match for strong-
flavoured foods, such as a robust cheese or even a curry.
Tasting Notes
A dark copper beer, combining fruit, silky, chocolatey
malt and hops in a good body. Malty, chocolatey,
orange fruit nose; dry, fruity, bittersweet finish.
Major stockist: local Waitrose

ORGANIC

**The Organic Brewhouse, Unit 1, Higher Bochym Rural
Workshops, Cury Cross Lanes, Mullion, Helston,
Cornwall TR12 7AZ. Tel. (01326) 241555
E-mail: a.hamer@btclick.com**

This entirely organic brewery was set up by Andy
Hamer in 2000 in a former slaughterhouse in the
shadow of Goonhilly Downs radio station in Cornwall.
It is the southernmost brewery in mainland Britain. The
first bottle-conditioned beer was brewed in 2001 and
three more have been added since. The beers are filled
from a cask or conditioning tank on site and have a
nine-month best before date.

LIZARD POINT

ABV 4%   **Bottle size** 500 ml   **Serve** cool
Ingredients Pale malt; crystal malt; Hallertau hops

Named after the most southerly point on the British
mainland (close to the brewery), Lizard Point was one
of Andy's first cask brews.

SERPENTINE

ABV 4.5%   **Bottle size** 500 ml   **Serve** cool
Ingredients Pale malt; crystal malt; chocolate malt; wheat
malt; Hallertau and First Gold hops

Taking its name from the local bedrock, which is often
shaped into decorative tourist souvenirs, this was
Organic's first regular bottled beer.
Tasting Notes
A ruby ale with a malty nose and a malty, sweet taste
countered by bitter roast grain. Bitter, roasted finish.

BLACK ROCK STOUT

ABV 4.7%   **Bottle size** 500 ml   **Serve** cool
Ingredients Pale malt; crystal malt; chocolate malt; wheat malt; Hallertau hops

A new stout. The hops used, as in the other beers, are imported from New Zealand.

WOLF ROCK

ABV 5%   **Bottle size** 500 ml   **Serve** cool
Ingredients Pale malt; crystal malt; wheat malt; Hallertau hops

Another new beer named after the famous Wolf Rock lighthouse that can be seen from the brewery.

OULTON ALES

Oulton Ales Ltd., Lake Lothing Brewery, Oulton Broad, Suffolk NR32 3LZ. Tel. (01502) 587905
E-mail: wayne@oultonales.co.uk
Web site: www.oultonales.co.uk
Mail order service

Oulton Ales brews on the site formerly used by Green Jack Brewery (former partner Tim Dunford now owns the Green Jack name). These beers, presented in swing-topped bottles, are hand-filled on site, after kräusening.

NAUTILUS

ABV 4.2%   **Bottle size** 500 ml   **Serve** cool
Ingredients Pearl pale malt; crystal malt; chocolate malt; caramalt; Challenger and Styrian Golding hops

Formerly Green Jack's Grasshopper, introduced in 1997.
Tasting Notes
A dark golden beer with a hoppy nose, a bitter, hoppy, sweet malt taste and a dry, hoppy finish.

GONE FISHING

ABV 5%   **Bottle size** 500 ml   **Serve** cool
Ingredients Pearl pale malt; crystal malt; chocolate malt; caramalt; Fuggle hops

A new strong, single-varietal hop bitter.

ROARING BOY

ABV 8.5%   **Bottle size** 500 ml   **Serve** cool
Ingredients Pearl pale malt; caramalt; maize; candy sugar;
Challenger and Styrian Golding hops

This the beer Green Jack used to call Ripper, which was
first produced in 1995. Prior to bottling, it is matured
for at least ten months.
Tasting Notes
A bronze beer with a strong hoppy nose with hints of
bitter orange. The flavour is sweetish, malty and fruity
(fruit cocktail), yet also hoppy and quite dry. It doesn't
taste its strength. Mostly bitter, hoppy finish.

PITFIELD

**Pitfield Brewery, The London Beer Company Ltd.,
14 Pitfield Street, Hoxton, London N1 6EY.
Tel. (020) 7739 3701
Web site: www.pitfieldbeershop.co.uk**
Mail order service

Pitfield was founded way back in 1981 and, after several
years out of production, was revived in 1996, next to
Hoxton's well-known Beer Shop. In 2000 the brewery
was certified to be an organic producer, but a new range
of historic re-creation beers are not organic (authentic
ingredients not being available in organic form). These
historic beers are listed separately at the end of the
Pitfield entry and are due to be augmented by an 1837
India Pale Ale and an 1896 XXXX Stock Ale. Through
such initiatives, the bottled beer range keeps on
growing, but, as Pitfield has a specialist off-licence
attached, it has the distinct advantage of being able to
bottle beers to demand (around 70 bottles at a time).
The beers are matured in cask for two–three weeks
before being racked mostly bright. New yeast is added
as required, with maltose syrup primings used to
encourage good secondary fermentation. The bottles are
then kept at the brewery for at least two weeks before
release. Six months are specified as a best before date.
Because finings (which are usually made from fish swim
bladders and are used to help clear beer of yeast) have
been omitted, the beers hold no fears for vegetarians or
vegans, but they may be a little hazy as a result. Special
one-off brews are occasionally produced, such as
Pumpkin Porter (5%) for Halloween and Valentine Ale
(5%) in February.

PITFIELD ORIGINAL BITTER

ABV 3.7%   **Bottle size** 500/750 ml **Serve** cool
Ingredients Maris Otter pale malt; crystal malt; wheat malt; Fuggle, Challenger and East Kent Golding hops

Pitfield's standard session bitter was one of its first ever brews. It was renamed 'Pitfield Original' in 1999.
Tasting Notes
An orange/gold-coloured beer with a hoppy nose. The taste is dry and hoppy with gentle malt behind. Very dry, hoppy finish.

SHOREDITCH STOUT

ABV 4%   **Bottle size** 500/750 ml **Serve** cool
Ingredients Maris Otter pale malt; roasted barley; flaked barley; Fuggle, Challenger and Target hops

Not as 'stout' as some, this brew was added in 1997.
Tasting Notes
A very dark brown beer with a smoky aroma. It is a little sour in the mouth but also fruity and malty. Gently roasty, bitter malt finish.

EAST KENT GOLDINGS

ABV 4.2%   **Bottle size** 500/750 ml **Serve** cool
Ingredients Maris Otter pale malt; crystal malt; wheat malt; flaked maize; East Kent Golding hops

This single-varietal hop beer, using the UK brewers' favourite aroma hop, was first produced in 1999 and is now a permanent part of the range.
Tasting Notes
An orange-gold ale with a fruity, peppery hop nose. Fruity hop is well balanced by smooth malt in the taste, which is not too bitter. Dry, gently bitter finish.

ECO WARRIOR

ABV 4.5%   **Bottle size** 500/750 ml **Serve** cool
Ingredients Chariot pale malt; sugar; Hallertau hops

This beer, launched in 1998, set the Pitfield organic ball rolling. It quickly found itself a niche and has been stocked by several health food shops.
Tasting Notes
A hazy golden beer with a fruity hop bouquet (hints of tinned peaches). In the mouth, the initially sweetish

taste is balanced by delicate, soft, orangey-peachy hops which provide slowly increasing bitterness. The fruity hop finish is dry.

HOXTON BEST BITTER

ABV 4.8%　　　**Bottle size** 500/750 ml **Serve** cool
Ingredients Maris Otter pale malt; crystal malt; dried pale malt; roasted barley; Northdown, Challenger and East Kent Golding hops

Designed as a pseudo-Scottish brew, with typically strong malty characteristics, this beer was formerly known as Hoxton Heavy. The use of a little dried malt adds a touch of sweetness and balances out the roasted barley flavours.
Tasting Notes
A dark copper beer with a malty, chocolatey nose, a malty but citrous taste, with balancing bitterness, and a bitter malt finish.

BLACK EAGLE

ABV 5%　　　**Bottle size** 500/750 ml **Serve** cool
Ingredients Maris Otter pale malt; crystal malt; black malt; wheat malt; Fuggle, Challenger and Styrian Golding hops

Black Eagle may ring a few bells with drinkers acquainted with Pitfield beers of old. It is reminiscent of the brewery's famous Dark Star, *Champion Beer of Britain* in 1987, which is now owned and produced by the Dark Star brewery, based in Brighton.
Tasting Notes
A dark ruby beer, with an aroma of ripe red berry fruits. The taste is smooth and fruity but with some dark malt flavour and good hop balance. Quite dry, it doesn't drink its strength. Dry, mostly bitter, lingering finish.

21ST ANNIVERSARY ALE

ABV 5.5%　　　**Bottle size** 500 ml　　　**Serve** cool
Ingredients Maris Otter pale malt; crystal malt; wheat malt; Challenger and Golding hops

A new strong ale introduced to commemorate the brewery's own coming of age. Like the historic beers that follow, this is not made from organic ingredients.
Tasting Notes
A copper-coloured ale with citrous hops leading over

malt in the nose. Juicy hop fruit is foremost in the well-balanced taste of this surprisingly light-drinking strong beer. Bittersweet, fruity finish.

1850 LONDON PORTER

ABV 5%   **Bottle size** 500 ml   **Serve** cool
Ingredients Maris Otter pale malt; brown malt; roasted barley; Golding hops

Pitfield had been producing this porter off and on for a few years before it decided to include it in the new range of beers based on historic beer styles. The recipes for these brews have been inspired by the work of the Durden Park Beer Circle, a dedicated and enthusiastic group of private brewers (one reluctantly uses the titles 'amateur' or 'home brewers', such is their proficiency and attention to detail). The Circle goes to extreme lengths to re-create beers that have long ceased to be part of the portfolio of brewers today, unearthing the truth about how beers used to taste.
Tasting Notes
A deep ruby beer with a coffeeish aroma. The taste is nutty and bittersweet with light roasted notes amidst the malt. Dry, nutty, coffeeish, gently bitter finish.

1830 AMBER ALE

ABV 6%   **Bottle size** 500 ml   **Serve** cool
Ingredients Maris Otter pale malt; amber malt; chocolate malt; Fuggle, Golding and Styrian Golding hops

In Victorian times, amber malt was widely used in brewing but it died out in the 20th century and is only now making a comeback among brewers who are looking to resurrect old-fashioned beers.
Tasting Notes
Actually ruby in colour, with soft, juicy pineapple and malt in the nose. Pineapple again features in the taste, overlaying plenty of malt, with nutty, toasted notes emerging on the swallow. Dry, roasted malt aftertaste.

1824 MILD ALE

ABV 6.5%   **Bottle size** 500 ml   **Serve** cool
Ingredients Maris Otter pale malt; black malt; wheat malt; Golding hops

Mild – an endangered species among beer styles – is most commonly found as a weak beer, around 3–3.5%

alcohol, these days. There are some stronger milds around, as this book illustrates, and Pitfield's new mild serves as a reminder that, in days gone by, mild was not only Britain's most popular brew but a rather potent drink, too.

Tasting Notes
Another ruby beer with some light fruit in the creamy, malty nose. Smooth malt leads in the mouth, with hints of darker malt and a suggestion of fruit. Dry, bitter, roasted malt finish.

1792 IMPERIAL STOUT

ABV 9.3%   **Bottle size** 500 ml   **Serve** cool
Ingredients Maris Otter pale malt; roasted barley; wheat malt; Northdown hops

Helping to fill a gap vacated by Courage's renowned Imperial Russian Stout, this strong, complex brew is typical of the beers that crossed the Baltic to warm the hearts of the imperial Russian court at the turn of the 19th century.

Tasting Notes
As black as night, this potent brew has a clean, slightly savoury aroma, with a hint of liquorice in its roasted notes and a light whiff of fruit. Smooth, oily malt leads in the taste, which is sweetish with a tinge of fruit and coffee notes. Very easy to drink for its strength. Mellow, sweetish, dark malt finish.

PLASSEY

Plassey Brewery, Eyton, Wrexham LL13 0SP.
Tel. (01978) 781111 Fax (01978) 781279
E-mail: plasseybrewery@globalnet.co.uk
Web site: web-nexus.com/plassey
Mail order service

Plassey Brewery was established in 1985 on the 250-acre Plassey estate, which also includes a caravan park, a golf course, craft shops and licensed premises. A new brewery was completed in 1996 and includes a shop.

FUSILIER

ABV 4.5%   **Bottle size** 500 ml   **Serve** cool
Ingredients Maris Otter pale malt; crystal malt; chocolate malt; carapils malt; Cascade, Styrian Golding, Saaz and Pacific Gem hops

Fusilier is the regimental ale of the Royal Welch Fusiliers, the oldest infantry regiment in Wales (raised in 1689). The bottle depicts Billy, the regimental goat mascot, and provides a little of his history. 'Serve with pride', instructs the label. Although brewed by Plassey, the beer is bottled by Hanby Ales.

Tasting Notes
A dark amber beer with a malty, fruity nose. The taste is sweetish and malty with a gentle hop seasoning. Bittersweet, malty, hoppy finish.

POACHERS

**Poachers Brewery, Unit 4, Camp Road,
Swinderby Industrial Park, Swinderby, Lincolnshire.
Tel. (01522) 510237
Web site: www.poachersbeer.co.uk**

Poachers was opened in May 2001 by former home brewer Ian Baker and ex-RAF man George Batterbee, which ties in nicely as their home is a unit on a former RAF base. The lads publicised their business by opening a real ale off-licence in Lincoln (see Beer Shops) but, as the brewery workload increased in summer 2003, this was placed on the market as a going concern. Their ever-expanding range of bottled beers are all matured in cask before being racked bright and kräusened ready for bottling.

TREMBLING RABBIT MILD

ABV 3.4%   **Bottle size** 500 ml   **Serve** cool
Ingredients Maris Otter pale malt; crystal malt; chocolate malt; Golding hops

Stuck for a name for their new mild, Ian and George threw it open to regulars at The Eight Jolly Brewers pub in Gainsborough, who took part in a competition to devise a suitable title.

POACHERS DEN

ABV 4.2%   **Bottle size** 500 ml   **Serve** cool
Ingredients Maris Otter pale malt; roasted barley; Styrian Golding, Golding and Hersbrucker hops

A best bitter named after Ian's father, Dennis Baker, who introduced the grateful Ian to cask ale. His cartoon features on the bottle.

Tasting Notes
A golden ale with a spicy hop-fruit aroma. The taste is also hoppy and fruity, but very dry. Dry, hoppy, fruity finish.

BLACK CROW STOUT

ABV 4.5%   **Bottle size** 500 ml   **Serve** cool
Ingredients Maris Otter pale malt; roasted barley; Challenger and Golding hops

The first beer Ian ever brewed was a stout (he was, at the time, a Guinness drinker). This one was named after the birds in the small wood behind the brewery, although it has been revealed since that they are actually rooks.

POACHERS DICK

ABV 4.5%   **Bottle size** 500 ml   **Serve** cool
Ingredients Maris Otter pale malt; crystal malt; Golding and Styrian Golding hops

This brew is named, in turn, after George's dad, Richard Batterbee, who is caricatured on the label.
Tasting Notes
An amber ale with a fruit aroma and a bittersweet, fruity taste. Dry, hoppy, increasingly bitter finish.

JOCK'S TRAP

ABV 5%   **Bottle size** 500 ml   **Serve** cool
Ingredients Maris Otter pale malt; roasted barley; Cascade and Mount Hood hops

A Scottish pun for a beer featuring American hops.
Tasting Notes
An orange-golden beer with an aroma of malt and hop pockets. The same hop pocket flavours continue in the fruity taste, while the finish is dry, bitter and hoppy with lingering fruit.

DER WILDERER

ABV 5.1%   **Bottle size** 500 ml   **Serve** cool
Ingredients Maris Otter pale malt; crystal malt; chocolate malt; smoked malt; Hersbrucker and Styrian Golding hops

A ruby-coloured, German-style smoked beer, named after the German words for poacher.

POTTON

**The Potton Brewery Co., 10 Shannon Place, Potton,
Bedfordshire SG19 2PZ. Tel. (01767) 261042
E-mail: info@potton-brewery.co.uk
Web site: www.potton-brewery.co.uk**

Reviving the Potton Brewery Co. name after it
disappeared following a take-over in 1922, this brewery
was set up in 1999, by two former Greene King
employees. The beers are conditioned in casks, decanted
bright, kräusened and then bottled at the brewery. One-
off, 'own label' beers are also produced and the brewery
also packaged four of its other cask ales as a one-off for
the Queen's Golden Jubilee in 2002.

BUTLERS' ALE

ABV 4.3%   **Bottle size** 330 ml   **Serve** cool
Ingredients Pearl pale malt; crystal malt; Target and First
Gold hops

Brewed for Wimpole Hall, a National Trust property in
Cambridgeshire, this beer is dedicated to the loyal
butler, who traditionally savoured a glass of home brew
downstairs after a hard day's service upstairs.
Tasting Notes
An amber ale with malt and fruit in the nose, a
pleasant, well-balanced, but mostly bitter and nutty
taste, and a dry, bitter aftertaste.

SHAMBLES BITTER

ABV 4.3%   **Bottle size** 500 ml   **Serve** cool
Ingredients Pearl pale malt; crystal malt; Target and
Styrian Golding hops

The Shambles – a series of trading stalls – in Potton's
market place were reconstructed in the late 18th
century by the Lord of the Manor, one Samuel
Whitbread. As the label of this beer reports, the stalls
were used by farmers and other merchants until the
end of the 19th century and were eventually
demolished in 1954. The beer is a bottled version of
Potton's cask best bitter of the same name.
Tasting Notes
An amber bitter with a fruit cocktail aroma. The fruit in
the mouth is slightly estery (hint of pear drop),
countered by crisp bitterness and balanced by malt
sweetness. Dry, bitter finish with some lingering fruit.

NO-ALE SPICED

ABV 4.8%   **Bottle size** 500 ml   **Serve** cool
Ingredients Pearl pale malt; crystal malt; carapils malt; roasted barley; Target and First Gold hops; seasonal spices

The festive bottle, this beer is based on the brewery's Christmas cask ale, but with added seasonal spices (including ginger, cinnamon, mace and cloves).

PRINCETOWN

**Princetown Breweries Ltd., The Brewery,
Tavistock Road, Princetown, Devon PL20 6QF.
Tel. (01822) 890789 Fax (01822) 890719**

Princetown Brewery was established in 1994 by former Gibbs Mew and Hop Back brewer Simon Loveless.

JAIL ALE

ABV 4.8%   **Bottle size** 500 ml   **Serve** cool
Ingredients Pipkin pale malt; crystal malt; wheat malt; Challenger and Progress hops

Based, as it is, just a short tunnelling distance from the famous prison, what else could the brewery call its premium beer? This bottled version of an award-winning cask ale is racked bright and re-seeded with yeast and fresh wort before bottling. Winner of the Tucker's Maltings bottled beer competition in 1999.
Tasting Notes
An amber beer with an aroma of fruity, floral hops. The taste is malty, sweet, fruity and flower-scented but has good hop balance. Bittersweet, malty finish.

Availability of Beers

Beers in this book are mostly sold locally, through farmers' markets, small grocers, craft shops and delicatessens. Some breweries also sell direct to the public, but this may be by the case only, and some offer a mail order service, which is mentioned if relevant. Otherwise beers can be obtained through specialist off-licences or mail order companies, many of which are listed in the Beer Shops section at the back of the book. If a beer has a listing with a major retailer (supermarket or off-licence chain), this is indicated at the end of the entry.

QUAY

**The Quay Brewery, Lapin Noir Ltd., Hope Square,
Weymouth, Dorset DT4 8TR.
Tel./Fax (01305) 777515 (call first to fax)
E-mail: mail@quaybrewery.com
Web site: www.quaybrewery.com**

Quay was set up in summer 1996 in buildings once
housing Weymouth's Devenish and Groves breweries,
bringing beer production back to the seaside town after
a ten-year absence. The brewery can now be visited as
part of the Timewalk tourist attraction, which includes
two on-site off-licences where Quay beers can be
purchased. The bottled beers come in swing-stoppered
glassware, which is filled on site from a conditioning
tank. There is no filtration and the beers are only
primed when required to boost the condition.

WEYMOUTH JD 1742

ABV 4.2%   **Bottle size** 500 ml   **Serve** cool
Ingredients Maris Otter pale malt; Challenger and Mount
Hood hops

Introduced in 2002, this beer commemorates the
founding of the Devenish Brewery in Weymouth by
John Devenish in 1742.

STEAM BEER

ABV 4.5%   **Bottle size** 500 ml   **Serve** cool
Ingredients Lager malt; black malt; wheat malt;
Cascade hops

Steam Beer is Quay's homage to the hybrid beers
created during the days of California's Gold Rush in the
19th century. These were brewed in the ale style with
lager ingredients, and enjoyed high carbonation levels
that provided a steamy hiss on dispense. (The style is
perpetuated today by San Francisco's Anchor brewery.)

JURASSIC

ABV 4.7%   **Bottle size** 500 ml   **Serve** cool
Ingredients Pale malt; crystal malt; Hallertau and
Saaz hops

Reflecting the brewery's position on the Jurassic Coast
of Dorset, this beer arrived in 2003 and is made from

mostly organic ingredients, including the malt and the
Hallertau hops from New Zealand.

ORGANIC GOLD

ABV 4.8%   **Bottle size** 500 ml   **Serve** cool
Ingredients Pale malt; Hallertau hops

Using organic pale malt and organic hops from New
Zealand, Organic Gold was introduced in 2001.
Tasting Notes
A copper-coloured ale with a fruity hop nose. The
bittersweet taste is also fruity, with a citrous hop
character. Bitter, hoppy, fruity finish.

OLD ROTT

ABV 5.4%   **Bottle size** 500 ml   **Serve** cool
Ingredients Maris Otter pale malt; crystal malt; Challenger
and Bramling Cross hops

Slightly stronger than its cask equivalent, bottled Old
Rott features a Rottweiler on the label.
Tasting Notes
A dark red/brown beer with a malty nose tinged with
lemon. Malty and rather sweet in the mouth, with
citrous hop bitterness for balance. Dry, bitter finish.

SILENT KNIGHT

ABV 5.9%   **Bottle size** 500 ml   **Serve** cool
Ingredients Maris Otter pale malt; chocolate malt; wheat
malt; Bramling Cross hops

This dark wheat beer, brewed in the style of a German
weizenbock, picked up the supreme accolade at SIBA's
Wheat Beer Challenge in 1997. At 5.9%, it is just a touch
stronger than its cask brother of the same name and,
like most wheat beers, is designed to be drunk hazy.

RCH

**RCH Brewery, West Hewish, Weston-super-Mare,
Somerset BS24 6RR.
Tel. (01934) 834447 Fax (01934) 834167
E-mail: rchbrew@aol.com
Web site: www.rchbrewery.com**

This brewery was originally installed behind the Royal

Clarence Hotel at Burnham-on-Sea in the early 1980s, but since 1993 brewing has taken place on a commercial basis on this rural site, a couple of fields away from the rumble of the M5 motorway. The beers are shipped in conditioning tanks to Wessex Craft Brewers for bottling, with the best before date for all brews set at six months. Pitchfork and Old Slug Porter are distributed by B United in the USA.

ON THE TILES

ABV 3.9%   **Bottle size** 500 ml   **Serve** cool
Ingredients Pale malt; crystal malt; Fuggle and Progress hops

On the Tiles is a bottled version of RCH's draught bitter, PG Steam, and was launched initially as part of a pack for sale in British Home Stores in 1998.
Tasting Notes
A pale brown beer with a fine hoppy nose, backed with fruit. The taste is immediately hoppy, with a hint of dark malt and some fruit. Hoppy, bitter finish.

PITCHFORK

ABV 4.3%   **Bottle size** 500 ml   **Serve** cool
Ingredients Pale malt; Fuggle and Golding hops

First produced in 1993, this beer's name was derived from the unsuccessful Pitchfork Rebellion against King James II by the followers of the Duke of Monmouth. They challenged the King's forces at nearby Sedgemoor in July 1685. The single malt beer is also available in cask (*Champion Best Bitter* at CAMRA's *Champion Beer of Britain* awards in 1998).
Tasting Notes
A golden beer with a mouth-wateringly fruity nose. Initially soft and fruity to taste, it soon gains a solid, slightly perfumed hop edge. The finish is hoppy, bitter and dry. A beer for hop-heads.
Major stockists Safeway, Sainsbury

OLD SLUG PORTER

ABV 4.5%   **Bottle size** 500 ml   **Serve** cool
Ingredients Pale malt; crystal malt; black malt; Fuggle and Golding hops

It took a brave brewery to name a beer this, but it doesn't seem to have deterred drinkers. Old Slug was named after the pesky little creatures that enjoyed the sandy soil around RCH's old brewery. The slugs are now a thing of the past, but the beer still has a dedicated following in both cask and bottle. Gold medalist in the Tucker's Maltings bottled beer competition in 1998.

Tasting Notes
A very dark red/brown porter with a deep coffee nose. Not too full-bodied, it nonetheless has bags of taste – good, bitter coffee with some sweetness, nuttiness and hops behind. Big, dry finish of bitter coffee.

ALE MARY

ABV 6%   **Bottle size** 500 ml   **Serve** cool
Ingredients Pale malt; chocolate malt; Progress and Target hops; ginger; cloves; cinnamon; coriander; nutmeg; pimento

Ale Mary is RCH's Firebox (see below), but with spice oils and essences added prior to bottling by Wessex Craft Brewers. It was first 'created' for Christmas 1998 and has remained a festive favourite. Voted CAMRA's champion bottle-conditioned beer in 2001.

Tasting Notes
Zesty fruit overlaid with exotic spice dominates the perfumed nose of this strong beer. The spices impart a very unusual taste, with the citrous qualities of Firebox exaggerated by the coriander in particular, and the other flavourings providing a peppery, gingery warmth. Dry, scented, bitter orange finish with a light ginger burn.

Major stockist Safeway

FIREBOX

ABV 6%   **Bottle size** 500 ml   **Serve** cool
Ingredients Pale malt; chocolate malt; Progress and Target hops

RCH's premium strength cask- and bottle-conditioned beer, distinctively red in colour. Its name reflects the steam-powered nature of the brewery, plus the fascination with the golden age of railways shared by director Paul Davey and brewer Graham Dunbavan.

Tasting Notes
A flavoursome, strong, red bitter with a hoppy and malty nose. The taste is very fruity, alive with zesty orange flavour, backed with hop bitterness and some dark malt. Dry, tangy, bitter orange finish, with a hint of dark malt.

Major stockist Waitrose

REBELLION

**Rebellion Beer Company, Bencombe Farm,
Marlow Bottom, Buckinghamshire SL7 3LT.
Tel. (01628) 476594 Fax (01628) 476617
E-mail: tim@rebellionbeer.co.uk
Web site: www.rebellionbeer.co.uk**
Mail order service

Rebellion was the company that brought brewing back
to Marlow, following the closure of Wethereds by
Whitbread. Opened in 1993, the brewery has since
moved locally and expanded, serving a sizeable pub
trade. Although the beer featured below is brewed in
Marlow, bottling takes place off-site, at Hepworth & Co
in Horsham.

WHITE

ABV 4.5%   **Bottle size** 500 ml   **Serve** cold
Ingredients Pale malt; wheat malt; First Gold and Cascade
hops; coriander; orange peel; lemon peel

This Belgian-style, spiced wheat beer was first brewed in
2001 and claimed that year's *Wheat Beer Challenge* top
award, followed up by a category gold medal in the
International Beer Competition in 2002. It's not available
on draught and, for bottling, the beer is filtered and re-
seeded with fresh yeast. The best before date is fixed at
12 months.
Tasting Notes
A hazy gold beer with a gingery spiciness to the nose,
along with a hint of perfumed, bitter orange and clove.
Crisp and easy-drinking, it tastes bittersweet with cloves
dominating and a backdrop of tart lemon. Scented
finish of bitter oranges.
Major stockists Safeway, Waitrose, local Unwins

REEPHAM

**Reepham Brewery, Unit 1, Collers Way, Reepham,
Norfolk NR10 4SW. Tel. (01603) 871091**

Reepham is one of the longest established breweries in
Norfolk, founded in 1983. Its contribution to the bottle-
conditioned beer scene is not entirely conventional, as
the beer mentioned overleaf is packaged only in 2-litre
PET bottles for sale in local off-licences, with a best
before date set at just six weeks after filling.

RAPIER PALE ALE

ABV 4.2%   **Bottle size** 2 litres   **Serve** cool
Ingredients Maris Otter pale malt; crystal malt; barley
syrup; Whitbread Golding Variety and Fuggle hops

Effectively fresh beer for quick consumption. Rapier, in
its cask form, is a former award-winner at the Norwich
Beer Festival.

REFRESH UK

55 Stallard Street, Trowbridge, Wiltshire BA14 8HH.
Tel. (01225) 715500 Fax (01225) 715570
E-mail: info@refreshuk.com
Web site: www.refreshuk.com

Refresh UK was founded by former Bass and Morland
sales executive Rupert Thompson as a marketing
company for the products of various breweries,
primarily the Ushers brands, following the closure of
the Trowbridge brewery in 2000. Refresh has since
purchased Wychwood's brewery and also the Brakspear
beer brands, which are now brewed under contract. The
Brakspear board decided to close the historic brewery to
cash in on the value of the central site in Henley-on-
Thames. Refresh hopes to open a new brewery close to
Brakspear's former home in the near future.

BRAKSPEAR LIVE ORGANIC

ABV 4.6%   **Bottle size** 500 ml   **Serve** cool
Ingredients Optic pale malt; crystal malt; Hallertau,
Golding and Target hops

Winner of the first ever *Organic Beer Challenge*, in 2000,
Live Organic has survived the depressing closure of
Brakspear and is now produced under contract for
Refresh UK by Brakspear's former head brewer, Peter
Scholey. He brews the beer personally at Hepworth &
Co in Horsham, using the old Henley yeast and filtering
the beer prior to re-seeding with fresh yeast of the same
strain. The beer is bottled at 4.3% alcohol, but ferments
in the bottle over three months up to its declared 4.6%.
The best before date is set at a year, after which, being
organic, says Peter, it may become hazy. He also
recommends it with spicy foods. The world's first
organic Golding hops were specially grown for
Brakspear in Belgium to produce this brew. Also

featured are organic German Hallertau and organic
Target hops, the latter used for dry hopping. Acceptable
to vegans.

Tasting Notes
A copper ale with a rich, orange and apricot aroma. The
taste is fairly bitter and crisp with lots of fruity, tangy
hops and a spicy overlay, but always a sweet malt
balance. Dry, bitter, hoppy finish.

Major stockists Safeway, Morrisons, Booths

RINGWOOD

**Ringwood Brewery Ltd., Christchurch Road,
Ringwood, Hampshire BH24 3AP.
Tel. (01425) 471177 Fax (01425) 480273
E-mail: info@ringwoodbrewery.co.uk
Web site: www.ringwoodbrewery.co.uk**
Mail order service

Ringwood was set up in 1978 and moved in 1986 to
attractive 18th-century buildings, formerly part of the
old Tunks brewery. It has since become one of the
stalwarts of the UK brewing scene, overtaking in size
many established regional brewers. The bottled beers
are brewed in the same way as the cask versions, except
that a week's cold-conditioning (3°C) is employed to
bring down the yeast count prior to bottling (which is
carried out under contract at Hop Back Brewery). The
beer is then kräusened. Nine months' shelf life is
indicated on the labels.

BOLD FORESTER

ABV 4.2%   **Bottle size** 500 ml   **Serve** cool
Ingredients Maris Otter pale malt; crystal malt; amber
malt; Challenger and Golding hops

Bold Forester was launched as a seasonal cask beer for
spring 2003, but was also bottled as a way of
commemorating the brewery's 25th birthday. There's a
possibility that it will now continue as an annual
bottled offering. Amber malt helps add dryness to the
brew while late and dry hopping (in the conditioning
tank) with Challenger hops adds to the spicy fruit
character.

Tasting Notes
An amber beer with chocolate notes in its malty nose.
The taste balances chocolate, malt, fruit and hops. Dry,
bitter finish with lingering chocolate.

XXXX PORTER

ABV 4.7%   **Bottle size** 500 ml   **Serve** cool
Ingredients Maris Otter pale malt; crystal malt; chocolate malt; Challenger, Progress and Golding hops

Cask XXXX Porter has been a favourite among local drinkers since 1981 but the brewery has only ever brewed it in the winter months. However, following its introduction in bottled form in November 2000, fans can now enjoy this dark brew at any time, as stocks bottled while the cask beer is in production should last through to the next winter run (October to March).
Tasting Notes
A near-black, dark ruby beer with an aroma of lightly roasted malt. Clean and tasty, it is easy to drink, with hints of orange and pleasantly bitter roasted notes, plus sweetness throughout. Dry, bittersweet, roasted malt and fruit finish.

FORTYNINER

ABV 4.9%   **Bottle size** 500 ml   **Serve** cool
Ingredients Maris Otter pale malt; crystal malt; Challenger, Progress and Golding hops

Fortyniner first appeared in cask form in 1978, taking its name from its 1049 original gravity. This bottled version only made its debut in 1996 and was increased in strength from 4.8 to 4.9% in 1998.
Tasting Notes
Orange gold in colour, this beer has a lovely, zesty aroma of oranges and hops. Malty orange fruit is prominent in the mouth, with some sweetness, although bitterness increases as the hops kick in. The body is good and solid, but this is an easy drinking and deceptively strong ale. Dry, bitter orange peel finish.
Major stockists Safeway, local Tesco and Sainsbury

ST AUSTELL

St Austell Brewery Company Ltd., 63 Trevarthian Road, St Austell, Cornwall PL25 4BY.
Tel. (01726) 74444 Fax (01726) 68965
E-mail: info@staustellbrewery.co.uk
Web site: www.staustellbrewery.co.uk

St Austell joined the band of bottle-conditioned beer brewers in spring 2000, when it won the *Tesco Beer*

Challenge with Clouded Yellow. The beer is brewed at St Austell but bottled by Hepworth & Co in Horsham.

CLOUDED YELLOW

ABV 4.8%   **Bottle size** 500 ml   **Serve** cold
Ingredients Maris Otter pale malt; wheat malt; Willamette hops; vanilla; cloves; coriander; maple syrup

St Austell stages an annual Celtic Beer Festival, for which it prepared two novel brews in 1999. This beer, known as Hagar the Horrible at the time, was one. Brewer Roger Ryman popped down to his local supermarket to pick up the ingredients to make his vision of a German-style wheat beer become reality. He didn't want foreign yeast strains in his brewhouse, where there might be a chance of St Austell's own prized yeast becoming contaminated, and so set about recreating weissbier flavours artificially, by adding various spices to the beer after the boil, as it strained through the hops in the hop back. Vanilla pods, whole cloves and coriander seeds are the key flavourings, as well as maple syrup which is used for priming, and they blended together so well that Roger decided to submit the beer for the Tesco contest. Rave reviews followed. In June 2003, the beer was re-formulated. The alcohol was dropped to 4.8% from 5%, the clove content was reduced and a touch more vanilla (four pods per barrel) completed the revamp. For a while, this new format beer – re-packaged in a slender green bottle – was exclusive once again to Tesco. The name is shared with a rare butterfly, which, just like German wheat beers, is a popular continental visitor to Britain in summer. Drink with a Thai curry or a dessert, Roger suggests.
Tasting Notes
A golden beer with soft banana and vanilla in the nose. Crisper and thinner than before, this new version still has plenty of banana and vanilla flavour, but noticeably less clove. Dry finish, with light banana and vanilla.
Major stockists Tesco, Safeway

SALOPIAN

The Salopian Brewing Company Ltd., The Brewery, 67 Mytton Oak Road, Shrewsbury, Shropshire SY3 8UQ. Tel. (01743) 248414 Fax (01743) 358866

Salopian began production in 1995. After closing briefly in 1997, it re-opened in new hands, retaining its inspiration, brewer Martin Barry. Bottle-conditioned beers were introduced in 1996 and were initially brewed on site. However, these are now brewed by Martin using the equipment at Hepworth & Co and are bottled there under contract, allowing the Shrewsbury brewery to focus on cask products.

PROUD SALOPIAN

ABV 4.5%   **Bottle size** 500 ml   **Serve** cool
Ingredients Maris Otter pale malt; crystal malt; Fuggle, Golding and Styrian Golding hops

This ale was one of Salopian's first cask beers and has been sold in bottled form since 1996 (albeit initially under the name of Minsterley Ale). The current title is a reference to legendary Shropshire brewer Thomas Southam, who was known as the 'Proud Salopian'.
Tasting Notes
A dark copper ale with a big, fruity, slightly peppery nose. The malty, fruity taste is fairly sweet, but also has hoppy bitterness. Dry, hoppy, bitter fruit finish.

GINGERSNAP

ABV 4.7%   **Bottle size** 500 ml   **Serve** cool
Ingredients Pale malt; crystal malt; pale chocolate malt; wheat malt; root ginger; East Kent Golding, Hersbrucker, Saaz and Styrian Golding hops

There's no mistaking the key ingredient of this brew. The ginger snaps out at you in the aroma and the initial taste but the acclaim the beer has received indicates that this is a better-balanced drink than most ginger-flavoured beers. It's actually a dark wheat beer (the mash is 40% wheat) with fresh root ginger added to the copper. Drink it cloudy and try it with chocolate or a dessert.
Tasting Notes
A bronze-coloured beer with a powerful ginger nose with some lemon in the background. The taste is surprisingly hoppy, a little citrous and ginger warm, with sound malt but little sweetness. Ginger warmth and bitterness fill the very dry finish.

ENTIRE BUTT

ABV 4.8%   **Bottle size** 500 ml   **Serve** cool
Ingredients Maris Otter pale malt; crystal malt; dark crystal malt; amber malt; pale chocolate malt; dark chocolate

malt; brown malt; black malt; lager malt; carapils malt;
wheat malt; malted oats; roasted barley; torrefied wheat;
Fuggle, Styrian Golding and Golding hops

Count the malts! This mammoth beer is a tribute to a
beer style which originated nearly 300 years ago. In the
early 1700s, drinkers favoured a blend of three beers –
pale ale, brown ale and stock ale – laboriously drawn
from three separate casks (or butts). A London brewer,
Ralph Harwood, hit upon the idea of combining the
three brews in one cask and gave it the name Entire
Butt (the brew being entirely in one butt, so to speak).
Its popularity with local street porters allegedly saw the
new brew re-christened 'porter'.

Tasting Notes
A very dark ruby porter with a mellow, lightly citrous,
coffee/chocolate aroma. Full and smooth on the palate,
it tastes deeply malty and fairly sweet, with citrous hop
notes. Dry, bittersweet, malty finish.

PUZZLE

ABV 4.8%   **Bottle size** 500 ml   **Serve** cool
Ingredients Lager malt; wheat malt; ginger; coriander;
orange peel; Saaz and Hersbrucker hops

According to brewer Martin Barry, Puzzle is the negative
version of Jigsaw, a black wheat beer that Salopian
produced for a few years, but which is not currently
available. No finings are used in this intriguing brew,
which is lagered for two weeks before bottling. Sixty per
cent of the grist is wheat.

Tasting Notes
A hazy yellow beer with a zesty nose of ginger, lemon
and bitter orange. Soft in the mouth, it features a
teasing citrus sharpness, peppery spiciness, an orange
peel bitterness and an underlying ginger warmth. Dry,
lemony, scented hop aftertaste, with a little burn from
the ginger.

FIREFLY

ABV 5%   **Bottle size** 500 ml   **Serve** cool
Ingredients Maris Otter pale malt; dark crystal malt;
peated malt; Golding and Styrian Golding hops

Peated malt, which gives this beer an unusual smoky
taste, is not liked by many brewers because, if used to
excess, it can give the beer an antiseptic, 'TCP' edge.
Martin seems to have hit the right balance in creating

an ale that has more than a hint of Scotch whisky. The beer is usually bottle conditioned but it has been seen on sale in filtered form, too.

Tasting Notes
A bronze beer with a peaty, smoky nose. The same attributes come through in the taste, which also has full malt, citrous sharpness and good, fruity hop bitterness. Tangy, smoky, dry finish.

SCARECROW

Scarecrow Brewery Ltd., c/o Dairyman's Daughter, Arreton Barn, Newport Road, Arreton, Isle of Wight PO30 3AA. Tel. (01983) 856161

Scarecrow Brewery – set up by the lads at Ventnor Brewery – is located at Arreton Craft Village, alongside the Dairyman's Daughter Inn. The 3.5-barrel brewery can be viewed from the adjacent Beer Emporium, which stocks beers from all over the UK, plus assorted breweriana.

BEST BITTER

ABV 4.2%   **Bottle size** 500 ml   **Serve** cool
Ingredients Pale malt; crystal malt; wheat malt; Bramling Cross hops

The only beer to date from the brewery that uses the punning slogan 'Outstanding in our field' to advertise its presence.

Tasting Notes
A red beer with a malty nose and a toffeeish, malty taste lightened by a gentle fruity edge. Sweet, malty finish with a pinch of hop.

SHOES

Shoes Brewery, The Three Horse Shoes Inn, Norton Cannon, Hereford HR4 7BH. Tel./Fax (01544) 318375

Three Horse Shoes landlord Frank Goodwin had been a home brewer long before deciding to brew for his own pub. His sole bottle-conditioned ale is sold in tiny numbers (no wholesaler calls, please!), and has smashed its way to the top of the list of the strongest beers featured in this book.

FARRIERS' BEER

ABV 15.1%   **Bottle size** 330 ml
Serve at room temperature
Ingredients Malt extract; sugar; Fuggle hops

Farriers is bottled and labelled by Frank himself in very small quantities. He has now managed to raise the strength to a mighty 15.1%, up from the 13.9% quoted in the last edition of this book, which itself was an increase on the modest 13.4% dealt out by the beer when it was first brewed in 2000. Beware, therefore: this is not a beer not for the faint-hearted. Even the brewery's yeast surrenders in the face of so much alcohol, which means Frank needs to finish off the fermentation with a wine yeast.

Tasting Notes
An amber beer with a powerful alcoholic nose. The taste is sweet and fiercely alcoholic, with estery almond notes and a persistent warmth. The warm, sweet, alcoholic finish has a sherry-like dryness.

SKINNER'S

Skinner's Brewing Co. Ltd., Riverside, Newham,
Truro, Cornwall TR1 2DP.
Tel. (01872) 271885 Fax (01872) 271886
E-mail: info@skinnersbrewery.com
Web site: www.skinnersbrewery.com

Skinner's was founded by Steve and Sarah Skinner, formerly of the Tipsy Toad brewery in Jersey, in 1997. Their beer names are mostly based on characters from Cornish folklore, but only one of their beers is now bottle conditioned. The brewery moved to new premises, close to its earlier Truro home, in 2003.

FIGGY'S BREW

ABV 4.5%   **Bottle size** 500 ml   **Serve** cool
Ingredients Optic pale malt; crystal malt; dark malts; Northdown hops

Launched in bottle in summer 2003, Figgy's Brew takes its name from the Cornish legend of Madgy Figgy, a local witch. Figgy's Chair is a pile of rocks at Land's End, where, it was reckoned, Figgy sat and lured sailors to their doom with her lamp. Her wild-eyed, toothless caricature now adorns the beer's label. The single-varietal hop brew is bottled at Wessex Craft Brewers in Gloucestershire, where it is filtered and re-pitched with fresh Skinner's yeast. The best before date is set at nine months.

SUTHWYK ALES

Suthwyk Ales, Offwell Farm, Southwick, Fareham, Hampshire PO17 6DX. Tel./Fax (023) 9232 5252
E-mail: mjbazeley@suthwykales.com
Web site: www.suthwykales.com
Mail order service

Suthwyk Ales does not brew itself. It is run by barley farmer Martin Bazeley, who decided to go the whole hog and complete the 'field to table' cycle by commissioning a beer brewed from malt kilned by Warminster Maltings from his own Optic barley. Produced by Hop Back Brewery, Skew Sunshine Ale proved to be a hit and was followed up by a second offering, Bloomfields. The beers – with best before dates set at 12 months – are still bottled by Hop Back but are now brewed by Oakleaf Brewing, just down the hill in Gosport. Both are also available in cask form. Incidentally, Martin reports that Montgomery and Eisenhower planned Operation Overlord (the D-Day offensive) in nearby Southwick House and used to enjoy a pint or two from the local Hunt's brewery, which closed in 1957, after their deliberations.

BLOOMFIELDS

ABV 3.8%   **Bottle size** 500 ml   **Serve** cool
Ingredients Optic pale malt; crystal malt; Challenger, Fuggle and Golding hops

Sidney Bloomfield was the man who tended Martin's land back in the 1920s, dying at the tender age of 40 in 1926 – a sad consequence perhaps of the fact that the 700 acres in his care were farmed only with horsepower. One field on the estate still bears his name and it is here that the barley that is turned into crystal malt for this session ale is grown (and, according to the label, blessed with evening sunshine and chalky soil). Try a bottled with some strong cheese, is Martin's recommendation.
Tasting Notes
A golden ale with spicy hop and malt leading in the aroma, but melon and citrous fruitiness emerging later.

Spicy and very drinkable, it tastes crisp and clean, with
good backing malt sweetness and a light fruitiness. The
dry, bitter and fruity finish turns hoppy.

SKEW SUNSHINE ALE

ABV 4.6%   **Bottle size** 500 ml   **Serve** cool
Ingredients Optic pale malt; Challenger hops

The barley malted for this premium ale is grown in
what is known as Skew Field, on Portsdown Hill. The
field faces south and catches the sun – hence the beer's
name.
Tasting Notes
A pale golden ale with a creamy, malty, lightly fruity
nose with a hint of sulphur. Light-bodied and fairly
spritzy, it tastes citrus-fruity with lightly scented hops
crisping up smooth malt. Bitter, fruity, hoppy finish.

SUTTON

**Sutton Brewing Company, 31 Commercial Road,
Coxside, Plymouth, Devon PL4 0LE.
Tel./Fax (01752) 205010**

This brewery was built alongside Plymouth's Thistle
Park Tavern in 1993 and began production the
following year. The first bottle-conditioned beer
appeared in spring 2001 and is bottled for Sutton by
Keltek Brewery.

MADIBA STOUT

ABV 5%   **Bottle size** 500 ml   **Serve** cool
Ingredients Maris Otter pale malt; crystal malt; chocolate
malt; black malt; roasted malt; wheat malt; Bramling Cross
hops

Nelson Mandela features on the label of this bottled
stout, the name 'Madiba' being an African word
meaning 'old father who is respected and wise'. The
South African connection is through the brewery's
owner, Quintin Style, who hails from Mandela's
country.
Tasting Notes
This dark ruby stout has a roasted, fruity-hoppy aroma,
followed by a nicely rounded, bittersweet, fruity taste,
with plenty of dark grain flavour, and then a
bittersweet, fruity, roasted finish.

TEIGNWORTHY

**Teignworthy Brewery, The Maltings, Teign Road,
Newton Abbot, Devon TQ12 4AA.**
Tel. (01626) 332066 Fax (01626) 330153
Mail order service (via Tucker's Maltings)

Teignworthy Brewery was founded in 1994 with a 15-barrel plant by former Oakhill and Ringwood brewer John Lawton, using part of the historic Victorian malthouse of Edward Tucker & Sons. (Tucker's Maltings is now an important and fascinating tourist attraction, enjoyed by thousands of Devon holidaymakers each year.) The bottled beers are the same as John's cask beers, except that usually they are filtered and re-pitched with new yeast. Sometimes, however, the beers are just fined and bottled from the cask. A 12-month best before date is marked on each bottle.

REEL ALE/EDWIN TUCKER'S DEVONSHIRE PRIZE ALE

ABV 4%   **Bottle size** 500 ml   **Serve** cool
Ingredients Maris Otter pale malt; crystal malt; Willamette, Golding, Bramling Cross and Challenger hops

Reel Ale is Teignworthy's standard cask bitter. When bottle conditioned, it is sold under the same name and also as Edwin Tucker's Devonshire Prize Ale in the Tucker's Maltings bottled beer shop, largely as an attempt to catch the eye of the many holidaymakers the Maltings attracts.
Tasting Notes
An orange/gold-coloured beer with a dry flavour of orange fruit, malt and hops, preceded by a gentle aroma of fruit, malt and orangey hops. The bitter orange finish is moderately dry.

SPRING TIDE

ABV 4.3%   **Bottle size** 500 ml   **Serve** cool
Ingredients Maris Otter pale malt; crystal malt; Willamette, Golding, Bramling Cross and Challenger hops

Named after the high tides which wash up the Teign estuary close to the brewery, this best bitter is brewed every four months or so.
Tasting Notes
A crisp, refreshing and enjoyable, copper beer with a zesty orange nose. Fruit and malt continue into the

taste which has a light, citrous hop balance and grassy, herbal notes. Dry, bitter orange finish.
Major stockist: local Tesco

OLD MOGGIE

ABV 4.4%   **Bottle size** 500 ml   **Serve** cool
Ingredients Maris Otter pale malt; crystal malt; wheat malt; torrefied wheat; Golding, Bramling Cross and Fuggle hops

Forget brewery cats: this beer, first brewed in January 2000, is named after the Morris Minor motor car owned by former underbrewer Mark Bayley and is a tribute to the heyday of the British motor trade. Mark has now left Teignworthy, but his legacy is this golden best bitter recipe. The beer may appear a little hazy in the glass, as it is not fined and is therefore acceptable to vegans.
Tasting Notes
An amber ale with a fruity, malty aroma. In the mouth it is toffeeish and malty-sweet with a fruity hop balance. The finish is also sweet and malty, with light hop-fruit.

BEACHCOMBER

ABV 4.5%   **Bottle size** 500 ml   **Serve** cool
Ingredients Maris Otter pale malt; Willamette, Golding, Bramling Cross and Challenger hops

Described as a lager on the label, Beachcomber was devised as a pale beer for swigging at barbecues on warm summer evenings. A bottom-fermenting yeast is used and bottles are prepared every four months.
Tasting Notes
A golden beer with a rich, citrous hop nose with sweet malt behind. The full taste combines light malt and excellent hoppiness with hints of blackcurrant. Bittersweet, hoppy, slightly tart finish.
Major stockist local Tesco

HARVEY'S SPECIAL BREW

ABV 4.6%   **Bottle size** 500 ml   **Serve** cool
Ingredients Pale malt; crystal malt; wheat malt; Golding and Fuggle hops

First brewed to celebrate the birth of John and Rachel Lawton's son, Harvey, on 8 April 2000 – hence the Baby Crockett lookalike on the blue label.

Tasting Notes
An orange-gold beer with an aroma of bitter orange
peel. The taste is fruity with silky malt and bitter orange
peel notes throughout. Dry, bitter fruit finish.

AMY'S ALE

ABV 4.8%   **Bottle size** 500 ml   **Serve** cool
Ingredients Pale malt; crystal malt; wheat malt; Bramling
Cross and Golding hops

A beer named after the Lawtons' first child (who drew
the label, by the look of it). Amy's Ale was brewed first
in March 2003.
Tasting Notes
A light amber beer with a big floral, honeyed aroma
backed with soft malt. The taste is equally flowery, with
hints of sweet tropical and citrus fruits. Pleasantly bitter
and gently fruity finish.

MALTSTER'S ALE

ABV 5%   **Bottle size** 500 ml   **Serve** cool
Ingredients Maris Otter pale malt; crystal malt; Willamette,
Golding, Bramling Cross and Challenger hops

This was a innovative brew when first prepared in 1996,
as it used the new barley strain Regina, but John has
now switched to Maris Otter. The beer is sold on
draught in winter and is bottled twice a year.
Tasting Notes
A mellow, bronze beer which lives up to its name with
a malty nose that features traces of treacle and citrus.
Richly malty in the mouth, it is finely balanced by
lemony hops and pear drop flavour. The pleasant
aftertaste is gentle, dry and bittersweet.

MARTHA'S MILD

ABV 5.3%   **Bottle size** 500 ml   **Serve** cool
Ingredients Pale malt; crystal malt; amber malt; chocolate
malt; wheat malt; Fuggle and Golding hops

Another baby celebration, this time for Martha, born on
27 March 2002. On the label, John declares that he
brewed it as a tonic for Rachel when she was feeding
the baby. The beer is now inked in as a regular brew for
May.
Tasting Notes
A deep ruby, strong mild with an aroma of coffeeish,

biscuity malt. The taste is smooth and quite sweet, with oily roasted malt notes and a hint of hop fruit. Bitterness increases and roasted flavour persists in the aftertaste.

EDWIN TUCKER'S MARIS OTTER

ABV 5.5%   **Bottle size** 500 ml   **Serve** cool
Ingredients Maris Otter pale malt; crystal malt; wheat malt; Willamette, Golding, Bramling Cross and Challenger hops

First produced in 1998, as a tribute to the most highly regarded strain of malting barley ('the master brewer's choice around the world'), Maris Otter is part of Edwin Tucker's 'Premium Malt Selection' series, although no other such beers have yet arrived.
Tasting Notes
A dark copper beer with an estery (bananas and pear drops), malty nose. Rich and malty in the mouth, with estery fruit and a hint of lemon, it is smooth and clean tasting. Bitter hops come through to provide a pleasant bittersweet finish with a hint of liquorice.

EDWIN TUCKER'S EAST INDIA PALE ALE

ABV 6.5%   **Bottle size** 500 ml   **Serve** cool
Ingredients East India malt; wheat malt; Bramling Cross and Golding hops

This well-researched replica of an authentic India Pale Ale – bursting with hops and packing the alcoholic punch such beers needed to cope with the long sea journey to India – includes malt that was specially kilned to match the colour of malt used in the days of the Empire (close to the colour of lager malt).
Tasting Notes
Although this copper ale has a relatively modest, orangey aroma, the taste is a revelation: zingy, orange hoppiness leads the way, crisp and well balanced with a little sweetness. The same orangey hops add bitterness in the lingering, dry, lipsmacking finish.

CHRISTMAS CRACKER

ABV 6%   **Bottle size** 500 ml   **Serve** cool
Ingredients Maris Otter pale malt; crystal malt; Willamette, Golding, Bramling Cross and Challenger hops

This strong seasonal brew is also sold in cask form.

Tasting Notes
A malty nose preludes a malty, fruity beer with
balancing bitterness. Malty, bitter finish. Red-brown in
colour.

EDWIN TUCKER'S CELEBRATED ARCTIC ALE

ABV 9%   **Bottle size** 275 ml   **Serve** cool
Ingredients Maris Otter pale malt; crystal malt; Bramling
Cross, Golding and Challenger hops

Like the other Edwin Tucker ales, this beer's label is
enhanced by a faded old photograph of the man
himself, his autograph adding authenticity. This beer is
indeed a throwback to Edwin Tucker's times, having as
its inspiration the creation of the first ever arctic ale in
1852. Brian Gates, who runs Tucker's excellent bottled
beer shop, discovered the beer in the records of 19th-
century brewing historian Alfred Barnard, who recalled
how Allsopp's in Burton had produced a special brew
for the voyage of *HMS Assistance* to the frozen North.
On the journey, despite freezing at one point, the beer
proved to be a 'great blessing' to the crew, according to
ship's captain Sir Edward Belcher. Brian and John
Lawton together came up with this recipe (which
involves a six-and-a-quarter-hour boil in the copper and
generous quantities of both crystal malt and hops) to
give some indication of how the arctic ale might have
tasted.

Tasting Notes
A cherry-coloured ale with hops giving a peppery
fruitiness to the malty aroma. Not as full bodied as
expected, the taste has a good smack of peppery, fruity
bitterness throughout, running on into the finish.

EDWIN TUCKER'S EMPRESS RUSSIAN PORTER

ABV 10.5%   **Bottle size** 275 ml   **Serve** cool
Ingredients Maris Otter pale malt; chocolate malt; oat
malt; roasted barley; Willamette, Golding, Bramling Cross
and Challenger hops

This re-creation of the Baltic porter style was inspired in
part by the failure to obtain stocks of the classic
Courage Imperial Russian Stout for the Tucker's beer
shop. It's the sort of strong, warming brew that was
shipped to Russia during the 18th and 19th centuries
and became known for its medicinal qualities.

Tasting Notes
(1998 vintage, tasted after one year) A wonderfully

mellow, very dark brown beer with caramel and fruit in the nose. Thick, smooth and sweetish on the palate, it has a creamy rum-and-raisin toffee taste with orange-citrus flavours and gentle roasted, bitter notes. Dry, lingering, deep and warming finish, with caramel, toffee and fruit balancing a gentle bitterness.
(2000 vintage, tasted after six months) A near-black beer with malt, polished leather and coffee in the nose. The taste is sweetish and deep: strong hops for bitterness, coffee and a little fruit, with persistent malt. Sweetish, roasted, hoppy finish.

TEME VALLEY

Teme Valley Brewery, The Talbot, Knightwick, Worcestershire WR6 5PH.
Tel. (01886) 821235 Fax (01886) 821060
E-mail: temevalley@aol.com
Web site: www.the-talbot.co.uk

The Talbot Inn at Knightwick is owned by the Clift family, who farmed hops locally from the 19th century to the year 2000. The hops they cultivated are still used in the pub's brewery, which was set up in 1997. Brewer Chris Gooch produces a range of cask and bottled beers to the same recipes, but beer for bottling is fermented with a dried, bottom-fermenting yeast which remains in the beer when it is bottled straight from cask by Wessex Craft Brewers. For Christmas 2002 Teme Valley's Christmas beer, Woss Ale (6%), was made available in bottle, but if this re-appears it is likely to be under a new title.

THIS

ABV 3.7%   **Bottle size** 500 ml   **Serve** cool
Ingredients Maris Otter pale malt; chocolate malt; wheat malt; Challenger, Fuggle and Golding hops

The Talbot Inn's own wine list has included, since spring 2003, a 'Beer and Food' page, suggesting ideal matches for Teme Valley beers. Here, THIS is recommended as the ideal accompaniment for sandwiches or a ploughman's lunch.
Tasting Notes
A dark golden beer with malt and hops in the nose, along with a strong hint of fruit. The taste nicely balances silky malt and crisp, moderately bitter hops before a dry, bitter, hoppy finish.

THE HOP NOUVELLE

ABV 4.1%   **Bottle size** 500 ml   **Serve** cool
Ingredients Maris Otter pale malt; wheat malt; Golding and
First Gold hops

Brewed once a year, time permitting, during the hop
harvest, this is an ale equivalent to wine's Beaujolais
Nouveau. The hops are plucked from bines less than
half a mile from the brewery and, within the hour,
without kilning, are cast green into the copper,
delivering a sappier, more resin-like flavour to the beer
than standard dried hops. The hops mentioned above
are the ones included in the 2002 vintage. Chris hopes
to make available three different Hop Nouvelles in
future, but cannot say which hop strains he is going to
use. The reason for this is that, when he has a
fermenting vessel free during the harvest, he will pop
down to the hopyard and collect whatever they are
picking that day.
Tasting Notes
(*2002 version*) A light golden beer with a citrous,
'sherbert lemons' aroma. The taste is richly hoppy, big
and tangy, with a green sappiness and, again, a hint of
sherbert lemon. Lipsmackingly hoppy finish.

THAT

ABV 4.1%   **Bottle size** 500 ml   **Serve** cool
Ingredients Maris Otter pale malt; chocolate malt; wheat
malt; roasted barley; Challenger and Fuggle hops

A perfect match for stews or game dishes, according to
The Talbot's beer menu, the hop bitterness lightening
rich sauces.
Tasting Notes
Hops and a hint of lemon pave the way in the aroma of
this amber ale. The hops continue in the taste over a
clean, nutty, malty base with lemon notes emerging.
Dry, hoppy, bitter finish with again a trace of lemon.

WOTEVER NEXT?

ABV 5%   **Bottle size** 500 ml   **Serve** cool
Ingredients Maris Otter pale malt; crystal malt; chocolate
malt; wheat malt; Northdown and Fuggle hops

The complex fruit and roasted malt flavours of Wotever
Next? are suggested as the ideal partners for a dessert
like a rich chocolate pudding.

Tasting Notes
A tawny ale with sharp fruit in the nose (lemon and blackcurrant). Hop fruit dominates the taste and runs into the drying, bitter finish where roasted malt lingers.

TINDALL

Tindall Ales, Toad Lane, Seething, Norfolk NR35 2EQ.
Tel. (01508) 483844
E-mail: greenangela5@aol.com

Tindall Ales is a family-run business founded in 1998 close to historic Tindall Wood (hence its name). In 2002, Tindall moved to new premises in a former stable block, just outside the village of Seething. Bottling began in 1999 and all the beers are kräusened before filling. Best before dates are set at four months later.

SUMMER LOVING

ABV 3.6%   **Bottle size** 500 ml   **Serve** cool
Ingredients Maris Otter and Fanfare pale malt; Mount Hood hops

Only brewed June–September, Summer Loving is designed as a refreshing summer beer, seasoned with American hops. The brewers suggest it's the sort of beer to drink with Mediterranean food.

BEST BITTER

ABV 3.7%   **Bottle size** 500 ml   **Serve** cool
Ingredients Maris Otter and Halcyon pale malt; Golding hops

Like the other bottled beers, Best Bitter – Tindall's first ever beer – is also available in cask form.
Tasting Notes
A very drinkable, copper ale with malt in the nose and a well-balanced bitter taste of hops and gentle malt. Hoppy, bitter, dry finish. Lots of flavour for its strength.

MILD

ABV 3.7%   **Bottle size** 500 ml   **Serve** cool
Ingredients Halcyon and Maris Otter pale malt; crystal malt; chocolate malt; Golding and Fuggle hops

A bottled equivalent of a popular cask dark mild.

Tasting Notes
Attractively ruby in the glass, Tindall's Mild has an
aroma of soft, dark malt with chocolate notes and some
light fruit. The smooth malt and gentle fruit continue
in the taste, with more fruit arriving on the swallow.
Dry, bittersweet finish, with fruit lingering. Moreish.

LIBERATOR

ABV 3.8%   **Bottle size** 500 ml   **Serve** cool
Ingredients Maris Otter and Pearl pale malt; Cascade hops

Tindall's new brewery stands opposite Seething USAAF
air base, home to the 448 Bombardment (H) Group and
their Liberator aircraft from 1943 to 1948 – hence the
name of this American-hopped bitter, which the brewer
thinks goes well with a curry.

RESURRECTION

ABV 3.8%   **Bottle size** 500 ml   **Serve** cool
Ingredients Halcyon pale malt; Cascade hops

A session beer infused with American hops, launched at
Easter 1999, as implied by its name.

ALLTIME

ABV 4%   **Bottle size** 500 ml   **Serve** cool
Ingredients Maris Otter and Halcyon pale malt;
Golding hops

An unusually-named beer, with a clock-face label. This
was a seasonal cask beer brought back permanently
because of demand, and hence now available 'alltime'.

CHRISTMAS CHEERS

ABV 4%   **Bottle size** 500 ml   **Serve** cool
Ingredients Maris Otter and Halcyon pale malt; crystal
malt; Golding hops

Available in December, Christmas Cheers is one of the
more quaffable festive beers, at a modest 4%.

DITCHINGHAM DAM

ABV 4.2%   **Bottle size** 500 ml   **Serve** cool
Ingredients Maris Otter pale malt; roasted malt; chocolate
malt; Golding and Mount Hood hops; liquorice; ginger

A spiced premium ale, taking its name from an area near the brewery. Ditchingham Dam was a scene of some controversy in 2000 when the local authority proposed to cull the wild chickens that roamed the area, considering them to be a danger to road users. (The chickens had lost their earlier home near Simpson's Maltings when it burned down.) The brewery stepped in and offered to give £5 for every firkin sold of this beer to provide signs to warn motorists of the hazard, and the chickens were saved. Note the picture of a rooster on the label.

Tasting Notes

A red beer with a fruity, herbal aroma. The taste is unusual, being fruity, herby and finely balancing bitterness and sweetness, with traces of lemon-ginger throughout. Dry, bitter, herbal finish.

EXTRA

ABV 4.5%   **Bottle size** 500 ml   **Serve** cool
Ingredients Maris Otter and Halcyon pale malt; Golding hops

The brewery's second beer, with extra colour, extra flavour and extra strength. It bears much the same label as Best Bitter, featuring a bird on a twig, except the border around the picture is red instead of green.

NORFOLK 'N' GOOD

ABV 4.6%   **Bottle size** 500 ml   **Serve** cool
Ingredients Halcyon pale malt; Cascade hops

Be careful how you ask for this stronger version of the 3.8% Resurrection! The risqué name is derived from a song popular with a local folk band, who have now written a new last verse specifically about the beer.

Tasting Notes

The big, hoppy nose – fruity, peppery and oily, like rummaging through a hop pocket – says much about this golden ale. Glorious hop flavours lead in the taste, with plenty of bitterness to boot, leaving a powerful, hoppy and bitter finish.

NORWICH DRAGON

ABV 4.6%   **Bottle size** 500 ml   **Serve** cool
Ingredients Halcyon pale malt; Cascade and Golding hops

A new premium ale named after Norwich's Dragon

Hall, a 13th-century merchant's hall that was rediscovered in the 1970s and is said to be the only building of its type still surviving in western Europe.

TITANIC

**The Titanic Brewery, Unit 5, Callender Place, Lingard Street, Burslem, Stoke-on-Trent, Staffordshire ST6 1JL.
Tel. (01782) 823447 Fax (01782) 812349
E-mail: titanic@titanicbrewery.co.uk
Web site: www.titanicbrewery.co.uk**

This brewery, named in honour of the *Titanic's* Captain Smith, who hailed from Stoke, was founded in 1985 but fell into difficulties until rescued by the present owners. A move to larger premises took place in 1992 and new brewing plant was installed in 1995. The brewery moved yet again in 2002. Beers are now bottled for Titanic by Wessex Craft Brewers (without filtration or the re-seeding of yeast) and each carries a best before date of six months.

STOUT

ABV 4.5%   **Bottle size** 500 ml   **Serve** cool
Ingredients Maris Otter pale malt; wheat malt; roasted barley; Northdown, Yakima Galena and Golding hops

Titanic Stout was the winner of *The Guardian's Best Bottle-Conditioned Beer* in 1994, although the recipe has been tweaked a little since, removing crystal malt and replacing it with a greater quantity of roasted barley. There are still American hops in the brew, but these are now Yakima Galena, instead of Willamette. A new, stylish 'ship's propeller' label was introduced in 2001. The brew is also available in cask.
Tasting Notes
A rich, near-black beer with an aroma of espresso coffee and liquorice. The taste has a light, malty, slightly fruity sweetness, roasted notes and bitter balance, and finishes with a smoky, roast grain, dry and bitter aftertaste.
Major stockist Sainsbury

CHRISTMAS ALE

ABV 7.2%   **Bottle size** 330 ml   **Serve** cool
Ingredients Maris Otter pale malt; crystal malt; wheat malt; invert sugar; Yakima Galena and Golding hops

Christmas Ale is a bottled version of Titanic's strong ale, Wreckage (7.2%). Only small runs are produced each year, with the bottle size likely to vary and some bottling carried out at the brewery itself.
Tasting Notes
A ruby beer with a deeply fruity, alcoholic nose. Slightly tart in the mouth, it is fruity, malty and fairly sweet, with a warming, sweetish, malt and fruit finish.

TOWNES

Townes Brewery, Speedwell Inn, Lowgates, Staveley, Chesterfield, Derbyshire S43 3TT.
Tel. (01246) 472252
E-mail: woodcurly@aol.com
Mail order service

Founded in 1994, in an old bakery on the outskirts of Chesterfield, Townes purchased The Speedwell Inn at Staveley and transferred production there in 1997. All the bottled beers are filled simply from casks and left unfined, making them acceptable to vegetarians and vegans.

STAVELEY CROSS

ABV 4.3%   **Bottle size** 500 ml   **Serve** cool
Ingredients Halcyon pale malt; pale crystal malt; wheat malt; Styrian Golding hops

A premium ale taking its name from an old part of Staveley, where a famous cross used to stand at a busy road junction.
Tasting Notes
A golden ale with a spicy aroma, a hoppy, spicy and dry taste and a dry, hoppy finish.

INDIA PALE ALE

ABV 4.5%   **Bottle size** 500 ml   **Serve** cool
Ingredients Halcyon pale malt; wheat malt; Cascade hops

An IPA in the American style, seasoned with Cascade hops.
Tasting Notes
A golden beer with a zesty, tangerine aroma. The full flavour balances tangy hops and supportive sweetness, with citrus fruit in evidence throughout. A dry, tangy hop aftertaste rounds off.

PYNOT PORTER

ABV 4.5%   **Bottle size** 500 ml   **Serve** cool
Ingredients Halcyon pale malt; crystal malt; black malt;
wheat malt; roasted barley; Bramling Cross and Styrian
Golding hops

Pynot is apparently another name for a magpie, a bird
that features on the Chesterfield coat of arms. Bramling
Cross is the main bittering hop, with Styrian Goldings
added late for aroma. Try with roast beef, suggests
brewer Alan Wood.
Tasting Notes
A ruby porter with sweet, dark malt and blackcurrant
fruit in the aroma. The reasonably full-bodied taste
features bitter, roasted barley and is not particularly
sweet. Bitter, roasted aftertaste.

MUFFIN MAN

ABV 4.6%   **Bottle size** 500 ml   **Serve** cool
Ingredients Halcyon pale malt; crystal malt; amber malt;
black malt; roasted barley; wheat malt; Northern Brewer
and Bramling Cross hops

A tribute beer: Alan is a big Frank Zappa fan and
'Muffin Man' is one of the Seventies rock star's best-
known tracks. Described as a 'best mild', with Bramling
Cross the aroma hop, it is only brewed in winter
months.
Tasting Notes
An amber premium ale with mostly fruit but also a little
malt in the nose. The taste is largely bitter, but with
plenty of malt support. Bitter, hoppy finish, with
roasted notes in the malt.

OATMEAL STOUT

ABV 4.7%   **Bottle size** 500 ml   **Serve** cool
Ingredients Halcyon pale malt; crystal malt; black malt;
roasted barley; malted oats; wheat malt; Challenger hops

Like the other bottled beers, Oatmeal Stout is also sold
in cask form.
Tasting Notes
A dark ruby stout with light fruit notes in the biscuity,
slightly coffeeish nose. Nutty, oaky malt leads in the
mouth, supported by plenty of bitterness and an
underlying creaminess. Dry, bitter finish with an oaky,
nutty maltiness.

STAVELEYAN

ABV 4.9%   **Bottle size** 500 ml   **Serve** cool
Ingredients Halcyon pale malt; crystal malt; wheat malt;
Styrian Golding hops

A strong, golden ale for the people of Staveley (known
as 'Staveleyans'). The label shows a photograph of the
Staveley Coal and Iron Company, which helped
develop the town into a major industrial area.

ESSENCE

ABV 5.1%   **Bottle size** 500 ml   **Serve** cool
Ingredients Halcyon pale malt; lager malt; wheat malt;
Liberty hops

Equal amounts of pale and lager malt go into this
golden ale, which highlights the American Liberty hop.

UNCLE STUART'S

**Uncle Stuart's Brewery, Antoma, Pack Lane,
Lingwood, Norwich, Norfolk NR13 4PD.
Tel. (07732) 012112
E-mail: stuartsbrewery@aol.com**
Mail order service

Stuart Evans has been brewing bottled beers in very
small quantities at his home in beautiful rural Norfolk
since spring 2002. His brewplant is only capable of
turning out 100 litres at a time and he didn't even start
selling cask beer until April 2003.

BREW NO.1

ABV 4%   **Bottle size** 500 ml   **Serve** cool
Ingredients Pale malt; crystal malt; black malt; chocolate
malt; Golding and Progress hops

A mild, brewed once a fortnight, like the other beers.

BREW NO.9

ABV 4.7%   **Bottle size** 500 ml   **Serve** cool
Ingredients Pale malt; crystal malt; Progress and Golding
hops

A ruby-coloured premium ale. Each of Stuart's bottled

beers is first matured in, and then filled from, a cask, with the addition of priming sugars to ensure good carbonation.

BREW NO.3

ABV 5.6%   **Bottle size** 500 ml   **Serve** cool
Ingredients Pale malt; crystal malt; Progress and Golding hops

A dark premium ale, given a 12-month best before period, as for all Stuart's beers.

BREW NO.2

ABV 5.7%   **Bottle size** 500 ml   **Serve** cool
Ingredients Pale malt; crystal malt; flaked maize; Golding and Progress hops

A pale, hoppy, strong bitter.

CHRISTMAS ALE

ABV 7%   **Bottle size** 500 ml   **Serve** cool
Ingredients Pale malt; crystal malt; black malt; Progress and Golding hops

A strong dark ale, sold only between October and January.

VALE

Vale Brewery Company, Thame Road, Haddenham, Buckinghamshire HP17 8BY. Tel. (01844) 290008 Fax (01844) 292505 E-mail: valebrewery@ntlworld.com Web site: www.valebrewery.co.uk Mail order service

Vale Brewery was opened in 1995 by brothers Mark and Phil Stevens, both of whom had previously worked for other breweries and related industries. Their brewery is housed in an industrial unit on the fringe of one of the most attractive villages in Buckinghamshire. The brewplant was expanded in 1996 and bottling began a year later. All the beers are matured in casks, filtered, primed with sweet wort and re-seeded with fresh yeast. Best before dates are set at six months. 'Own label' bottles are also supplied for individual customers.

BLACK SWAN DARK MILD

ABV 3.3%   **Bottle size** 500 ml   **Serve** cool
Ingredients Maris Otter pale malt; crystal malt; roasted
barley; Golding and Fuggle hops

Bottle-conditioned milds are extremely rare, as
conventional wisdom has it that more alcohol is
needed for the beer to mature and survive in the bottle.
However, the Stevens brothers have taken the plunge
with this version of an award-winning cask brew. The
name and the label play on the brewery logo (actually
based on the Buckinghamshire county emblem) of a
swan, but making it black to match the beer.
Tasting Notes
Pouring ruby, with a white foam collar, Black Swan has
a light, chocolatey malt nose and a gentle fruitiness in
the taste, balanced by soft, sweetish malt and bitterness
from both hops and roasted barley. Dry, bitter aftertaste.

WYCHERT ALE

ABV 3.9%   **Bottle size** 500 ml   **Serve** cool
Ingredients Maris Otter pale malt; crystal malt; Fuggle and
Challenger hops

'Wychert', meaning 'white earth', is the substance from
which many of the oldest buildings in the lovely village
of Haddenham (the brewery's home) were constructed.
You see them all around the sprawling village green.
Tasting Notes
An amber ale with orange fruit and a little toasted malt
in the aroma. The taste is nutty and lightly fruity, with
a good, hoppy, bitter balance. Dry, bitter, hoppy finish.

BLACK BEAUTY PORTER

ABV 4.3%   **Bottle size** 500 ml   **Serve** cool
Ingredients Maris Otter pale malt; roasted barley; Fuggle
and Golding hops

A dark horse. Unlike the other beers, there are no Saxon
or local connections: the name's just a good description
of the beer inside.
Tasting Notes
Another ruby-coloured beer, this time with subtle dark
malt and juicy fruit leading in the nose. The lightish
body supports a slightly tropical fruitiness from the
hops, roasted barley and gentle bitterness. Dry, bitter,
roasted finish.

EDGAR'S GOLDEN ALE

ABV 4.3%   **Bottle size** 500 ml   **Serve** cool
Ingredients Maris Otter pale malt; Fuggle and
Golding hops

Edgar is a Stevens family name, traditionally passed
down to the first son of the first son over the
generations. The beer was formerly sold also as Halcyon
Daze.
Tasting Notes
A clean and tasty, golden beer with a hoppy aroma of
fruit cocktail. The same juicy fruit cocktail flavours
continue in the mouth, tempered by a crisp, spicy hop
bitterness. Fruity, bitter, hoppy finish.

GRUMPLING PREMIUM

ABV 4.6%   **Bottle size** 500 ml   **Serve** cool
Ingredients Maris Otter pale malt; crystal malt; roasted
malt; Challenger and Golding hops

Grumpling stones are the large, foundation stones upon
which wychert houses are constructed (see Wychert Ale,
on the previous page).
Tasting Notes
Amber in colour, Grumpling Premium is a bitter but
fruity beer with excellent malty body and a bitter,
hoppy finish. The aroma offers both soft, juicy fruit and
malt.

HADDA'S HEAD BANGER

ABV 5%   **Bottle size** 500 ml   **Serve** cool
Ingredients Maris Otter pale malt; crystal malt; Challenger
and Fuggle hops

Hadda was the Saxon king who settled in (and gave his
name to) the village of Haddenham and Hadda's Head
Banger is just one of a range of seasonal cask beers Vale
produces under his banner. This, however, is the only
Hadda in bottle. The label shows a Saxon warrior,
complete with axe.
Tasting Notes
Soft malt and a hint of fruit combine in the nose of this
amber ale. There's a slightly salty note behind the main
taste of hops, fruit, malt and lightly roasted bitterness,
making it rather moreish for a 5% beer. The same
savoury note lingers along with fruit in the dry, bitter
aftertaste.

GOOD KING SENSELESS

ABV 5.2%   **Bottle size** 500 ml   **Serve** cool
Ingredients Maris Otter pale malt; crystal malt; chocolate malt; Fuggle and Golding hops

This Christmas warmer is bottled each November and stocks generally last until spring.

VENTNOR

Ventnor Brewery, 119 High Street, Ventnor, Isle of Wight PO38 1LY. Tel. (01983) 856161 Fax (01983) 856404 Web site: www.ventnorbrewery.co.uk
Mail order service

The former Burts Brewery was put back into production by new ownership in 1996 and now supplies up to 100 pubs on the Isle of Wight with cask beers. The first bottle-conditioned beer was St Boniface Golden Spring Ale (ABV 6%), which was produced in 1997 as a limited edition in antique quart bottles discovered on the site. However, apart from Old Ruby, featured below, the brewery's wide-ranging bottled output is no longer naturally conditioned. See also Scarecrow Brewery.

OLD RUBY BITTER

ABV 4.7%   **Bottle size** 500 ml   **Serve** cool
Ingredients Pale malt; crystal malt; wheat malt; Golding and Challenger hops

Designed as an old-style beer, Old Ruby is bottled for Ventnor by Wessex Craft Brewers.
Tasting Notes
Not really ruby in colour, more a light red/brown, this premium ale opens with a malty, fruity aroma (hint of blackcurrant). The palate has lots of clean, nutty malt but is not particularly sweet, and a light fruitiness persists. Toasted malt provides bitterness in the finish.

WARCOP

Warcop Brewery, 9 Nellive Park, St Brides Wentlooge, Gwent NP10 8SE. Tel./Fax (01633) 680058

Brewery established in September 1998 by chemist and experienced home brewer Bill Picton, who renovated a former milking parlour just outside Newport for the purpose. The six-barrel plant came from the Ross Brewery brew pub in the town and the name of the brewery is derived from Bill's family's initials. The quoted address is the home/office; the brewery is a few miles away. The bottled beers are produced whenever Bill is running short of stock and may include any of his extensive draught range. What follows is a listing of the bottled beers the *Guide* has been able to track down. Each is bottled straight from the cask and primed with sugar. Bottled beers are also brewed to order for private celebrations and other events.

DRILLERS

ABV 4%   **Bottle size** 500 ml   **Serve** cool
Ingredients Maris Otter and Halcyon pale malt; crystal malt; Golding hops

Local industry features strongly in the names of most of Warcop's cask and bottled beers, hence the title of this dark golden ale.

STEELERS

ABV 4.2%   **Bottle size** 500 ml   **Serve** cool
Ingredients Maris Otter and Halcyon pale malt; crystal malt; chocolate malt; Golding hops

A amber-coloured tribute to the steel workers of Llanwern, on the eastern side of Newport.

YA No. 3

ABV 4.3%   **Bottle size** 500 ml   **Serve** cool
Ingredients Maris Otter pale malt; Fuggle hops

'YA' stands for Yellow Ale – to avoid confusion with Bill's other beer, 'YB' ('Yellow Bitter')! It's called No. 3 because it weighs in at 4.3% ABV.

ZEN

ABV 4.4%   **Bottle size** 500 ml   **Serve** cool
Ingredients Maris Otter and Halcyon pale malt; crystal malt; Golding hops

One more golden brew, this one's name is derived from the contemplation given by Bill Picton over what to call the beer.

RIGGERS

ABV 4.5%   **Bottle size** 500 ml   **Serve** cool
Ingredients Maris Otter and Halcyon pale malt; crystal malt; Golding hops

Riggers is a less potent version of the 5% Dockers (see below).

ROCKERS

ABV 4.8%   **Bottle size** 500 ml   **Serve** cool
Ingredients Maris Otter and Halcyon pale malt; lager malt; Fuggle hops

The flippant counterpart to Rollers (another beer that Bill produces with name origins in the steel industry).

DEEP PIT

ABV 5%   **Bottle size** 500 ml   **Serve** cool
Ingredients Maris Otter and Halcyon pale malt; crystal malt; chocolate malt; Golding hops

The title Deep Pit clearly reflects the mining heritage of South Wales.
Tasting Notes
A red-brown ale with a malty, roasty, hoppy aroma. Malt, roast malt and citrous hops feature in the taste, too, before a dry, roasty, bitter finish.

DOCKERS

ABV 5%   **Bottle size** 500 ml   **Serve** cool
Ingredients Maris Otter and Halcyon pale malt; crystal malt; Golding hops

Newport has long been an important docks town – hence the name of this premium ale.

BLACK AND AMBER EXTRA

ABV 6%   **Bottle size** 500 ml   **Serve** cool
Ingredients Halcyon pale malt; crystal malt; chocolate malt; Golding hops

Locals will need no reminding that the Black and Ambers is the nickname of Newport Rugby Football Club. This 'Extra' is stronger than Warcop's 4% cask beer called simply Black and Amber.

Tasting Notes
A reddish brown ale with an alcoholic, malty, fruity
aroma. The taste is malty, fruity and strong. Dry, bitter
fruit and malt finish, with a hint of roast.

QE2

ABV 6%   **Bottle size** 500 ml   **Serve** cool
Ingredients Maris Otter and Halcyon pale malt; lager malt;
Fuggle hops

A beer initially brewed in 2002 for The Queen's Golden
Jubilee.
Tasting Notes
An appropriately golden beer with light spice and fruit
in the nose. The taste is also lightly fruity and the finish
is dry and hoppy.

RED HOT FURNACE

ABV 9%   **Bottle size** 330 ml   **Serve** cool
Ingredients Maris Otter and Halcyon pale malt; crystal
malt; chocolate malt; Golding hops

Newport's steel connections (Llanwern again) provide
the inspiration for this powerful winter beer.
Tasting Notes
A ruby beer with a spicy, fruity, malty aroma. Although
malty, sweet and fruity in the mouth, it is well balanced
and tastes nothing like its strength. Dry, bittersweet,
fruit finish, with a hint of roast.

WENTWORTH

**Wentworth Brewery Ltd., The Powerhouse,
The Gun Park, Wentworth, Rotherham,
South Yorkshire S62 7TF.
Tel. (01226) 747070 Fax (01226) 747050
Web site: www.wentworthbrewery.co.uk**

Wentworth opened in 1999 on the site of the former
anti-aircraft gun positions on the Wentworth
Woodhouse estate. The impressive, 18th-century facade
of Wentworth Woodhouse (the longest in England) is
depicted on the labels of all three bottled beers, which
were introduced in November 2000 and are filled on
site after kräusening. The brewery's Whistlejacket, at a
powerful 8.4%, may be the next beer to find its way
into the bottle.

WENTWORTH PALE ALE

ABV 4%   **Bottle size** 500 ml   **Serve** cool
Ingredients Maris Otter pale malt; lager malt; wheat malt;
Cascade and Fuggle hops

Light and refreshing, says the label, about Wentworth's
standard bitter, commonly known as WPA or 'Woppa'.
Tasting Notes
A golden beer with an aroma of toffee-malt and hop
fruit. The taste is crisp, bitter and aggressively hoppy,
with fruit throughout. Bitter, hoppy finish.

OATMEAL STOUT

ABV 4.8%   **Bottle size** 500 ml   **Serve** cool
Ingredients Maris Otter pale malt; black malt; wheat malt;
roasted barley; oatmeal malt; Golding hops

The cask equivalent of Oatmeal Stout was bronze
medallist in CAMRA's 2003 *Champion Winter Beer of
Britain* contest.
Tasting Notes
A near-black stout with a softly roasted, biscuity,
slightly toffeeish aroma. The complex taste is crisp, dry,
roasted and toasted, leathery, biscuity, creamy and
bitter. Nicely bitter, long roasted grain finish.

MOORE'S MAGIC

ABV 5.5%   **Bottle size** 500 ml   **Serve** cool
Ingredients Maris Otter pale malt; wheat malt; Cascade
hops

This pale, hoppy strong ale is one of the few bottle-
conditioned beers to be on sale at a football stadium
(why can't more sporting venues offer decent bottled
beers if they feel they aren't able to handle cask ale?). It
was named after Rotherham United's manager, Ronnie
Moore, and replaces an earlier beer for the club which
was called Miller's Red Ale.

RAMPANT GRYPHON

ABV 6.2%   **Bottle size** 500 ml   **Serve** cool
Ingredients Maris Otter pale malt; crystal malt; wheat
malt; Challenger and Golding hops

A gryphon stands atop the coat of arms of the
Wentworth estate and lends its name to two of the

brewery's strong ales. Gryphon, at 5.1%, is not bottled however, only this even more potent – hence 'rampant' – brew.

Tasting Notes

An orange-gold ale with a malty, orangey aroma. The taste is crisp and bitter but reveals the beer's strength, bursting with tangy, fruity hops, yet with lots of thick malt behind. The bitter, hoppy aftertaste has some lingering fruit.

WEST BERKSHIRE

**The West Berkshire Brewery Company Ltd.,
The Old Bakery, Yattendon, Thatcham,
Berkshire RG18 0UE.
Tel. (01635) 202968 Fax (01635) 202638
E-mail: davemaggs@wbbrew.co.uk
Web site: www.wbbrew.co.uk**

Dave and Helen Maggs set up West Berkshire Brewery in a barn behind the idyllic Pot Kiln pub (a separate business), near Frilsham in Berkshire in 1995. They still brew there but have also opened a second, larger site in an old bakery in the estate village of Yattendon, a few miles away. They have been dabbling in bottled beers for some time, producing occasional and trial brews, but only Full Circle is a regular product (now bottled about four times a year).

FULL CIRCLE

ABV 4.6%   **Bottle size** 500 ml   **Serve** cool
Ingredients Maris Otter pale malt; crystal malt; wheat malt; hops not declared

Brewed first as West Berkshire's 1,000th brew (and still also available as a cask ale), Full Circle initially incorporated locally-grown Northdown hops alongside local barley, but replacements from further afield have now had to be found. The beer is re-seeded with fresh yeast (the brewery's regular strain) prior to bottling. Bottles are kept for a month to condition before release and the best before date is set at nine months. Contracting out bottling is a possibility for the future and the strength of the beer may be increased to 5%. Full Circle may also be found in carbonated form, so look out for the words 'bottle-conditioned' when you come across a bottle. A beer to enjoy with a steak and kidney pie, according to Dave.

WICKWAR

**The Wickwar Brewing Co., The Old Brewery,
Station Road, Wickwar, Gloucestershire GL12 8NB.
Tel./Fax (01454) 294168
E-mail: bob@wickwarbrewing.co.uk
Web site: www.wickwarbrewing.co.uk**

Wickwar brewery was launched in 1990. Although its
bottled beers are brewed at Wickwar, bottling is carried
out by Wessex Craft Brewers after the beer has been
fined in a conditioning tank. All bottles carry a nine-
month best before date.

BOB (Brand Oak Bitter)/DOG'S HAIR

ABV 4%   **Bottle size** 500 ml   **Serve** cool
Ingredients Maris Otter pale malt; crystal malt; chocolate
malt; Fuggle and Challenger hops

BOB has always been one of Wickwar's most popular
beers, and took its name from Brand Oak Cottage,
where one of the founders was living at the time. The
beer has also been packaged by Wessex Craft Brewers
under the light-hearted name of Dog's Hair.
Tasting Notes
An amber ale with a fruity, malty nose. The taste is a
dry, lightly apple-fruity mix of malt and hops, rounded
off by a dry, bitter, malt and hops finish.

COTSWOLD WAY

ABV 4.2%   **Bottle size** 500 ml   **Serve** cool
Ingredients Maris Otter pale malt; crystal malt; chocolate
malt; Fuggle and Challenger hops

A new beer, added to the range in December 2002.
Tasting Notes
There are traces of chocolate behind the malt and hop
in the nose of this dark golden beer. Malt is well in
evidence in the taste, but so are fruitiness and dry, soft
bitterness, which come to dominate the moreish finish.

INFERNAL BREW

ABV 4.8%   **Bottle size** 500 ml   **Serve** cool
Ingredients Maris Otter pale malt; crystal malt; chocolate
malt; Fuggle and Challenger hops

Another Wessex Craft Brewers re-badge, Infernal Brew,

for all its devilish red and black packaging, is actually the brewery's rather more humbly-named Olde Merryford Ale in a bottle.

Tasting Notes
An amber ale with a hoppy aroma. The taste is also hoppy and fruity, but the malt renders it bittersweet rather than bitter, and it rounds off with a bittersweet, hoppy aftertaste.

OLD ARNOLD

ABV 4.8%   **Bottle size** 500 ml   **Serve** cool
Ingredients Maris Otter pale malt; crystal malt; chocolate malt; Fuggle and Challenger hops

This premium ale was named after a Mr Arnold who founded the original brewery in Wickwar in 1800 and who merged his business with that of Mr Perrett, his near neighbour, in 1826. The stone tower brewhouse they constructed was employed for cider making from the 1920s and was eventually closed in 1969, remaining so until it was occupied by the current brewery in 1990. The recipe for this brew is based on Mr Arnold's 'Strong Old Beer', which, so the label reveals, was sold for 12/- a firkin.

Tasting Notes
A reddish brown ale with a malty, chocolatey aroma, enhanced by citrous notes. Initially malty in the mouth, it becomes increasingly fruity as the hops kick in. Gently bitter, hoppy finish.

MR PERRETT'S

ABV 5.9%   **Bottle size** 500 ml   **Serve** cool
Ingredients Maris Otter pale malt; crystal malt; chocolate malt; Fuggle and Challenger hops

A *Tesco Beer Challenge* winner in 2001, Mr Perrett's Traditional Stout, as it was then more fully known, was at first only available in cruelly small 330 ml bottles. Since the exclusive contract with Tesco ended, a standard half-litre bottle has been introduced. The beer has been twice voted *Champion Beer of Gloucestershire* in its cask form.

Tasting Notes
A very dark red/brown brew with coffee and tart dark fruits in the nose. The same flavours continue on the palate, but with a light liquorice bitterness poking through. Roasted malt leads in the dry finish. Gently smoky throughout.

STATION PORTER

ABV 6.1%   **Bottle size** 500 ml   **Serve** cool
Ingredients Maris Otter pale malt; crystal malt; chocolate
malt; Fuggle and Challenger hops

An award-winning cask beer (including two silver
medals at CAMRA's Great Winter Beer Festival), named
after Wickwar village's long-lost railway halt, Station
Porter was first bottled in 1997. The simple, almost
child-like, stencilled label design hasn't always worked
to the beer's advantage (one supermarket rejected the
beer, considering it likely to tempt underage drinkers),
but it has become a distinctive trademark.
Tasting Notes
An extremely dark ruby beer with a fruity, chocolatey
nose. The taste is smooth, sweetish and fruity (hints of
bitter orange), with bitter roast character to balance.
Lightish body; roasted, bitter orange finish.

WOLF

**The Wolf Brewery Ltd., 10 Maurice Gaymer Road,
Attleborough, Norfolk NR17 2QZ.**
Tel. (01953) 457775 Fax (01953) 457776
Web site: www.wolf-brewery.ltd.uk
Mail order service

Founded in 1996 by Wolfe Witham, former owner of
Norfolk's Reindeer Brewery, this brewery is housed in an
industrial unit on the site of the former Gaymer's cider
orchard. The beers are kräusened prior to bottling,
ensuring fresh Wolf yeast is carried forward into each
bottle.

CAVELL ALE 9503

ABV 3.7%   **Bottle size** 500 ml   **Serve** cool
Ingredients Pearl pale malt; crystal malt; wheat malt;
Fuggle and Challenger hops

Brewed primarily for the Norwich lodge of The
Buffaloes – number 9503, the Edith Cavell Lodge – this
beer is largely sold at The Beehive, the lodge's meeting
place in the city. The label includes a picture of the
World War I nursing heroine, who was executed by the
Germans.
Tasting Notes
Toasted malt and fruity hops dominate the aroma of

this amber ale, which has a fruity, mostly bitter taste, but also some malt sweetness. The aftertaste is dry and bitter.

FESTIVAL ALE

ABV 3.7%   **Bottle size** 500 ml   **Serve** cool
Ingredients Pearl pale malt; crystal malt; wheat malt; Fuggle and Challenger hops

Festival Ale is an annual brew for Norwich and Norfolk's Arts Festival, but with the recipe changed from year to year. Versions have included lavender honey and blackcurrants.

NORFOLK LAVENDER

ABV 3.7%   **Bottle size** 500 ml   **Serve** cool
Ingredients Optic pale malt; crystal malt; wheat malt; Golding, Styrian Golding and Cascade hops; lavender honey

An unusual beer – 'Brewed for Norfolk Lavender Ltd., Heacham', according to the label – with the scented inclusion of local lavender honey.
Tasting Notes
A golden beer with a perfumed, honeyed aroma. In the mouth, it is scented, citrous and bittersweet, with a light honey softness. A perfumed, bitter, hoppy finish rounds off.

WOLF IN SHEEP'S CLOTHING

ABV 3.7%   **Bottle size** 500 ml   **Serve** cool
Ingredients Pearl pale malt; crystal malt; chocolate malt; wheat malt; Golding and Cascade hops

From its name, you'd think that this beer had something to hide, but it's essentially just a fruity session ale.
Tasting Notes
Toffee notes to the malt and a raisin fruitiness feature in the aroma and taste of this ruby ale, which also has a moreishly dry, slight saltiness and finishes with bitter fruit and hops.

BEST BITTER

ABV 3.9%   **Bottle size** 500 ml   **Serve** cool
Ingredients Pearl pale malt; crystal malt; amber malt; Fuggle and Golding hops

This version of the brewery's cask Best Bitter barks out the Wolf slogan, 'Howlin' good beer!', on its label.

Tasting Notes
A dark amber beer with hop fruit in the aroma, a hoppy, bitter, toasted malt taste and a toasted bitterness in the finish.

WOLF ALE

ABV 3.9%   **Bottle size** 500 ml   **Serve** cool
Ingredients Pearl pale malt; crystal malt; wheat malt; Golding, Challenger and Styrian Golding hops

Another cask beer that is bottled from time to time.

COYOTE BITTER

ABV 4.3%   **Bottle size** 500 ml   **Serve** cool
Ingredients Pearl pale malt; crystal malt; wheat malt; Golding, Styrian Golding and Cascade hops

Cascade hops lend an American accent to this award-winning brew, which explains the presence of the Americanised wolf in the name. The coyote is featured howling at a desert moon on the colourful label.

Tasting Notes
This amber beer has a powerful fruity aroma, laced with hints of pears and juicy oranges. Big, peppery hops, more juicy fruit and a good malt base feature in the taste, before a dry, bitter, peppery-hop finish.

BIG RED

ABV 4.5%   **Bottle size** 500 ml   **Serve** cool
Ingredients Pearl pale malt; crystal malt; amber malt; chocolate malt; wheat malt; Styrian Golding, Golding and Challenger hops

A new, ruby-coloured beer, brewed for cask and bottle.

Tasting Notes
A tasty, fruity beer with a deep malt background and good, balancing bitterness. The aroma highlights fruit and dark malt, while the aftertaste is mostly bitter but with a nagging fruity maltiness.

LUPINE

ABV 4.5%   **Bottle size** 500 ml   **Serve** cool
Ingredients Pearl pale malt; crystal malt; amber malt; wheat malt; Styrian Golding and Golding hops

Another Wolf beer added to the range since the last edition of the book.

Tasting Notes
Orange fruit emerges in the aroma of this ruby beer, along with light, biscuity malt. Robust and full-bodied, its taste has bitterness to the fore, but also malt and a little fruit for balance. Long, bitter, hoppy finish.

GRANNY WOULDN'T LIKE IT!!!

ABV 4.8%   **Bottle size** 500 ml   **Serve** cool
Ingredients Pearl pale malt; crystal malt; chocolate malt; wheat malt; Golding and Challenger hops

Particularly popular at Christmas, as a novelty gift for granny (to see if she would!!!), this is another acclaimed Wolf ale. Taking the fairy story as its inspiration, the label pictures Little Red Riding Hood and a menacing, red-eyed wolf.

Tasting Notes
A red-amber ale with a slightly piney, vinously fruity aroma. The taste is mostly bitter, but with plenty of malt, pepper, roasted malt and a little vinous fruit. Dry, roasted, bitter finish.

PRAIRIE

ABV 5%   **Bottle size** 500 ml   **Serve** cool
Ingredients Pearl pale malt; wheat malt; Golding and Styrian Golding hops

A strong ale introduced in summer 2003.

TIMBER WOLF

ABV 5.8%   **Bottle size** 500 ml   **Serve** cool
Ingredients Pearl pale malt; crystal malt; chocolate malt; wheat malt; Golding and Challenger hops

A warming ale for the winter months.

Tasting Notes
A ruby beer with a fruity, vinous aroma. Light winey notes continue through this fruity, tangy drink to the finish, with dark malt lurking in the shadows.

PORTED TIMBER WOLF

ABV 5.8%   **Bottle size** 500 ml   **Serve** cool
Ingredients Pearl pale malt; crystal malt; chocolate malt; wheat malt; Golding and Challenger hops; port

Bearing the descriptive sub-title of 'Falling Down Water', this is a doctored version of Timber Wolf, in the style of an Irish stout-and-fortified-wine cocktail. A whole bottle of port is added immediately after fermentation to every firkin, and the beer is then left to age for at least nine months before it is bottled.

Tasting Notes
A ruby beer with an appetising, mellow fruit aroma. The taste is strong and bitter, but the fruitiness of the port shines through amid some roasted malt flavour. Very dry, bitter, roasted finish, with teasing hints of winey fruit.

WOOD

The Wood Brewery Ltd., Wistanstow, Craven Arms, Shropshire SY7 8DG.
Tel. (01588) 672523 Fax (01588) 673939
Web site: www.woodbrewery.co.uk

This village brewery was founded by the Wood family in 1980, in buildings next to The Plough Inn in Wistanstow. Its first bottled brews came out over a decade ago and bottling is now carried out by Wessex Craft Brewers. Primary fermentation is halted slightly earlier than for the cask brews. The beers are then fined before the bottles are filled. Nine months are allowed in the shelf life date. The beers have also appeared in pasteurised format, but the bottle-conditioned versions will continue. Check for sediment in the bottles!

SHROPSHIRE LAD SPRING BITTER

ABV 5%   **Bottle size** 500 ml   **Serve** cool
Ingredients Pale malt; crystal malt; chocolate malt; torrefied wheat; Fuggle and Golding hops

Wood introduced this beer in 1996, to commemorate the 100th anniversary of the publication of AE Housman's well-known poem *A Shropshire Lad*. The ale is also available in cask form but the bottled version is subtly different, weighing in at 5% ABV as opposed to 4.5. The labels (re-designed in recent years but still quoting Housman's noble declaration that: 'Ale man, ale's the stuff to drink') carry the subtitle 'Spring Bitter', although the beer is sold all year.

Tasting Notes
A reddish brown beer with an initially sweetish, yet crisp and fruity character and good hop bitterness. The

aroma combines hops, dark malt and a hint of lemon, whilst the bitter fruit finish is dry and hoppy.
Major stockists Safeway, local Tesco

HOPPING MAD

ABV 4.7%   **Bottle size** 500 ml   **Serve** cool
Ingredients Halcyon pale malt; crystal malt; torrefied wheat; Progress hops

A new bottled beer for 1998, Hopping Mad was already a success in cask form, having collected a silver medal at the *Beauty of Hops* awards in 1997. The draught version is only available at Easter (hence the bunny on the label), but the bottled beer is produced all year.
Tasting Notes
An amber beer with a hoppy nose featuring hints of orange and lemon. Tangy hop bitterness and soft lemon lead the way in the taste, but these are nicely backed up by malt, before a hoppy, very dry, bittersweet finish.

CHRISTMAS CRACKER

ABV 6%   **Bottle size** 500 ml   **Serve** cool
Ingredients Halcyon pale malt; crystal malt; chocolate malt; Fuggle and Golding hops

Though Wood's Christmas Cracker has been warming the hearts of local drinkers for some years, this bottled version is a relative newcomer, first clinking its way off the bottling line at Christmas 1996. It's the same beer as cask, brewed several times in November. Not surprisingly, Wood considers it to be the perfect match for the rich foods of Christmas.
Tasting Notes
A ruby beer with a malty, fruity nose. Rich, malty and fruity to taste, it is well-balanced by crisp bitterness and some roast malt. Not too full-bodied. Dry, generally bitter finish.

WOODFORDE'S

**Woodforde's Norfolk Ales (Woodforde's Ltd.),
Broadland Brewery, Woodbastwick, Norwich,
Norfolk NR13 6SW.
Tel. (01603) 720353 Fax (01603) 721806
E-mail: info@woodfordes.co.uk
Web site: www.woodfordes.co.uk**
Mail order service

Woodforde's was founded in 1981 in Drayton, near Norwich, and moved to a converted farm complex in the picturesque Broadland village of Woodbastwick in 1989. It brews a wide range of award-winning beers (including two former CAMRA *Champion Beers of Britain*), many of which are now also bottled (racked bright and re-seeded with fresh yeast). The bottles were upgraded in size in 2002 to 500 ml across the range (with the exception of Norfolk Nip) and new stylish labels were added at the same time.

WHERRY

ABV 3.8%   **Bottle size** 500 ml   **Serve** cool
Ingredients Maris Otter pale malt; crystal malt; Golding and Styrian Golding hops

This is a bottled version of CAMRA's *Champion Beer of Britain* of 1996 and well it reflects the success of its cask-conditioned equivalent. A wherry is a type of boat once commonly seen on the Norfolk Broads.
Tasting Notes
An orange gold beer with a fruity, hoppy and slightly peppery nose. Bitter, zesty, hoppy orange fruit fills the mouth (like digging a fingernail into the peel of an orange) before a dry, bitter fruit finish rounds off.

GREAT EASTERN

ABV 4.3%   **Bottle size** 500 ml   **Serve** cool
Ingredients Maris Otter pale malt; lager malt; Progress hops

'A special brew to commemorate 150 years of the Great Eastern Railway in Norfolk', declares the label, confirming that Great Eastern was first brewed in 1994 in cask form as a souvenir beer for railway enthusiasts.
Tasting Notes
A pale golden beer with an appetising aroma of fruit. The taste is dry and fruity with a little peppery hop and a bitter, hoppy finish.

NELSON'S REVENGE

ABV 4.5%   **Bottle size** 500 ml   **Serve** cool
Ingredients Maris Otter pale malt; crystal malt; Golding hops

Nelson's Revenge reflects the famous admiral's associations with Norfolk (he was born in the county).

Tasting Notes
With an appealing citrus fruit and pears aroma, this copper ale has bags of character right from the first sniff. A fine balance of zesty fruit, malt and hop bitterness follows, with a dry, moreish, bittersweet finish.

NORFOLK NOG

ABV 4.6%   **Bottle size** 500 ml   **Serve** cool
Ingredients Maris Otter pale malt; crystal malt; chocolate malt; Fuggle and Golding hops

Pre-dating the success of the brewery's Wherry by four years, Norfolk Nog was CAMRA's *Champion Beer of Britain* in 1992. To earn the supreme CAMRA accolade with two different ales is a remarkable achievement, especially for a small brewery. (For the record, only one other brewery, Fuller's, has claimed the top prize with more than one beer.) The only caveat when citing this achievement is that drinkers should be gently reminded that cask beer and bottled beer are not quite the same thing, even if the beer leaves the same cask, as in this case. The level of carbonation can make a difference to the nature of the beer, as can the maturing process in the bottle.

Tasting Notes
This is a ruby-coloured, strong mild, without the deeper bitterness of a stout or the cloyingness of a heavy old ale. Its aroma is coffeeish and chocolatey, characteristics which continue in the taste, alongside soft malt sweetness and a little fruit. Roasted malt features in the bittersweet finish.

ADMIRAL'S RESERVE

ABV 5%   **Bottle size** 500 ml   **Serve** cool
Ingredients Maris Otter pale malt; crystal malt; rye crystal malt; Golding hops

First brewed in April 2002 to commemorate Woodforde's 21st anniversary, Admiral's Reserve – a strong bitter – is now a permanent member of the bottled range and is also available in cask form. The best before date is set at nine months.

Tasting Notes
A dark amber strong ale with creamy malt in the nose and nutty malt in the taste, together with a little sweetness, fruit and a robust but balanced bitterness. Bitter, roasted malt notes hog the finish.

HEADCRACKER

ABV 7%   **Bottle size** 500 ml
Serve at room temperature
Ingredients Maris Otter pale malt; caramalt; Golding hops

Clearly in the first division of the appropriate names league, Headcracker is not a beer to treat lightly. Its origins are in the barley wine school. In fact, you could say it is now one of the class leaders, having won CAMRA's *Best Barley Wine* award on no less than three occasions (in cask form). This is one beer to experiment with over a longer period than the prescribed 12 months' shelf life to see how it matures and how the flavours mellow out in the bottle.

Tasting Notes
This complex barley wine has an orange-gold colour and a fruity (oranges and peaches) nose. The powerful, fairly sweet taste features fruit and a robust hop bitterness, while bitter fruit tingles away in the dry aftertaste.

NORFOLK NIP

ABV 8.2%   **Bottle size** 330 ml
Serve at room temperature
Ingredients Maris Otter pale malt; crystal malt; chocolate malt; roasted barley; Golding hops

Norfolk Nip closely follows a recipe dating from 1929 for a beer (also called Norfolk Nip) from the defunct Steward & Patteson brewery in Norwich. The original beer was phased out by Watney's in the early 1960s, but the brew was revived by Woodforde's in March 1992 to commemorate the tenth anniversary of the local CAMRA news journal, *Norfolk Nips*. Brewing now takes place annually on or around St Valentine's Day. Although 12 months are suggested as the best before time, the strength and high hop rate should enable this beer to mature well beyond a year after bottling. Indeed, it has already enjoyed at least six months of maturation in the cask at the brewery prior to bottle filling.

Tasting Notes
Very dark ruby in colour, this barley wine has tropical fruit (pineapple) in its aroma, over a leathery, lightly treacly base. Sweetness, dark malt, raisin fruit, pineapple, orange and fine hop bitterness combine in the complex taste, although it is not as full-bodied as expected. Gum-tingling, warm finish.

WYE VALLEY

**Wye Valley Brewery, Stoke Lacy, Herefordshire
HR7 4HG. Tel. (01885) 490505 Fax (01885) 490595
E-mail: wvb@freeuk.com
Web site: www.wyevalleybrewery.co.uk**
Mail order service

Wye Valley Brewery began production in 1985 and, growing substantially, has since moved premises twice, taking up residence in Stoke Lacy in 2002. Wye Valley seasonal cask beers all roll out under the 'Dorothy Goodbody' title. There is not, and never has been, a real Dorothy: she is just a figment of the brewery's fertile imagination, a computer-generated 1950s blonde bombshell dreamt up to market the seasonal range. Three of these seasonal beers are regularly available in bottle-conditioned form, complete with a picture of the seductive Miss Goodbody on the front. Like the other offering, they are now bottled by Hop Back, having been filtered and then re-seeded with fresh bottling yeast. If necessary, the beers may be kräusened to ensure good natural carbonation. Occasionally, draught seasonal and celebration beers may be bottled, too. Best before dates are set at 12 months.

DOROTHY GOODBODY'S GOLDEN ALE

ABV 4.2%   **Bottle size** 500 ml   **Serve** cool
Ingredients Maris Otter/Optic pale malt, crystal malt; wheat malt; East Kent Golding and Fuggle hops

Available in cask-conditioned form March–August, Golden Ale was initially a filtered beer in bottle. However, it has been 'real' now for a number of years.
Tasting Notes
As its name suggests, a dark golden ale with malt and fruit in the nose, a bittersweet, hoppy taste and a soft, malty mouthfeel, plus a dry, bitter hop finish.

BUTTY BACH

ABV 4.5%   **Bottle size** 500 ml   **Serve** cool
Ingredients Maris Otter/Optic pale malt, crystal malt; Golding and Fuggle hops

Mainly aimed at the brewery's Welsh customers, 'Little Friend' has been one of Wye Valley's most successful beers, its cask equivalent voted top beer at the Cardiff Beer Festival in the year it was first brewed, 1998.

WYE VALLEY

Tasting Notes
A golden ale with a hoppy, malty aroma. On the palate there's a strong, clean hoppiness over a sweet, malty base, and the finish is also hoppy.

DOROTHY GOODBODY'S WHOLESOME STOUT

ABV 4.6%   **Bottle size** 500 ml   **Serve** cool
Ingredients Maris Otter/Optic pale malt; roasted barley; flaked barley; Northdown hops

The label of this dark brew claims that Dorothy discovered the recipe in her grandfather's brewing books. The truth is that brewery founder, Peter Amor, once worked for a famous Irish brewery and was duly inspired to create this award-winning stout.
Tasting Notes
A very dark red/brown stout with an aroma of chocolate, coffee and fruit. In the mouth it feels rich and nourishing, with an excellent smooth balance of chocolatey malt sweetness, fruit and crisp, bitter roast flavours. Roast and bitterness dominate the dry finish.

DOROTHY GOODBODY'S COUNTRY ALE

ABV 6%   **Bottle size** 500 ml   **Serve** cool
Ingredients Maris Otter/Optic pale malt, crystal malt; amber malt; wheat malt; flaked barley; roasted barley; Bramling Cross and Fuggle hops

Ruby-hued Country Ale is a version of Wye Valley's Christmas Ale and is mostly exported to the USA.
Tasting Notes
A fruity, malty aroma leads to lots of malt, hops and fruity flavours in the taste, including light pineapple. Big, malty finish with hops and bitterness.

Availability of Beers
Beers in this book are mostly sold locally, through farmers' markets, small grocers, craft shops and delicatessens. Some breweries also sell direct to the public, but this may be by the case only, and some offer a mail order service, which is mentioned if relevant. Otherwise beers can be obtained through specialist off-licences or mail order companies, many of which are listed in the Beer Shops section at the back of the book. If a beer has a listing with a major retailer (supermarket or off-licence chain), this is indicated at the end of the entry.

YATES'

Yates' Brewery, The Inn at St Lawrence, Undercliff Drive, St Lawrence, Ventnor, Isle of Wight PO38 1XG.
Tel. (01983) 854689
E-mail: info@yates-brewery.fsnet.co.uk
Web site: www.yates-brewery.co.uk

Dave Yates used to work for Burts Brewery on the Isle of Wight and also joined the shortlived Island Brewery. Since 2000, he's been brewing on his own, with a five-barrel plant based at The Inn at St Lawrence pub. The bottled beers were launched in summer 2003 and are bottled from cask after being kräusened. Nine-month best before dates are applied.

UNDERCLIFF EXPERIENCE

ABV 4.1%   **Bottle size** 500 ml   **Serve** cool
Ingredients Optic pale malt; crystal malt; chocolate malt; torrefied wheat; Golding and Fuggle hops

The brewery's flagship bitter – taking its name from the brewery's address – is primarily seasoned with Golding hops, but a charge of Fuggles is added late in the boil. This is contrary to the method of most brewers who use this classic combination: the Goldings are usually added last for aroma.

HOLY JOE

ABV 4.9%   **Bottle size** 500 ml   **Serve** cool
Ingredients Optic pale malt; crystal malt; torrefied wheat; Cascade hops; coriander

A glance at the ingredients listing suggests that this is going to be a citrus beer, with the zesty inclusion of American Cascade hops and powdered coriander added late into the copper. The beer is named after a local character from the 1860s and is brewed through the summer months.

WIGHT WINTER

ABV 5%   **Bottle size** 500 ml   **Serve** cool
Ingredients Optic pale malt; crystal malt; roasted malt; torrefied wheat; Northdown hops

This is the brewery's seasonal warmer, described by Dave Yates as a stout-like, very dark bitter.

BROADWAY BLITZ

ABV 5.5%   **Bottle size** 500 ml   **Serve** cool
Ingredients Optic pale malt; torrefied wheat; Fuggle and Cascade hops

A strong ale brewed in its cask form only for The Broadway Inn at Totland and enjoying the cheerful local nickname of 'Wobble Gob'.

YOUNG'S

Young & Co.'s Brewery PLC, The Ram Brewery, Wandsworth, London SW18 4JD.
Tel. (020) 8875 7000 Fax (020) 8875 7100
Web site: www.youngs.co.uk

This popular London brewery has claims to being the oldest in the country, having been founded in 1675. The Young family first took an interest in 1831 and is still involved today, although Young's has been a publicly quoted company since 1898. The company now produces a wide range of bottled beers, two of which are bottle conditioned. In autumn 2002, it also brewed a special, one-off bottle-conditioned beer called GBG 30, to commemorate the 30th edition of CAMRA's *Good Beer Guide*.

CHAMPION LIVE GOLDEN BEER

ABV 5%   **Bottle size** 500 ml   **Serve** cool
Ingredients Lager malt; Styrian Golding hops

Lagered for five whole weeks at the brewery before being filtered, re-seeded with fresh yeast and kräusened with ale yeast, this new beer was the winner of the *Tesco Beer Challenge* in spring 2003 (hence the name).
Tasting Notes
A pale golden ale with spicy, citrus hops in the nose. The taste is floral and fruity-hoppy (elderflower notes), with plenty of buttery malt sweetness for balance. Dry, hoppy finish with lingering creamy malt sweetness.
Major stockist Tesco

SPECIAL LONDON ALE

ABV 6.4 %   **Bottle size** 500 ml   **Serve** cool
Ingredients Maris Otter pale malt; crystal malt; Fuggle and Golding hops

Special London Ale is the current name for Young's
Export, an award-winning, originally filtered beer once
targeted at the Belgian market and, for a while, brewed
under licence in Belgium. This bottle-conditioned
version was a few years in the planning, eventually
arriving in off-licences in summer 1998. The non-
bottle-conditioned equivalent is still sold in Young's
pubs, if you'd like to compare the two. The beer is
fermented for seven days in open fermenters and then
warm conditioned for up to three weeks over a bed of
whole Golding hops. A cold stabilisation period follows
before the beer is filtered. The beer is then primed with
a hopped wort extract and re-seeded with fresh yeast
prior to bottling. A 12-month best before date is marked
on the label, with the beer said to be at its prime
three–four months after bottling. The high condition
and heavy alcohol content allow it to be served with
most foods. CAMRA's *Champion Bottle-Conditioned Beer*
1999 and overall champion at the 2002 *International
Beer Competition*.
Tasting Notes
A bronze ale with a malt nose enlivened by hints of
pineapple and orange. Smooth, rich and malty on the
palate, it has a fine tangy hop balance with bitter
orange fruit notes. Good, bitter, fruity-hop finish.
Major stockists Safeway, Tesco, Sainsbury, Budgens,
Waitrose, Morrisons, Booths, Oddbins, Bottoms Up,
Unwins.

The Champions

Below is a list of all the winners of CAMRA's *Champion Bottle-Conditioned Beer of Britain* contest, which is now sponsored by *The Guardian* newspaper. Judging takes place at the Great British Beer Festival in August.

1991
1st Bass Worthington's White Shield
2nd Guinness Original Stout
3rd Eldridge Pope Thomas Hardy's Ale

1992
1st Gale's Prize Old Ale
2nd Eldridge Pope Thomas Hardy's Ale
3rd Bass Worthington's White Shield

1993
1st Eldridge Pope Thomas Hardy's Ale
2nd Courage Imperial Russian Stout
No 3rd place declared.

1994
1st Courage Imperial Russian Stout
2nd King & Barnes Festive
3rd Shepherd Neame Spitfire

1995
1st King & Barnes Festive
2nd Gale's Prize Old Ale
3rd Bass Worthington's White Shield

1996
1st Marston's Oyster Stout
2nd Bass Worthington's White Shield
3rd Courage Imperial Russian Stout

1997
1st Hop Back Summer Lightning
2nd King & Barnes Festive
3rd Fuller's 1845

1998
1st Fuller's 1845
2nd Burton Bridge Empire Pale Ale
3rd Hampshire Pride of Romsey

1999
1st Young's Special London Ale
2nd Salopian Entire Butt
3rd Hampshire Pride of Romsey

2000
1st King & Barnes Worthington's White Shield
2nd Hampshire Pride of Romsey
3rd King & Barnes Festive

2001
1st RCH Ale Mary
2nd Hop Back Summer Lightning
3rd Fuller's 1845

2002
1st Fuller's 1845
2nd Brakspear Live Organic
3rd Hop Back Summer Lightning

At **Safeway**

we work in partnership

with brewers large

and small and are proud

to offer the finest,

most innovative and

most comprehensive

range of beers

from around the world.

For your nearest

store call:

01622 712987

Beer Shops

The variety of bottled beers sold in British supermarkets has increased dramatically in recent years. No longer do you visit your local store and expect to find only bland national beers in ugly, cheap cans. Safeway is foremost among the national supermarket giants in supporting bottled beers, including many bottle-conditioned beers, while Booths supermarkets in the North-West are also great advocates of real ale in a bottle.

For an even wider selection, it may pay to seek out a specialist independent off-licence. The following shops all have a reputation for stocking bottle-conditioned beers and should prove a useful starting point. Some of these also offer mail order services, as indicated by the abbreviation *(MO)* after the address. There are also a small number of internet-based companies that offer mail order beer sales. The most prominent of these are listed at the end of this section.

Bristol:
The Bristol Wine Company, Transom House, Victoria Street, Bristol. *(MO)*
Tel. (0117) 373 0288
www.thebristolwinecompany.co.uk

Humpers Off-Licence, 26 Soundwell Road, Staple Hill.
Tel. (0117) 956 5525

Cambridgeshire:
Bacchanalia, 79 Victoria Road, Cambridge.
Tel. (01223) 576292

Jug & Firkin, 90 Mill Road, Cambridge. *(MO)*
Tel. (01223) 315034

Wadsworth's, 34 The Broadway, St Ives.
Tel. (01480) 463522

Cheshire:
deFINE Food & Wine, Chester Road, Sandiway, Northwich. *(MO)*
Tel. (01606) 882101
www.definefoodandwine.com

Cornwall:
Waxies Dargle, 10 High Street, Falmouth.
Tel. (01326) 311691

Cumbria:
Open All Hours, 5 St Johns Street, Keswick. *(MO)*
Tel. (0176 87) 75414
www.personalbeer.co.uk

Derbyshire:
Chatsworth Farm Shop, Pilsley, Bakewell.
Tel. (01246) 583392
www.chatsworth.org

Goyt Wines, 1A Canal Street, Whaley Bridge.
Tel. (01663) 734214
www.goytwines.co.uk

The Original Farmer's Market Shop, 3 Market Street, Bakewell.
Tel. (01629) 815814

Devon:
Green Valley Cider at Darts Farm, Topsham, Exeter.
Tel. (01392) 876658

Tucker's Maltings, Teign Road, Newton Abbot. *(MO)*
Tel. (01626) 334734
www.tuckersmaltings.com

Durham:
Binns Department Store, 1–7 High Row, Darlington.
Tel. (01325) 462606

Essex:
Beers Unlimited, 500 London Road, Westcliff-on-Sea.
Tel. (01702) 345474

Hampshire:
Bitter Virtue, 70 Cambridge Road, Portswood, Southampton. *(MO)*
Tel. (023) 8055 4881
www.bittervirtue.co uk

Liquid Pleasures, Unit R10, Festival Place, Basingstoke. (Wed–Sat only)
Tel. (020) 7394 8601
www.utobeer.co.uk

Herefordshire:
Orchard, Hive & Vine, 4 High Street, Leominster. *(MO)*
Tel. (01568) 611232
www.orchard-hive-and-vine.co.uk

Hertfordshire:
Boxmoor Vintners, 25–27 St John's Road, Boxmoor.
Tel. (01442) 252171

Isle of Wight:
Scarecrow Brewery and Beer Emporium, Arreton Craft
Village, Arreton.
Tel. (01983) 856161 (Ventnor Brewery)

Kent:
The Bitter End, 107 Camden Road, Tunbridge Wells.
Tel. (01892) 522918
www.thebitterend.biz

The Cask & Glass, 64 Priory Street, Tonbridge.
Tel. (01732) 359784

Lancashire:
Rainhall Drinks, 18 Rainhall Road, Barnoldswick. *(MO)*
Tel. (01282) 813374
www.rainhalldrinks.co.uk

Real Ale Shop, 47 Lovat Road, Preston.
Tel. (01772) 201591

Leicestershire:
The Offie, 142 Clarendon Park Road, Leicester. *(MO)*
Tel. (0116) 270 1553
www.the-offie.co.uk

Lincolnshire:
Poachers Off-Licence, 457 High Street, Lincoln.
Tel. (01522) 510237

Greater London:
The Beer Shop, 14 Pitfield Street, Hoxton, N1. *(MO)*
Tel. (020) 7739 3701
www.pitfieldbeershop.co.uk

The Bitter End, 139 Masons Hill, Bromley. *(MO)*
Tel. (020) 8466 6083
www.thebitterend.biz

Bottles, 349 Commercial Road, E1. *(MO)*
Tel. (020) 7265 8388
www.onlyfinebeer.co.uk

Cave Direct, 40 Parkview Road, Welling.
Tel. (020) 8303 5040

Hops 'n' Pops Wine Merchant, 538 Holloway Road, Holloway, N7.
Tel. (020) 7272 1729

Nelson Wines, 168 Merton High Street, Merton, SW19.
Tel. (020) 8542 1558

Utobeer: The Drinks Cage, Unit 24, Borough Market, London Bridge, SE1. (Fri pm and Sat only)
Tel. (020) 7394 8601
www.utobeer.co.uk

Greater Manchester:
The Bottle Stop, 136 Acre Lane, Bramhall, Stockport.
Tel. (0161) 439 4904

Carringtons, 322 Barlow Moor Road, Chorlton.
Tel. (0161) 881 0099

Carringtons, 688 Wilmslow Road, Didsbury.
Tel. (0161) 446 2546

Unicorn Grocery, 89 Albany Road, Chorlton-cum-Hardy. (organic beers only)
Tel. (0161) 861 0010
www.unicorn-grocery.co.uk

Norfolk:
Beers of Europe, Garage Lane, Setchey, King's Lynn. *(MO)*
Tel. (01553) 812000
www.beersofeurope.co.uk

Breckland Wines, 80 High Street, Watton.
Tel. (01953) 881592

Oxfordshire:
Classic Wines and Beers, 254 Cowley Road, Oxford.
Tel. (01865) 792157

SH Jones & Co. Ltd., 27 High Street, Banbury. *(MO)*
Tel. (01295) 251179

SH Jones & Co. Ltd., 9 Market Square, Bicester. *(MO)*
Tel. (01869) 322448

The Grog Shop, 13 Kingston Road, Oxford.
Tel. (01865) 557088

Shropshire:
The Marches Little Beer Shoppe, 2 Old Street, Ludlow. *(MO)*
Tel. (01584) 878999
www.beerinabox.co.uk

Suffolk:
Barwell Foods, 39 Abbeygate Street, Bury St Edmunds.
Tel. (01284) 754084

Memorable Cheeses, 1 The Walk, Ipswich.
Tel. (01473) 257315

Surrey:
Hogs Back Brewery Shop, Manor Farm, The Street,
Tongham. *(MO)*
Tel. (01252) 783000
www.hogsback.co.uk

Sussex (East and West):
The Beer Essentials, 30A East Street, Horsham.
Tel. (01403) 218890

Southover Wines, 80–81 Southover Street, Brighton.
Tel. (01273) 600402

Trafalgar Wines, 23 Trafalgar Street, Brighton.
Tel. (01273) 683325

Warwickshire:
SH Jones & Co. Ltd., 121 Regent Street, Leamington
Spa. *(MO)*
Tel: (01926) 315609

West Midlands:
Alexander Wines, 112 Berkeley Road South, Earlsdon,
Coventry. *(MO)*
Tel. (024) 7667 3474

Bernie's Real Ale Off-Licence, 266 Cranmore Boulevard,
Shirley.
Tel. (0121) 744 2827

Da'Costa Wines and Beers, 84–86 Edgewood Road,
Rednal, Birmingham.
Tel. (0121) 453 9564

Global Wines, 2 Abbey Road, Smethwick, Birmingham.
Tel. (0121) 420 3694

Global Wines, 243 Eachelhurst Road, Sutton Coldfield.
Tel. (0121) 351 4075

Laurel Wines, 63 Westwood Road, Sutton Coldfield.
Tel. (0121) 353 0399

Stirchley Wines and Spirits, 1535–37 Pershore Road,
Stirchley, Birmingham.
Tel. (0121) 459 9936

Wiltshire:

Magnum Wines, 22 Wood Street, Old Town, Swindon.
Tel. (01793) 642569

Worcestershire:

Weatheroak Ales, 25 Withybed Lane, Alvechurch.
Tel. (0121) 445 4411
www.weatheroakales.co.uk

Yorkshire:

Ale Shop, 79 Raglan Road, Leeds.
Tel. (0113) 242 7177

Archer Road Beer Stop, 57 Archer Road, Sheffield.
Tel. (0114) 255 1356

Beer-Ritz, 17 Market Place, Knaresborough. *(MO)*
Tel. (01423) 862850
www.beerritz.co.uk

Beer-Ritz, Victoria Buildings, Weetwood Lane,
Far Headingley, Leeds. *(MO)*
Tel. (0113) 275 3464
www.beerritz.co.uk

Beer-Ritz, 31 Goodramgate, York. *(MO)*
Tel. (01904) 628344
www.fabeers.com

Dukes of Ingleton, Albion House, 6 High Street,
Ingleton. *(MO)*
Tel. (0152 42) 41738

Jug and Bottle, Main Street, Bubwith.
Tel. (01757) 289707

Wells Wine Cellar, 94–100 St Thomas Street,
Scarborough. *(MO)*
Tel. (01723) 362220
www. wellswinecellar.co.uk

York Beer and Wine Shop, 28 Sandringham Street, York.
Tel. (01904) 647136
www.yorkbeerandwineshop.co.uk

Scotland:
Peckham's (licensed delicatessen with several branches
in Glasgow, Edinburgh and Stirling: *MO)*
Tel. (0141) 445 4555
www.peckhams.co.uk

Peter Green and Co., 37A/B Warrender Park Road,
Edinburgh.
Tel. (0131) 229 5925

The Wine Basket, 144 Dundas Street, Edinburgh.
Tel. (0131) 557 2530

Wales:
R&V Wines, 17 Bridge Street, Aberystwyth, Ceredigion.
Tel. (01970) 625040

Thirst for Beer, Unit 2, Y Maes, Pwllheli, Gwynedd.
Tel. (01758) 701004

Northern Ireland:
The Vineyard, 375 Ormeau Road, Belfast.
Tel. (028) 9064 5774
www.vineyardbelfast.co.uk

The Vintage, 33 Church Street, Antrim.
Tel. (028) 9446 2526

Internet Sites:
The following internet companies sell beer via the web,
but check also the web sites of the shops listed above.

www.beernetwork.net
www.euro-beer.co.uk
www.tavernontap.co.uk

Bottled Beer Dictionary

A quick reference to the technical terms used in this book and to the language of bottled beer labels.

ABV: Alcohol by Volume – the percentage of alcohol in a beer.

Abbey beer: a strong beer brewed in the fashion of monastic beers but by commercial companies rather than monks. Only authentic Trappist monasteries have the legal right to call their beers 'Trappist'; others producing beers in a similar style under licence from a clerical order have adopted the term 'Abbey'.

adjuncts: materials like cereals and sugars which are added to malted barley, often to create a cheaper brew but sometimes for special flavours or effects.

aftertaste/afterpalate: see finish.

ale: a top-fermenting beer (the yeast generally sits on top of the wort during fermentation).

aroma: the perfumes given off by a beer.

barley: the cereal from which malt is made, occasionally used in its unmalted form in brewing, primarily to add colour.

barley wine: a very strong, often sweetish beer.

bitter: a well-hopped ale.

body: the fullness of the beer, generally indicative of the malt content.

bottle-conditioned: beer which undergoes a secondary fermentation in the bottle ('real ale in a bottle').

bouquet: the hop aroma of a beer.

brewery-conditioned: beer with a fermentation completed at the brewery and usually pasteurised.

bright: filtered (and usually pasteurised) beer.

burtonise: to adjust the salts in brewing water to emulate the natural, hard waters of Burton upon Trent.

cask: container for storing unpasteurised beer.

cask-conditioned: beer which undergoes a secondary fermentation in a cask ('real ale').

condition: the amount of dissolved carbon dioxide in a beer. Too much condition and the beer is gassy; too little and the beer is flat.

decoction: a continental mashing system in which parts of the mash extract are transferred into a second vessel and subjected to a higher temperature, before returning to the original vessel. The aim is better starch conversion into sugar.

dubbel: a Belgian/Dutch Trappist or Abbey ale traditionally of 'double' strength. Dubbels are generally dark brown and malty, with low hop character. Tripel ('triple' strength) beers are stronger, fruity and often pale in colour.

esters: organic compounds comprised of an alcohol and an acid which are produced during fermentation. These have unusual – often fruity – aromas and flavours.

filtered: a beer with its yeast and other sediment extracted.

fine: to clear a beer by adding an amount of glutinous 'finings'. Finings attract yeast particles like a magnet and draw them to the bottom of a cask of beer (or a conditioning tank in the case of many bottled beers), leaving the beer clear. Finings are usually made from the swim-bladder of a tropical fish. Also known as isinglass.

finish: the lingering taste in the mouth after swallowing beer.

grist: crushed malt ready for mashing. The term also refers to a mix of cereals, or hops, used in the brew.

head: the froth on top of a beer.

hop: fast-growing plant, a relative of the nettle and cannabis. Its flowers are used to provide bitterness and other flavours in beer. Hops also help preserve beer.

keg: a pressurised container for storing usually pasteurised beer. Brewery-conditioned beers are known as 'keg' beers and need gas pressure to give them artificial fizz.

kräusen: to add a small quantity of partially fermented wort to a beer in order to provide fresh sugars for the yeast to continue fermentation. It helps generate extra condition.

kriek: a spontaneously fermented (using wild yeasts) Belgian beer undergoing a secondary fermentation with the addition of cherries or cherry juice. Similar beers incorporate raspberries ('framboise'/'frambozen'), peaches ('pêche'), blackcurrants ('cassis') and other fruits.

lager: a bottom-fermented beer (the yeast sinks to the bottom of the wort during fermentation) that is matured for several weeks (months in the best instances) at low temperatures before going on sale.

malt: barley which has been partially germinated to release vital sugars for brewing, then kilned to arrest germination and provide various flavours.

malt extract: commercially-produced concentrated wort, used by some brewers to save mashing, or to supplement their own wort.

mash: the infusion of malt and water in the mash tun which extracts fermentable materials from the grain.

mild: a lightly hopped, usually lowish-strength ale, often dark in colour.

mouthfeel: the texture and body of the beer.

nitrokeg: keg beer dispensed with a mix of carbon dioxide and nitrogen gas, to soften the gassiness associated with previous keg beers. Such beers are filtered and pasteurised, 'dead' products.

nose: see aroma.

OG: Original Gravity – a reading taken before fermentation to gauge the amount of fermentable material in a beer. The higher the OG, the more fermentables and the greater the likely strength of the finished brew.

old ale: a strong, dark beer.

original gravity: see OG.

palate: the sense of taste.

pasteurised: beer which has been heat treated to kill off remaining yeast cells and prevent further fermentation.

porter: a lighter-bodied predecessor of stout, usually dry, with some sweetness in the taste.

rack: to run beer from a tank into a cask or bottles.

real ale: an unpasteurised, unfiltered beer which continues to ferment in the vessel from which it is dispensed ('cask-conditioned' or 'bottle-conditioned').

sediment: solids in beer, primarily yeast but also possibly some proteins.

single-varietal: a beer using just one strain of hops or one type of malt.

stock ale: traditionally a very strong beer intended to be kept and matured for several months.

stout: a heavy, strongish beer, usually dark in colour and tasting dry and bitter, often with roasted barley flavour.

sunstruck: beer which has been over-exposed to bright light. This can cause a chemical reaction, leading to unsavoury aromas and flavours.

Trappist ale: a bottle-fermented strong beer brewed by certain monks in Belgium.

tripel: see dubbel.

wheat beer: a style of beer originating in Germany and Belgium, brewed with a high percentage of wheat and often served cloudy with yeast in suspension.

wort: the unfermented sweet liquid produced by mashing malt and water.

yeast: a single-celled micro-organism which turns sugar in wort into alcohol and carbon dioxide – the cause of fermentation.

Real Ale in a Bottle Index

Breweries Index

Join CAMRA

If you like good beer and good pubs you could be helping to preserve, protect and promote them as a member of the Campaign for Real Ale. CAMRA was set up in the early 1970s to fight the mass destruction of a part of Britain's heritage by the giant brewers.

The big producers and pub groups are still pushing through takeovers and closing small breweries. They are still trying to impose poor quality national beer brands on their customers whether they like it or not, and they are still closing down town and village pubs or converting them into grotesque 'theme' outlets.

CAMRA wants to see genuine free competition in the brewing industry, fair prices, and, above all, a top quality product brewed by local breweries for local tastes, served in pubs that maintain the best features of a tradition that goes back centuries.

As a CAMRA member you can make your voice heard and fight back against the dumbing down of pub life. You will also be able to enjoy generous discounts on CAMRA books and products and will receive the monthly newspaper, *What's Brewing*. You will be able to take part in local social events and brewery trips.

To join, complete the form below (or a copy) – and, if you wish, arrange for direct debit payments by filling in the form overleaf – and return it to CAMRA. To pay by credit card, just call CAMRA on (01727) 867201.

Full membership £16; Joint (living partners') membership £19; Single under-26, senior citizen, student, registered disabled, unemployed £9 (joint £12)

Please delete as appropriate:
I/We wish to become members of CAMRA.
I/We agree to abide by the memorandum and articles of association of the company.
I/We enclose a cheque/p.o. for £   (payable to CAMRA Ltd.)

Name(s)

Address

Postcode

Signature(s)

Please return to: CAMRA, 230 Hatfield Road, St Albans, Hertfordshire AL1 4LW.

Instruction to your Bank or Building Society to pay by Direct Debit

Please fill in and send to the Campaign for Real Ale Limited, 230 Hatfield Road, St Albans, Herts AL1 4LW

DIRECT Debit

This Guarantee should be detached and retained by the payer

Name and full postal address of your bank or building society

To The Manager .... Bank/Building Society

Address ....

.... Postcode ....

Name of Account Holder(s)

....

Bank/Building Society account number

Branch Sort Code

Reference Number

Banks and Building Societies may not accept Direct Debit instructions for some types of account

Originator's Identification Number

9	2	6	1	2	9

FOR CAMRA OFFICIAL USE ONLY

This is not part of the instruction to your Bank or Building Society

Membership Number

Name

Postcode

Instructions to your Bank or Building Society

Please pay CAMRA Direct Debits from the account detailed on this instruction subject to the safeguards assured by the Direct Debit Guarantee. I understand that this instruction may remain with CAMRA and, if so, will be passed electronically to my Bank/Building Society

Signature(s)

Date

Direct Debit

This Guarantee should be detached and retained by the payer

- This Guarantee is offered by all Banks and Building Societies that take part in the Direct Debit Scheme. The efficiency and security of the Scheme is monitored and protected by your own Bank or Building Society.

- If the amounts to be paid or the payment dates change CAMRA will notify you 7 working days in advance of your account being debited or as otherwise agreed.

- If an error is made by CAMRA or your Bank or Building Society, you are guaranteed a full and immediate refund from your branch of the amount paid.

- You can cancel a Direct Debit at any time by writing to your Bank or Building Society. Please also send a copy of your letter to us.